Iris Murdoch

Figures of Good

SUGUNA RAMANATHAN
Lecturer in English
St. Xavier's College, Ahmedabad, India

St. Martin's Press   New York

First published in the United States of America in 1990

Printed in Hong Kong

ISBN 0–312–04504–2

Library of Congress Cataloging-in-Publication Data
Ramanathan, Suguna
    Iris Murdoch: figures of good/Suguna Ramanathan.
        p.   cm.
    Includes bibliographical references.
    ISBN 0–312–04504–2
    1. Murdoch, Iris—Criticism and interpretation.   2. Characters and
characteristics in literature.   3. Good and evil in literature.
4. Ethics in literature.   I. Title.
    PR6063.U7Z83   1990
    823'.914—dc20   89–70289
                                                                  CIP

In loving memory of my father and mother

Contents

Preface

In examining the religious and moral preoccupations of Iris Murdoch's later fiction, this study seeks to bring them into clearer focus by concentrating on a single 'good' figure from each of the six novels which preceded the latest. Each of these novels provides, for the space of that novel, a concept of good that seems to be the answer. But the next novel provides another answer regarded with the same degree of absorbed attention. Her most recent novel, *The Message to the Planet*, contemplates an intimately related category – that of the holy. For this reason it has been included in this study. Taken all together it can be seen that they are all really part of the same evolving answer, and that in turning over different moral codes, she moves, Alice-like, from point to point in a process of denudation and discarding while standing all the while on the same central ground. Images are retained only to awaken sensitivity to something 'other', but then point away from themselves to that different 'other' which is itself subjected to critical scrutiny. The effect is different from the insights of her essays and lectures for only art can simultaneously offer contradictory positions. Her novels form a many-faceted conglomerate, rather like an immense crystal drop mirroring innumerable possibilities.

In narrowing down, separating, and projecting only one important element, this study has bypassed Murdoch's marvellous Shakespearian breadth and blend. With a sad sense of leaving out much of the richness of Murdoch's world, and a fearful sense of treading unfamiliar moral and theological ground, I have limited myself to the religious–ethical dimension of a writer who seems to me to be the most important English novelist writing today.

SUGUNA RAMANATHAN
St Xavier's College
Ahmedabad

Acknowledgements

Many people helped in the writing of this book. A British Council grant-in-aid enabled me to visit Britain to meet Iris Murdoch, and to use libraries in London and Oxford. Dr Willy Engineer of the Bombay British Council was the moving spirit behind this and I am especially grateful to her. Iris Murdoch answered many letters, generously provided books and articles, and talked fascinatingly of many things on the two occasions that we met. I cherish the memory of her kindness and am grateful for permission to quote from her books. Thanks are also due to Chatto & Windus for their kind permission to print extracts from the novels. Conversations with Dr Peter J. Conradi were helpful and illuminating; his book, *Iris Murdoch: The Saint and the Artist*, is indispensable to anyone writing on Iris Murdoch.

This book was written in the basement-library of Premal Jyoti, Ahmedabad. My thanks to its Rector, Fr Martin Patrao SJ, for providing an ambience so absolutely right that it became impossible to work anywhere else, and for allowing me to use the resources of the library. Fr M. Irudairaj SJ, also of Premal Jyoti, took great trouble to educate me on the question of suffering in the Judaeo-Christian tradition and to comment on the chapter on Anne.

Fr J. Munitiz SJ, Master, Campion Hall, Oxford supplied biblio-graphical help with great promptness.

Fr Donald Dias SJ, Principal, St Xavier's College, Ahmedabad, provided chapter and verse for any text I vaguely remembered. Fr J. M. Heredero SJ, Behavioural Science Centre, St Xavier's College, spoke to me about Liberation Theology and reinterpreted faith. Dr F. Franco SJ, St Xavier's College, not only provided valuable critical comments on the Introductory chapter and the chapters on Brendan, James and Marcus, but also shaped and modified my views on Christ. His ideas, even his words, have worked their way into the text.

Shama Chowdhury offered insights which I have used, and talked about some of the novels in such a way as to force me to rethink and recast some points. Sarvar V. Sherry Chand, St Xavier's College, endlessly discussed the novels with me, helped me out at every step, and provided more ideas than I can well remember.

It is impossible to acknowledge through end-notes, or notes of any kind, the extent of her contribution.

My daughter Vaidehi lovingly supplied me with articles from distant America and was much missed in the course of writing this book. My son Vikram provided the lighter moments. My husband, Krishna Ramanathan was, as usual, a rock of support.

S.R.

List of Abbreviations

The following abbreviations and editions have been used:

BB   *The Book and the Brotherhood* (London: Chatto & Windus, 1987)
FHD *A Fairly Honourable Defeat* (Harmondsworth: Penguin, 1987)
GA   *The Good Apprentice* (New York: Viking, 1986)
HC   *Henry and Cato* (New York: The Viking Press, 1977)
MP   *The Message to the Planet* (London: Chatto & Windus, 1989)
NS   *Nuns and Soldiers* (New York: Penguin Books, 1982)
PP   *The Philosopher's Pupil* (London: Chatto & Windus, 1983)
SS   *The Sea, the Sea* (London: Chatto & Windus, 1978)
SG   *The Sovereignty of Good* (London: Routledge & Kegan Paul, 1970)
RDL *Revelations of Divine Love*: Julian of Norwich, (ed.) Grace Warrack (London: Methuen, 1927)
Dh   *Dhammapada*, trans. Buddharakita Thera (Bangalore: Buddha Vacana Trust, 1979)

And when he was demanded . . . when the kingdom of God should come, he answered them and said, The kingdom of God cometh not with observation; Neither shall they say, Lo here! or lo there! for behold, the kingdom of God is within you.

Luke 17:20–21

1

Introduction

Iris Murdoch's twenty-four novels, offering a huge world capable of multiple interpretations, move from an early sophisticated inquiry through a dark phase in which little can redeem nature, to a partial reconciliation, and thence, with her latest novels, into a macabre dance and a contemplation of the technological nightmare. She refuses finality with all her strength.

A preoccupation with the importance of good manifests itself with a new insistence in *A Fairly Honourable Defeat*, though a growing moral seriousness has been in evidence, as most critics agree, since *The Nice and the Good*. Tallis Browne, the good figure in *A Fairly Honourable Defeat*, has an authorial centrality that makes him a prototype for the figures who form the subject of this book. That novel, as Murdoch has herself said in an interview, is an allegory of the struggle between good and evil, and the title refers to the defeat of good by evil in the world. For this reason it has been taken as a paradigm and used as a point of departure for the discussion of the good in this introductory chapter. Tallis is the early version of the clearly defined good figure. He is the literary ancestor of Brendan Craddock in *Henry and Cato*, James Arrowby in *The Sea, the Sea*, Anne Cavidge in *Nuns and Soldiers*, William Eastcote in *The Philosopher's Pupil*, Stuart Cuno in *The Good Apprentice* and Jenkin Riderhood in *The Book and the Brotherhood*, each of whom is the subject of a chapter in the present work.

It must be noted, however, that between the publication of *A Fairly Honourable Defeat* and *Henry and Cato*, there appeared four novels in which the good figure does not receive the same attention. These novels are *An Accidental Man*, *The Black Prince*, *The Sacred and Profane Love Machine*, and *A Word-Child*. In the last named novel, for instance, though there is a scene in which Arthur Fisch speaks simple, good words that throw Hilary Burde's confusion into sharp relief, he lacks significance in the overall design of the novel.

But with *Henry and Cato* and the novels that follow thereafter, the good figures, however peripheral in terms of the action, form a centre of their own. They provide henceforth a sort of 'deep structure' on which the novel rests, despite the fact that the world

1

around is as dark as ever. They show how immensely difficult it is to be or to do good in a world increasingly mad despite, or because of, increasing scientific rationalism. They quietly continue doing it anyway. These later novels offer a precarious zig-zagging between an overhanging amoral world that looms and threatens in a most disturbing way, and a path beaten out by these marginal good figures as they make their way through the jungle of self and society.

Murdoch's novels have been widely regarded as disturbing, unsatisfying and uncomfortable-making; as resorting to the lurid and exaggerated – wild scenes of disaster and rescue, sexual interactions regardless of sex and kin, 'unrealistic' twists, and so on. When this happens in what is apparently a realistic novel, her critics are thrown off their pivot. She goes beyond the ordinary and normal, they say. I suggest that these improbable possibilities which she chooses to present are actually externalisations of the endless combinations, often mutually exclusive and contradictory, that lie at the bottom of consciousness. Anything and everything may be entertained there; behaviour is regulated and made decorous only through socialisation. Exclusion, choosing, acting in certain ways rather than others, are constructs placed over a seemingly bottomless, surging inner sea. It is this innermost, interior seascape that Murdoch is disclosing; it is, therefore, hardly surprising that it seems unrealistic to the socially conditioned consciousness. On the other hand, from the moral point of view, it appears as inescapably and profoundly true because moral principles lie like bridges over the swirl, and derive their importance and strength from the dark flux they span.

It is not enough to say that Murdoch is deeply interested in goodness. Goodness is not just one of her preoccupations, it is the central preoccupation of the later novels. While the novels create rich and densely-peopled worlds where lots of things are going on, and express freely the fun, the horror, the sadness and joy of life, they quietly call attention to an unselfing process which alone has any real value. For this reason the novels are centrally and deeply moral works. But they are not *moralistic*, for good is subjected, as will be discussed later in this chapter, to overwhelming attack; the damages and traumatic injuries inflicted on the idea of the good in the present time are exhibited in elaborate detail. But these figures of good, simultaneously minor and un-ignorable, show how goodness 'operates' in the world: it is absolutely central and by far the most important idea, but it is not often recognised.

The marginality of these figures is crucially connected with the nature of good. It is as if good can be itself only if it is on the periphery of the world of behaviour. The centre of the stage is where self and self-willed action flourish. Julius King in *A Fairly Honourable Defeat*, for instance, is centrally there or not there; his absence or presence sets off ripples because his selfhood obtrudes so strongly. But the marginality of Tallis, his near-invisibility (nicely suggested by his voice and his colourless eyebrows) is linked with his being forever accessible whenever required. At all other times he must be not just in the background, but the background itself; his hardly being there is essential to his always being there. Brendan Craddock and James Arrowby likewise remain on the edge and appear only after events have taken disastrous turns. And none could be more peripheral than William Eastcote. Quite clearly, strong visibility has something to do with the importance of self, and marginality with its effacement. Good can be sovereign only by being a 'powerless', non-intervening source. This is the point that emerges from Murdoch's unmasking of the madness beneath our idea of an all-sufficient, completely secular and rationalised society.

This study also examines Murdoch's de-mythologising of religion. Can religion survive without a mythology? On the other hand, to what extent does religious myth obstruct clear understanding of the truth it encloses? Such questions are under the surface as Murdoch moves by slow degrees from a goodness which is named God to a concept which is seamless, simple and very rare. There is a progressive discarding of images and magic, and a simultaneous loving retention of the images as reminders of purity and excellence. Instead of seeing goodness as emanating from God, Murdoch's later novels, taken together, explore God as an image of good, sometimes necessary, always to be critically re-examined for possible spurious accretions. T. R. Wright says that 'the hidden presence of God in an atheistic world' is the subject of the novels of Greene and Waugh.[1] While this is not literally true of Iris Murdoch's novels, his phrase is useful. The hidden presence of good in a world which tilts away from it is her theme. The good exists necessarily and absolutely, and Murdoch implies that once this is seen, there is no option. We are not volunteers, we are conscripts.

An 'other' order of reality is posited as real. While the entire weight of the novels falls on an order indifferent, if not hostile, to this 'other', it is clearly judged by the 'other'. Of these two orders of reality, the unseen one provides the criterion by which the material one in which we live may be measured and shaped.

Such a position derives, of course, from Plato. Plato's influence on Iris Murdoch's thought has been widely recognised and openly acknowledged by herself. Her 'certainty of a standard' (SG 60) which cannot be reduced is related to the notion of Forms, and the life of Christ so central to her moral picture seems to be, for her, a powerful projection of the Idea of perfection. It is worth noting that Plato's Idea and Christ's life form the parameters within which her picture of the good grows and evolves. Both are necessary – the Platonic concept for realisation at the intellectual level, and the Christian myth for its emotional regenerative power. They constantly modify each other. Plato's Good undergoes, in Murdoch's hands, a distinct Christian transmutation. The selfless loving which connects us with Good is not Greek but Christian. In turn, as discussed in a later chapter on Stuart Cuno, Christ by himself will not do either, because the romantic softness of Christian tradition comes between us and the idea of perfection Christ embodies. The Platonic concept controls the potential for debilitating sentimentality latent in the Christian myth of regeneration through suffering. This is why Plato is a pervasive presence in the background of Murdoch's mental world. Finally, with her latest novel, she turns her attention to the holy.

I

Human existence is a task, a vocation, demanding an endless, ongoing clarification. Jan Walgrave says we exist in the truth before we think it explicitly, that even before reflection takes place, man is already aware of the mystery in which he lives.[2] Every genuine encounter and dialogue is expressive of a call to grow towards generosity and love. This call to an authentic morality appears to be a basic human experience, common to human beings everywhere in the world. However determined by cultural differences, certain patterns of thought and behaviour seem to be universally recognised as good. Murdoch takes the deontological stand when she asks in *The Sovereignty of Good*:

Are we not certain that there is a 'true direction' towards better conduct, that goodness really matters, and does not that certainty about a standard suggest an idea of permanence, which cannot be reduced to psychological or any other set of empirical standards? (SG 60)

An independent imperative calls us to be moral and good. Hence the human recognition of the good.

However difficult to be, or do good, it is even more difficult to ignore its presence altogether. There is a curious reaction here, difficult to define. On the one hand, we act selfishly and badly largely because we do not see clearly what the good is, or are unwilling to see it because it interferes with selfish pleasures – all of which implies a willing suspension of what we half-know. On the other hand, it is next to impossible to ignore it altogether. In *A Fairly Honourable Defeat*, Julius is haunted by Tallis; it is only by an effort of will, propelled by selfish enjoyment, that he succeeds in not surrendering to him. It is difficult to be good, and it is difficult to be altogether bad. Murdoch's position implies an inescapable recognition of good together with the difficulty of the moral task. To *see* it; then to *be* it; then to *do* it: all of this requires a life of unceasing effort.

In the novels there is no unquestioned assumption made about the good's easy sovereignty. On the contrary, the novels themselves seem to be a strong attack on any intuitively grasped justification. Stuart Cuno facing challenges from materialists and scientific reductionists in *The Good Apprentice* is only one concrete illustration of the implicit attack on good contained in the bulk of the later novels. Julius triumphant in Paris; Cato out of the order and Henry settling down; Charles Arrowby's buzzing schemes; Gertrude's blindly happy arrangements with Tim *and* Peter; George's murderous attempts and subsequent quietening down; Stuart's puzzlement, even at the end, about the different meanings of good; Gerard and Rose and Jean and Duncan ensconced in easy settlements and Jenkin dead – this list indicates the defeat (the fairly honourable defeat) of good in the world. In the world's terms, good is not powerful or sovereign; yet the good figures stubbornly haunt the memory as it contemplates the Murdochian universe.

While the present study concentrates on what it takes to be Murdoch's projection of good, it recognises that the novels have implicit contradictions that discourage categorical statements of any kind. The ambivalence goes deeper than the marginalisation of the few who see and try to be good and the domination of the many who do not. Even those who see and know are not wholly in the clear. In *The Book and the Brotherhood*, the more Gerard knows and desires and tries to do good, the less he succeeds. As for Brendan Craddock, one of the figures of this study, what is one to make of the fact that he intellectualises quite as much as Rozanov in *The Philosopher's Pupil*? It is impossible for him – or for Anne in *Nuns and Soldiers*, or for James in *The Sea, the Sea* – to be like Jenkin. The earlier figures, I suggest, are earlier stages in an evolving concept of good, and Murdoch grows increasingly convinced that discussion and conceptualising of the sort in which Brendan engages are obstacles, and must be dropped. Even charm is an obstacle, which is why the movement is from beautiful, clever Brendan to stodgy, unspectacular Jenkin.

But while a backward-looking survey of the novels provides such a perspective as can be called a 'movement', the writing in each novel has a disruptive effect, containing within itself all the ingredients necessary for the demolition of her thesis. It is this overflow, this 'more' than the expected projection, that is responsible perhaps for the unease many readers of her novels feel. They do not know where they are or what stand they should take. *The Book and the Brotherhood* illustrates the quandary quite nicely. In the absurd and macabre dance of the novel, the call to change partners sounds repeatedly and mockingly. Jenkin lived – is there, therefore, hope? But then he died – is there therefore no hope? And what is the meaning of Gerard's parrot Grey, all-knowing, beautiful bird, wise in its cage, where it walks upside down? If it was good for Tamar to break away from her mother (and Western reason and notions of freedom declare that it was), why is she so much less likeable at the close than she was at the beginning? Crimond himself shrinks and dwindles till, in the end, the unfissured strength he suggested is diminished and cut down to ordinary size. The force of these disruptions cracks the earth on which Jenkin stands; there is a sense of both play and disaster which more than threatens the message of good he embodies. If one were to use Barthes' terms, Jenkin coincides with the linguistic, rhetorical units which support reason and meaning, but the text, while not contradicting these, flows in the interstices and ensures what Foucault calls 'a ludic denial' of them.[3] I suggest that 'transgressions' of this kind necessarily occur because Murdoch's mind constantly moves back on itself, questioning the assumptions of her moral base, of its genuineness, its possible falseness, its inevitable inefficacy in the world, and its exhaustion. Her novels create a space for such circling and retracing through actions and characters. Take for instance, the shocking end of *A Fairly Honourable Defeat*: Rupert dead; the sisters Hilda and Morgan finally together in a semi-incestuous union; Julius at large in Paris; Tallis writing his interminable letters. After the convoluted plot-manipulation and human interactions, this is the end. *Such is the world*. Tallis, so clearly a Christ figure, has no victory here. It is true that Tallis leads Julius to the telephone to undo his evil; there is a clear indication at the symbolic level of evil's submission to good. But the tide of events set going by Julius's wickedness is too strong to be contained, and undercuts the meaning. Reason recognises that Rupert dies because of damaged telephone-wires, that accident prevents the saving of his life, but the underground impression, beyond the rational level, is the horror of Rupert's body bobbing in the water and the inappropriateness of the sisters in California.

The point to be stressed is that while the figures of good may indeed be interpreted as forming the most significant centre, they are not, from another point of view, significant at all. They make nothing happen. The important thing is to go on trying. That seems to be her 'message', but the 'text' evokes the futility of such effort. The contradiction is deeply inscribed in the later novels, so much so that William Eastcote in *The Philosopher's Pupil* passes virtually unnoticed. Criticism dealing with that novel rarely mentions him.

The Philosopher's Pupil provides several examples of the mixed nature of things and the difficulty of clarification. For instance, Gabriel McAffrey. Her overflowing love for things outside herself is one of the marks of goodness, of the ethics of love. But she is, as suggested later in the chapter on William Eastcote, mixed and confused, and what should be a flow of clear gold is a turbid stream. Frankena in his *Ethics* says that morality rests on a basis of conscious choice and willed effort; it must have adequate internal sanctions.[4] By this measure, Gabriel's instinctive love is adventitious, not based on willed fostering of moral dispositions. But if, at the level of discourse, the message is that one must make a willed effort, Fr Bernard Jacoby, who makes such an effort in the same novel, is caught in his own circuitous toils. Anne in *Nuns and Soldiers* tries strenuously, and Murdoch has said she is on her side,[5] but her morality evokes a dour dullness compared with Gertrude's self-centred gaiety. Murdoch's stand, the rhetorical, linguistic unit, is clear, but the 'text' of *Nuns and Soldiers* lets in doubt at every point. The doubleness of effects in *Henry and Cato* is another case in point. True, Brendan is the type of the good, and Henry sinking into the country-squire pattern has the light of irony playing over him. But at some deep level, there is a reification of a class-structure which makes us glad to see Henry married to Colette. Or is there, here, an irony directed at the reader whose expectations are known and 'satisfied'? Different possibilities are open.

This study proposes to examine Murdoch's conscious, worked-out moral position against a background of rich ambivalence. Frankena, speaking of ethical judgements, says that an ethical judgement claims that it will stand up under scrutiny by oneself and others in the light of the most careful thinking and the best knowledge, and that rival judgements will not stand up under such scrutiny.[6] Murdoch's presentation of her good figures, and her readiness to let the reader watch their near-submergence and judge for himself whether they still have any validity, invite this kind of scrutiny.

II

It needs to be clearly stated that there is a theological as well as a moral slant to Murdoch's later work, but that the theological dimension does not involve the positing of an absolute. In her rejection of an absolute creator and her refusal to abandon the notion of contingency she may be regarded from the orthodox point of view as an atheist. She says in *The Sovereignty of Good*:

> I can see no evidence to suggest that human life is not something self-contained. There are properly speaking many patterns and purposes within life, but there is no general and as it were externally guaranteed pattern or purpose of the kind for which philosophers and theologians used to search. We are what we seem to be, transient, mortal creatures subject to necessity and chance. This is to say that there is, in my view, no God in the traditional sense of that term; and the traditional sense is perhaps

the only sense. . . . Our destiny can be examined but it cannot
be justified or totally explained. We are simply here.   (SG 79)

This is an acceptance of contingency as the ultimate. Her novels
too underscore the fundamental ambiguity – an ambiguity that
would be destroyed by the assertion of 'God in the traditional
sense of the term'. She offers no *docta spes*, learned hope, which
can give a direction to history or to the future of mankind.

On the other hand, she clearly offers something that can be
offset against the cyclical nightmare of a human life. This is her
concept of good – affirmed and denied before the world and
between the rocks – an eternal recurrence within the subjective
consciousness that can lighten the stay here.

Is this principle of good purely terrestrial, or is it something
more? She is, it seems to me, offering something more. The
paragraph quoted above from *The Sovereignty of Good*, in which she
says there is no God in the traditional sense of that term, concludes
with a sentence that invites careful attention:

And if there is any kind of sense or unity in human life, and the
dream of this does not cease to haunt us, it is of some other
kind and must be sought within a human experience.   (SG 79)

While, at the syntactical level, the sentence asserts the primacy of
the human experience, at the emotional level it suggests something
very different. Such words as 'the dream of this does not cease to
haunt us' effectively cancel out the conviction of 'must be sought
within a human experience'. The conditional 'if there is any kind
of sense or unity in human life', evokes such a simultaneous
longing for unity and readiness for contingency as indicate a
metaphysical openness well beyond the average 'human
experience'.

Elsewhere in *The Sovereignty of Good* she says that the idea of the
transcendent, in some form or other, belongs to morality (SG 58).
Making her way with fastidious scrupulosity to avoid falling into
vague generalisations and wished-for consolations, she argues for
a sense of separateness from the temporal process, for an idea of
perfection which has immense psychological power, and escapes
reductive explanations.

In fact, speaking of good as transcendent, she remarks, 'One
might be tempted to use the word "faith" here if it could be purged

of its religious associations.' (SG 60) One may say that the later novels are concerned with the affirming of faith in a milieu which thwarts it. The novels evoke simultaneously both those regions where nothingness holds sway, and those regions where goodness creates a magnetic field. If the proper function of a metaphysical attitude is to be constantly alive to the paradox of this situation – the impossibility of either affirming or denying, and the absolute necessity both to affirm and to deny – if this is the metaphysical attitude, no English novelist has expressed it so profoundly and so continuously as Murdoch.

Such an attitude is essentially a religious attitude. The faith it expresses is a wholly tentative but hopeful affirmation of the possibility of good, bound to be disappointed and frustrated, and forever in suspense in a world of process.

For this reason, in one novel after another, the good figure appears again and again, establishing no victory, but never annihilated. Is this hope or despair? That there is no conquering of evil and no conclusion possible points to despair. But the very fact of a continuous, undetermined life makes openness to this good a perpetual possibility, and that points to hope. That the good is frustrated is sad; that it is never arrested is a matter of joy. It is precisely this presentation, such an articulation of just such a kind of faith that makes her satisfying from a religious point of view.

Her preoccupation with specific religious attitudes, Christian and Buddhist, will be dealt with separately in section V of this chapter. At this point it suffices to say that Murdoch has little use for the 'religious' notions of salvation as reward for virtue, and salvation through a saviour.

The first of these is a species of ethical egoism or enlightened prudentialism built into the moral life. It is a curious fact, as Frankena notes, that the Judaeo-Christian tradition, which regards self-love as immoral ('he who shall save his life shall lose it'), holds out the prospect of the great reward of salvation. Are we to be good for the sake of something which will promote our own good?

Murdoch's answer is a clear *no*. First, the promise of ultimate salvation in some other kingdom would involve the acceptance of finality in human life. This, as explained earlier, is not her picture. Second, such a reward makes its appeal to the self seeking its welfare. As a strategy for keeping people in order it might work, and has been so used, but in itself, it is a non-moral picture, a teleological stand. A teleological theory says that the ultimate criterion of what is morally right, or wrong, or obligatory, is the non-moral value that is brought into being.[7] Iris Murdoch rejects this and refuses to make the morally good a function of what is non-morally good (even if this means joy in the kingdom of heaven). Her stand is that something is good or right because of its own nature. One must be, and do, good for its own sake, and for nothing else. She says:

> The Good has nothing to do with purpose, indeed it excludes the idea of purpose. 'All is vanity' is the beginning and end of ethics. The only genuine way to be good is to be good 'for nothing' in the midst of a scene where every 'natural' thing, including one's own mind, is subject to chance, that is to necessity. (SG 71)

The second 'religious' concept of saviour is equally unacceptable to her. Christ and Buddha are of immense importance to her delineation of the good, but as human prototypes, not as divine redeemers. There is absolutely no substitute for doing all the work oneself – the work of saving one's soul, that is. The responsibility is wholly one's own. Obviously, such a phrase as 'saving one's soul' would have a special connotation here. It would mean working for the sake of an a-temporal, non-natural reality called good, through moral means out of love.

III

Murdoch conducts a critical examination of her own stand on the sovereignty of good through Julius in his exchange with Rupert in *A Fairly Honourable Defeat* (FHD 218–26). Julius's voice is the voice of the naturalist and scientist, dismissing vague notions of the ineffable as nonsense and non-existent. Rupert puts the case for goodness, but is far less convincing than Julius.

Julius's several remarks, scattered over eight pages, fall into three main groups. First, he is a spokesman for the theory of psychological egoism which maintains that self-love is the only basic principle in human nature, that ego-satisfaction is the only aim, and that the 'pleasure principle' is the basic drive in every individual. It denies that we can ever have any concern or desire for the welfare of others except as a means to our own, any concern

or desire in their welfare for its own sake. When he tells Rupert
that most of us prefer our friends in tears, he hints at our secret
superiority and vitality renewed and nourished by the misfortunes
of others. Any desire to promote good, he adds, is rooted in the
need to be complacent. (If we want anyone to be happy, it
must be as a result of our own busybodying: FHD 221.) Modern
psychology indicates that there are no saints; their sacrifices have
nothing to do with goodness but a lot to do with ego. Helping
other people, and letting oneself be imposed on, proceed from
self-interested motives. So much for human nature.

Second, the case for a transcendent good is effectively demolished
by scientific, materialistic arguments. We cannot *know* reality, for
one thing; there is no reality other than the material one, for
another. The top of the structure, he tells Rupert, is completely
empty. Human beings have dreamed of the extension of goodness
beyond their level, 'but it is precisely a dream' – therefore, not
real. Even as an idea, it is not a coherent concept; it is unimaginable;
there is no notation with which to indicate it; it is simply not there.
He dismisses the empirically unverifiable as nonsense. To Rupert's
weak remonstrance that one can at least attempt to be truthful, he
flatly declares it impossible to be truthful about these things.
Interestingly, in a later conversation with Tallis (FHD 337), when
asked to explain why stealing is wrong, he proves, in the manner
of linguistic philosophers, that to 'steal' being a concept with a
built-in pejorative significance, the statement 'stealing is wrong'
simply amounts to 'wrong is wrong', and is therefore empty.
Furthermore he claims, like the emotivists, that such a statement
cannot be true or false; instead, it is a cry or a plea based on an
unexpressed emotional response: 'Please don't steal.' 'Ought' is
shown to have nothing to do with 'is', and to be based in personal
preference.

The third argument against good follows from Julius's understanding of the way in which such concepts have been found
useful in sustaining existing social structures by providing consolation. They have been propagated far and wide in most societies
all over the world as a consequence of their usefulness in serving
certain ideological ends.

Julius's remarks establish that goodness is not good because it
is a mask for selfishness; that goodness is either un-knowable or
non-existent; and that the concept as it exists has been formulated
and spread for purposes of expediency.

Against such an onslaught (delivered, incidentally, with nonchalance, as interspersed casual remarks), belief in good can only stammer; it cannot provide the sort of proofs required, and finally has to fall back on faith. Stuart Cuno's stuttering defence in *The Good Apprentice* is of the essence.

Julius cannot be answered on his own terms. Another set of assumptions, extending the real to possibilities outside the natural world, has to be called up before the argument can proceed further. A survey of theological literature will at once make clear that certain assumptions may be chosen and held and justified only with the help of non-logical terms. In a recent issue of *The Heythrop Journal*, for instance, Daniel Helminiak, presenting four viewpoints on the human – the positivist, the philosophic, the theist and the Christian – can only relate them to one another by using such terms as 'higher viewpoints' and 'lower viewpoints', and declaring openly: 'The *shift* to any of the higher viewpoints depends on a choice.'[8] The point at issue is that Julius has also made a *choice* of certain assumptions about what is real and true, and in so doing is not as free from preference nor as neutral as he thinks himself, as analytical scientist, to be.

Murdoch herself, in *The Sovereignty of Good*, openly makes a choice, and so do all her 'good' characters. But through the Julius–Rupert conversation in *A Fairly Honourable Defeat* the case against her own choice is given the fullest possible hearing.

The ground of such a choice is faith, shorn of its usual religious associations; and faith itself rises from love – of the world, of human life, of individuals. It is interesting to note that Julius rejects love ('I have no general respect for the human race. They are a loathsome crew and don't deserve to survive': FHD 218), and gives up research in biological warfare not for humanitarian reasons but because he is bored. Murdoch is finally making the Pauline assertion, that love is the greatest of all the virtues. This will be examined in the next section.

IV

One might begin a discussion of Murdoch's ethics by saying that it is an ethics of love. According to Frankena, this ethical code states that there is only one basic ethical imperative – to love – and that all the others are derived from it.

Thou shalt love the Lord thy God with all thy heart, and with
all thy soul, and with all thy mind. This is the first and great
commandment. And the second is like unto it, thou shalt love
thy neighbour as thyself.[9]

Taken together the two commandments establish the link between
religion and morality. The first commandment addresses itself to
the religious impulse, and the second to the moral. It must be
stated here that while morality has long been linked with religion,
there is no inevitable connection. It is entirely possible to adhere
strictly to moral principles and have no belief whatsoever in
anything transcendent. However, a link very readily and naturally
establishes itself. S. Radhakrishnan speaks of the connection
persuasively:

When man realises his essential unity with the whole of being,
he expresses this unity in life. Mysticism and ethics, other-
worldliness and worldly work go together.[10]

Murdoch is clearly interested in the link, and speaks of religion as
being the love and worship of the good (*Acastos* 109), and again of
religion as our love of virtue, lightening the present moment
(*Acastos* 119). She also speaks of morality as needing a background,
a central assertion. Recognising the capacity for reverence as a
separate capacity, she sees it as related, though not necessarily, to
the moral faculty. When she says, in *Acastos*, that out at the very
end of our imagination the spirit is eternally active (*Acastos* 119),
perhaps what she means is that the two impulses frequently flow
into one another. The moral faculty helps itself along with religious
images; the religious object focuses attention that gets drawn away
from self (a moral movement). Simultaneously, as the imagination
broods on a beautiful, transcendent image (God), it becomes
'eternally active', i.e. it initiates and undergoes a regenerative,
purifying process, resulting in a better moral state of mind and
better moral acts.

To restate it in terms of the Biblical commandment to love
mentioned earlier, loving God helps in the loving of one's neighbour. In Murdoch's later novels, the first part of this commandment
is subjected, as will be discussed below, to a demythologising
process till it eventually merges, in *The Book and the Brotherhood*,
with the second commandment and disappears from sight. That

is, the second commandment is the same now as the first, or the only meaningful manifestation of the first.

If Murdoch is positing an ethics of love, seeing human existence as a task to grow in love, it must be asked what sort of love this is which is to be nurtured. She specifically says in *The Sovereignty of Good*, 'Love is knowledge of the individual' (SG 28), and again, 'the central concept of morality' is 'the individual thought of as knowable by love'.

The novels plentifully illustrate the falsification to which this loving is susceptible. Most interactions in love – erotic, fraternal, filial – are shown to be narcissistic and possessive. While they are imagined so intensely from the inside that we are within the cocoon spun by, say, Harry and Midge in *The Good Apprentice*, the awareness that such a path is a dead end, a limiting and imprison-ing, is never allowed to die down altogether. In *An Unofficial Rose*, Randall and Lindsay are at last rich and free in Paris, in the land of heart's desire, but there is an unmistakable taste of let-down. Or take from *The Sacred and Profane Love Machine*, Blaise and Emily, interknit sexually by the strongest chains – why does a desolating light fall on them as they set out to live happily ever after? These are only three random examples from a huge number of loving pairs in twenty-three novels. Almost all are shown to be travellers lured by the enchantment of a mirage.

If the individual as knowable by love is the central concept of morality, then the love expended by the people mentioned above does not turn on knowledge of the other individual, but is rooted in their own need.[11] Knowing the individual 'other' entails denial of one's own need and concentrating on the need of the other. Proper loving requires recognising the *separateness* of the other. 'Love thy neighbour *as* thyself' implies recognising and cherishing the other's autonomy as carefully as one cherishes one's own. The temptation to swallow lover or child or friend into one's greedy centre is the temptation to be resisted. Individuals known through love must be allowed to stand independently, breathing freely the air around them. Only such separateness can make complete, free loving possible. The power element in human relationships has to be constantly checked; proper loving precludes use of the other for any purpose whatsoever. As one looks over the large Murdochian canvas, very few of the characters show any understanding of this. Ann Perronet and Tallis Browne are two early figures who love powerlessly. Thereafter, the figures who form the subject of this study are the only ones who understand the nature of love. Only they attempt to see others around them with patience and accuracy and have the necessary control to let them be.

Murdoch's good figures think and act in a way that leads one to formulate the following general statement:

> Proper loving does not seize or use the object of its love in any way, but attends to the object with growing knowledge and care.

Such a statement, though nowhere made, may be said to describe an important part of Murdoch's ethical system.

Even if it cannot, properly speaking, be made into a universal moral rule to be acted on by everyone, that would not make it less moral. There are certain attitudes which seem to be innately moral. Murdoch says in 'Vision and Choice in Morality':

> I want now to consider whether there are not positive and radical moral conceptions which are unconnected with the view that morality is essential universal rules. I have in mind moral attitudes which emphasise the inexhaustible detail of the world, the endlessness of the task of understanding, the importance of not assuming that one has got individuals and situations 'taped', the connection of knowledge with love and of spiritual insight with apprehension of the unique.[12]

In the light of this one may go back to one's earlier general statement and recognise it as innately moral, and possibly capable of being made into a universal moral law. The statement falls into two parts: (i) proper loving is attention to the object without self-interest; (ii) proper loving means attending to and promoting the interests of the other.

In other words, there must be both unselfing and loving concern. The exact nature of these two requirements will be discussed later in this chapter. Here it may be said that the double task is very difficult and endless since it must be observed faithfully in every human relationship. The question arises whether it is possible to follow one part of the proposed moral law and not the other, or whether they are inextricably linked. For instance, in *Henry and Cato*, Cato's love for Beautiful Joe as expressed in finding money to educate Joe meets the second requirement about care for the needs of the other, but not the first of attention without regard for self. Cato's plan to look after Joe is rooted in his desire to be with him and possess him, to use Joe to appease his aching need. Since his plan to find money for Joe's support arises from this, it ceases to be genuine attention to the other's interest, and becomes instead a disguised attention to his own.

What about love that observes only the first part of the moral law and not the second, that is, *attends* to the other without self-interest, but does not (or cannot) promote the other's interest – a purely contemplative love? Tallis in *A Fairly Honourable Defeat* appears at first sight to be an instance. Tallis writing letters at the close to his wife Morgan who, having injured him over and over, never replies, seems to be an example of purely contemplative loving. However, in this case, such standing aside and letting Morgan go is the only way of promoting Morgan's interest; so Tallis is actually living out the second part of the law as well.

In an article entitled 'L'Amour et L'Ascèse', Claude Flipo under-lines the importance of self-denial in love and asserts the need in human interactions for an ascesis comparable with the renunci-ations required by 'l'amour de Dieu'. He says:

> Seul un amour dépouillé de tout retour narcissique peut se défaire de la prétention au pouvoir, que celui-ci s'exerce par la pression persuasive ou par la captation possessive. Reconnaître l'autre, c'est vouloir qu'il existe pour lui-même, c'est-à-dire, différent de soi. Cette conversion ne s'opère pas sans l'accepta-tion de certaines frustrations affectives, d'une certaine solitude du coeur.[13]

Tallis at the end is acquainted with the heart's solitude mentioned above. Seeing Morgan as different from himself, remaining absol-utely there if she wants to return, but refusing to persuade her to return – all three attitudes are part of his twofold task of loving unselfishly and being concerned. His passivity is misunderstood by the others as weak-kneed ineffectuality. Hilda and Rupert chafe against his inert attitude in the matter of Morgan who is, after all, his wife. ('I think he's completely spineless', says Rupert: FHD 220.)

However, when promoting the interests of others unequivocally requires action, none shows himself quicker to act than Tallis. In the scene in which the Jamaican is at the mercy of the white youths, he springs into the fight on the Jamaican's behalf, while

Simon and Axel hesitate, and Julius looks on with bright-eyed interest. Tallis's passiveness concerning Morgan, and quickness to act in the matter of the Jamaican are entirely consistent with each other, both being expressions of love or concern for the other at the expense of self.

The point about a purely contemplative, non-possessive love is that it is the background or state of mind out of which action – promoting the interests of the other – arises. The first part of the moral statement about proper loving describes the right and moral state of mind, and the second the right and moral kind of action. They are not separate. However, the first exists by itself and waits upon a situation before it is made manifest in action. That is, it can exist without anyone ever knowing. The second part of the moral statement cannot stand separately. One may of course do what is good for the other, but with entirely the wrong motive. Tallis might come to the defence of the Jamaican but out of desire for personal revenge on the attacker, in which case it would not be, properly speaking, a loving act, though the effect may be to increase good and inhibit evil. When good is increased as a result of action not in itself rooted in right feeling, that is not a moral action.

The requirements of loving and of unselfing must be examined since they are so central to Murdoch's vision of the good. One might go further back in the argument and ask why it is necessary to love; why it is the only principle of righteousness in the human soul; why it is, as Rupert says, the secret name of all the virtues. Here one must have recourse finally, not to logical reasons, but to felt experience.

Our experience tells us that there is in us a sense of insufficiency, what the Second Vatican Council called *radicalis insufficientia mundi huius*, the radical insufficiency of this world. Simone Weil, discussing Plato's *Symposium*, speaks of a desire coming from the very sources of our being to be reintegrated into the state of completion. Love, she says, is the great reconciler, the principle by which we escape from our duality to the unity which is our end:

> Love is thus the right physician for our original illness. We need not ask ourselves how to have love, it is in us from birth to death, imperious as hunger. We need only know in what direction to direct it.[14]

It is only on the basis of this felt insufficiency and the consequent reaching out – the birth and movement of love – that one can affirm that there is a unity or a good to be sought. The good things in life do not compose that good; they only intoxicate and appease temporarily, and the hunger revives. Nor can carnal love be the goal; it too is a temporary remedy, though perhaps the most uplifting and beautiful one. There is a greater good than anything that can be known here, and we know of it because love makes us aware of it and takes us towards it. Julius in *A Fairly Honourable Defeat* has denied love outright. He also denies that there is anything at 'the top of the structure'. The first denial leads to the second, for it is love that turns the viewer to the top of the structure which is out of sight.

Murdoch describes love as the tension between the imperfect soul and the magnetic perfection which lies beyond it. Admitting that it is the source of our greatest errors, and capable of infinite degradation, she says:

> when it is even partially refined it is the energy and passion of the soul in its search for Good. Its existence is the unmistakable sign that we are spiritual creatures, attracted by excellence and made for the Good. It is a reflection of the warmth and light of the sun. (SG 103)

The first assertion that must be made is that there is love. Also, love is both the way and the end. That is, it acts upon the self, increasing the capacity for loving, making more room for itself. Simultaneously, it brings an awareness that there is more of itself which is a unity, a completeness, and that the way to experience that completeness is to let this work in the soul. The religious articulation of this would say both that love takes the soul towards God, and that God *is* love.

Simone Weil remarks that love is the only faculty of the human soul which might cannot touch, from which no brutality of any sort can proceed.[15] Julius King can be what he is (the allegorical interpretation casts him as Satan) because he allies himself with might and refuses love. He uses other people, manipulates them for his own enjoyment and does not love them. He has repeatedly told Morgan that he cannot love her.

Julius would dismiss the felt radical insufficiency and the felt presence of love as assertions induced and maintained by vested powers to preserve certain power-structures. But all his impressive arguments are simply and quietly negated by the fact of Tallis's existence. Tallis exists, loves powerlessly, and steadily refuses to assume power. How is this to be explained away? Tallis is, as has been generally recognised, a Christ figure. He not only shows what proper loving is; he is indubitably *there*. Morgan, fly about as she will, cannot efface him. He is the capacity for love. The human soul, typified by Morgan, recognises this and embraces it, and then, of course, because of muddle and selfishness, abandons it and strays, but is not herself abandoned at any point by Tallis.

The concept of unselfing or selflessness is also important in Murdoch's moral scheme. One may ask why this should be so, why it is not enough to do merely what is required by duty for one's neighbour. In seeking an answer to this question, one runs up against a good greater than self, and a capacity for love directed towards this 'greater good'.

Morality has to do with society and social rules which are necessary. Right and wrong are usually related to the observance or violation of these rules. But the good is greater than right, and whatever it is that loves the good, while including the performance of righteous acts, recognises the existence of a beautiful 'something' towards which it orients itself. Simone Weil says in *Gravity and Grace*:

> Intention directed towards obedience to God saves us, whatever we do, if we place God infinitely above us, and damns us, whatever we do, if we call our own heart God.[16]

The key phrase here is 'if we place God infinitely above us'. The term 'God' may be replaced by 'good' if necessary. The point to be stressed is that something beyond demands disciplined self-denial and keeps us closer to the true and real. This is necessary because there is a real danger of calling our own heart God. For instance, we may say that religious belief restricts Harijans (Untouchables) from entering Hindu temples, a clear case of calling our own heart (in this case an assumption concerning caste purity which in turn conceals a vested social interest) God.

If, however, we disregard the self and place something (God or good) above it, and deny any self-interested dictate of the heart, then there is a greater chance of not being mistaken about the true and real, of seeing the object as in itself it really is.

Loving something which is other than ourselves seems insepa-rable from the good and the dissolving of the self seems written into the process of loving. The ego appears in the last light to be a contrived, built, and blocking construct in the way of something intuitively grasped as both true and precious. With the ego's dissolution, that 'other' something – it may be given different names – enters the space with an expanding, releasing movement, and the painful death of the self brings a joyous sense of freedom. Love is an extension away from self towards the other, and loving the good which is greater than self amounts to moving away from self towards that which is more than self. Thus both good and that which loves good are linked with *what is not self.*

If asked why this is so, one must go back to the answer that love has to do always with 'the other', is a movement towards something outside. Love moves, as said earlier, out of a radical insufficiency towards 'the other'. As soon as 'the other' becomes more important than self, there is a sense of loving. One knows that one loves. Of course, this 'other' can take many forms. The Platonic ladder of ascent takes us through some of them. Also, as indicated earlier, there are degraded selfish ways of loving which require proper unselfing. In loving people, especially (as Brendan says in *Henry and Cato*), illusion readily falsifies and the narcissistic streak returns again and again.

The central fact, however, is that love is love of 'the other', and that at its finest, that other is the good. Love is what asserts the certain presence of the good and lies at the basis of the ontological affirmation.

This good is above the good–evil opposition. Simone Weil observes that if good is the union of opposites, then evil is not the opposite of good.[17] The good above the good–evil opposition is sovereign and inviolate. It can transform evil and is therefore more powerful. Evil can change and *become good*; but the good remains itself, however many fall away from it and however frequently. As an idea, evil seems not to have that sovereign power; while it flourishes everywhere, it can always be transfigured because of the capacity for love.

Jenkin Riderhood in Murdoch's 1987 novel, *The Book and the Brotherhood*, is hardly conscious of good. But he is conscious of justice. Murdoch's point implies that justice – recognising the existence and rights of others – is even more important than loving the good, for this may be (as illustrated by Gerard) a way of selfishly loving oneself. Loving one's neighbour necessitates a self-forgetting. Justice is more important than benevolence, perhaps? Or perhaps it is nearer the mark to say that justice *is* benevolence. As long as the rights of others are upheld, there is no need for much more.[18]

An interesting point here is the fact that Jenkin's actions proceed out of a state of mind which is aware but not self-consciously so. He does not act out of pure instinct (that would be a reduction); he faces his temptations and thinks about them, but without fuss. Dialectical inquiry into the nature of good has been reduced to a minimum, a point hinted at in *The Good Apprentice* when Stuart refuses to talk further about this because 'talking spoils things'.

If 'more' is dangerous because it leads to what Murdoch calls 'the warm, messy' regions of the empirical psyche, are we to conclude that a stern sense of morality is enough for anyone and that anything more is unnecessary and undesirable? Through Jenkin, however, Murdoch presents no stern picture. Jenkin flies about wherever called without a second thought, suggesting not only the imperative of duty but also something more. It is clear then that there must be something more, but not very much more, if the quagmire of self-regard is to be avoided.

Frankena in his *Ethics* establishes the connection between mere duty and something more:

> I wish to contend that we do not have any moral obligations, *prima facie* or actual, to do anything that does not directly or indirectly, have some connection with what makes somebody's life good or bad, better or worse . . . . all of our duties, even that of justice, presuppose the existence of good and evil and some kind of concern about their existence and incidence. To this extent, and only to this extent, is the old dictum that love is what underlies and unifies the rules of morality correct. It is the failure to recognise the importance of this point that makes so many deontological systems unsatisfactory. To say (that love underlies all moral rules) is to say not only that we have no obligations except when some improvement or impairment of someone's life is involved, but also that we have a *prima facie* obligation *whenever* this is involved. To quote William James's inimitable way of putting it:
>
> > Take any demand, however slight, which any creature, how-

ever weak, may make. Ought it not, for its own sole sake, to be satisfied? If not, prove why not.[19]

V

It will be obvious from the discussion thus far that Murdoch's thesis has a quasi-religious slant, that she inhabits a region where religion and ethics meet. Her attitude to religious traditions and to the religious spirit have to be taken into account in any consideration of her concept of the good. Her novels and interviews indicate that the religions which interest her most deeply are Christianity and Buddhism.

Very alive to the accretions of Christianity which obstruct the central purity, she is haunted by Christ to an extraordinary degree. He recurs in novel after novel, modified each time as she takes a new turn in her exploration, but unquestionably there.

However, she is not a Christian novelist like Greene or Waugh. That is, she is not to be identified with any one religious faith or any one religious tradition. She cannot, strictly speaking, be called a Christian because she does not believe in the Resurrection and the Atonement. But she penetrates to the very heart of Christianity and reinterprets it to the contemporary world in terms which it will find acceptable.

In order to do this with the greatest authenticity she needs to stand *outside* the crystallised form of any faith. If she were to be inside as the complete believer, she would be cut off from the truth as it presents itself differently in different parts of the world. As she examines different religious traditions – Roman Catholic, Quaker, Buddhist – she speaks as one who is an insider, but only for the space of that work. She remarks in the Dialogue on Religion in *Acastos* that it is as if truth has been cast into a particular form, but that the truth itself requires criticism of that form, the seeing of it as provisional and only one of different ways. That frame must then be set aside, the picture left behind, an attempt made to do without a picture or to form another picture. She says:

> The truth has to be put into a conceptual picture because we feel it can't be expressed in any other way; then truth itself forces us to criticise the picture. (*Acastos*, 85)

The provisional nature of the picture and the need to assemble it over and over again is indispensable to the task of seeing the truth. With crystallisation, the thing itself gets lost in intricacies; mystification and power may then enter in veiled disguise.

Her attitude in these matters is close to that of Simone Weil who, though seized by Christ, refused baptism because it would hinder the perpetually re-formed and re-forming picture needed for the truth. But in the moment of contemplating a particular picture of the truth, the entire attention must recognise it and surrender to it:

> When a thing is beautiful, as soon as we fix our attention upon it, it represents unique and single beauty. Two Greek statues: the one we are looking at is beautiful, the other not. The same is true of the Catholic faith, Platonic thought, Hindu thought, etc. The one we are looking at is beautiful, the others not. Thus those who proclaim that such and such a faith alone is true and beautiful, although *they are wrong*, are in a sense more right than those who are right for they have looked at it with their whole soul.[20]

Murdoch's complete attention to the religious tradition she examines in any given novel accounts for the authenticity of the religious colouring.

The search for authenticity also leads her to a sustained and resolute demythologising, a freeing of the truth from the prison of its myth, especially in her engagement with Christianity. Its central tenet of unselfish love is at the heart of Murdoch's moral world, but she needs to separate it from the surrounding coloured and emotion-filled atmosphere, and also from the powerful social institutions that have grown around it. The history of Christianity comes between us and Christ, and Murdoch's piercing through the rich fabric to the pure essence affords a contemporary version of faith.

Christ is important because he is the most intense picture of love, of that in us which loves a good greater than ourselves. The reinterpreted meaning of Christ is thrown into relief by the traditional response to him as an object of attention. Cato's mistaken emotionalism; Fr Bernard Jacoby's elaborate worship; Barney's tearful masses; Anne's need for a miracle, and Fr McAlister's brooding over the mysteries are all shown as obstructions in the way of clear understanding. The clearly-perceived Christ is Christ as example.

Murdoch's evolving interpretation of Christ as perfected man, the perfect model and incarnation of powerless love, is part of the demythologising process. This is an attitude she shares with Simone Weil whose influence upon herself she has openly acknowledged. Simone Weil says:

> With those who have received a Christian education the lower parts of the soul become attached to those mysteries when they have no right at all to do so. That is why such people need a purification of which St. John of the Cross describes the stages. Atheism and incredulity constitute an equivalent of such a purification.[21]

The last sentence is specially relevant in Murdoch's case. Her 'atheism' is of this sort, a vigilant incredulity that guards against the transformation of a transcendent good into a religious object.

The process has begun in *Henry and Cato*, with Fr Brendan Craddock's replies to Cato in the last pages of the novel. To Cato's insistent questions about belief in a personal God, Brendan's reply is that we deal in the idea of persons because we have to, but that God is unimaginable and incomprehensible and nameless. Brendan's being a Roman Catholic priest charges this reply with a special significance. Brendan cannot give up the name and the idea of a person even though he recognises that truth cannot be localised there. When Cato asks

> 'If you don't know whether God is a person what happens to your Christology?'

Brendan replies, 'I let Christ look after my Christology.' (HC 372)

At this stage in Murdoch's work Christ is not merely perfect model; he is also transcendent good evoking love. Brendan needs the resonances that go with the beloved name; for him the passage from the named to the nameless and back again is a way of keeping close to the truth.

The Christ figure is stripped in each succeeding novel in a movement from the mytho-poetic Jesus to the historical Jesus. Christ in *Nuns and Soldiers* openly rejects the beautiful and powerful Christian stories of sacrifice and atonement and declares himself to be only the principle of love in the human heart. The capacity for love not only reaches out to the divine (Anne's impassioned plea), it *is* the transcendent end as well as the transcending movement towards that end. The love that shakes Anne in the presence of Christ is very much to the point. But he is not the Redeemer; he is that quality in herself that can alter her consciousness and make her more capable of proper loving.

In the next novel, *The Philosopher's Pupil*, Christ as a model to be imitated is indicated by William Eastcote's attentive obedience. The magic of his name (for Brendan) and the beauty of the idea (for Anne) have disappeared. Eastcote's internalisation of Christ is so complete that this Quaker is spoken of after his death in phrases originally used for Christ.

The phrases used in connection with him after his death ('innocent substitute', 'Something's all washed away – washed away in blood . . . . Bill the Lizard dead') suggest a reinterpretation of the Atonement doctrine. The orthodox Christian concept of the Atonement has to do with the process by which reconciliation with God is accomplished through the death of Jesus Christ. The simplest and best-known expression of it in English may be the hymn 'There is a green hill far away' which has the following stanza:

> He died that we may be forgiven;
> He died to make us good,
> That we might go at last to heaven
> Saved by his precious blood.

This is Christ as the once-for-all sacrifice making it possible for the sinner to be at one with God (hence Atonement). Such an interpretation has already been seen as unacceptable in *Nuns and Soldiers* in the light of Christ's words to Anne that she must do all the work herself.

The point then of using these Atonement-associated phrases when speaking of William Eastcote's death is to reinterpret the meaning of the Atonement and carry forward the Christ-as-example theme. The death of the pure and good person, by drawing attention to the purity and goodness vanishing with his death, can effect a kind of dying to evil in the hearts of those among whom he lived. The lacuna caused by his death stabs the consciousness awake to its degenerate condition by acting as a sharp reminder of a lost but attainable good. Eastcote's death as influence, worked out through the temporary blinding of George in a scene suggestive of St Paul's experience on the road to Damascus, reinforces the fact that Eastcote's life has been an imitation of Christ's.

From henceforth, this is Christ's relevance, and the two novels that follow *The Philosopher's Pupil* have Christ figures who instinctively follow his example. In *The Good Apprentice* Stuart Cuno steadfastly refuses religious affiliation, but his actions, some of his experiences, and several phrases used of him (all of which are considered at length in a later chapter) bring in the Christ reference very clearly. The point to be stressed is that Stuart, at the level of articulation and rationality, stands apart from orthodox religion in order to live the life prescribed by religion. His interlocutors ask him why he does so since the necessary structures exist within which he can do what he wants to do. But Stuart wants to have nothing to do with these. Collectivities of any kind obstruct the good that has to be lived out.

Christ is the great example, but he is not for Stuart what he is for Brendan. The role has been significantly modified. Stuart is spoken of from time to time as if he is Christ. He is the son of a 'girl'; he goes about doing good, is asked whether he has the stigmata, and openly mocked and reviled; and has a kind of agony in the London Underground. All this implies that Stuart can be Christ. It is necessary to see that Christ must have once been (like) Stuart in order that Stuart, or anyone, may be (like) Christ.

References to Christ appear in Stuart's conversation with Thomas MaCaskerville in the course of which Stuart says Christ is to be associated with an awful, pointless suffering – the Auschwitz horrors, for example. This remark is not elaborated, but Jurgen Moltmann's unforgettable phrase about 'the scattering or *diaspora* of the spirit – its dissemination in the openness of history'[22] helps to explain the implications of this kind of suffering. The 'beautiful' suffering – beautified by Christian art – has to be openly rejected (as it is by Christ when he appears to Anne in *Nuns and Soldiers*). It is in the 'awful' suffering of the powerless, the criminal, and the condemned, in suffering wholly disassociated from prestige or cause, that Christ lives on.

Simone Weil speaks of the great difficulty of turning from the prestige 'for the prestige which one really cares about is not recognised as such'. Christ's prestige was wholly torn away after the Last Supper; even his disciples abandoned him. Simone Weil observes:

> man is not truly stripped of all participation in social prestige
> until penal justice has cut him off from society. No other type
> of suffering has this characteristic of irreducible, ineradicable
> degradation which is essential to the suffering inflicted by penal
> justice.[23]

She implies that there can be a completely true, just and good man
only when there is *no appearance* of justice. The appearance of
justice, fidelity to a cause or an idea, national or religious or
political, prevents a complete spiritual nakedness and total loss of
prestige. Christ was completely true, good and just because nothing
protected him:

> He was ridiculed like those madmen who take themselves for
> kings; then he perished like a common criminal. There is a
> prestige belonging to the martyr of which he was entirely
> deprived. Also he did not go to his martyrdom in joy, but in a
> swoon of all the powers of the soul, after having vainly implored
> his Father to spare him and having vainly asked men to console
> him.[24]

In the light of this, Stuart's remarks about associating Christ with
pure awful suffering seem relevant. Stuart's reference to Auschwitz
makes sense when degradation is seen as a necessary spiritual
condition for absolute spiritual purity. This is what Christ stands
for now: love in powerlessness.

In *The Book and the Brotherhood*, Murdoch has moved a step
further. Unlike Stuart, Jenkin never mentions Christ, but is clearly
the type of Christ: phrases used of him, as of Stuart, establish this
beyond a doubt, however unlikely a Christ-figure he may seem at
first. The secularisation of Christ is complete in this novel. The fact
that Jenkin never thinks of him or speaks of him – but *is* him –
makes the internalisation even more total than in the case of Stuart.

The thought 'He died for me', recurring after Jenkin's death in
the minds of several characters in *The Book and the Brotherhood*
(explained in detail in a later chapter) develops the Atonement
doctrine in the direction of an even greater simplicity. Jenkin dies
because of his readiness to help anyone in need. He rushes to
Crimond's house in answer to Jean's appeal for help, and he goes

to that fatal encounter from the middle of an appeal for help from Tamar. Having comforted one, he responds to the call of the next. The emphasis here is on the practical help he extends, and on the manifestation of love in such giving and in so allowing himself to be used. The Atonement-associated phrase is thus stripped and pared till Christ is seen, not as one who died once and for all for the world, but as the birth, again and again, of love, expressed as love of neighbour. The second commandment has clearly become the only way of living out the first commandment. What is needed to express this new picture is not a conjunction joining two separate injunctions but a single one of the following kind: 'Love your neighbour as yourself so that your love of God becomes a meaningful thing'. Or something to that effect.

The faith Christ preached and exemplified implies, in the final analysis, something different from what is set out in the Nicene Creed. Rather, it has to do with a growing realisation of the non-power-seeking capacity within the self that grows in love and awareness. It may not be consciously known or speculated on. Jenkin Riderhood beautifully illustrates Christian faith though he has nothing whatever to do with Christian doctrine. His faith in himself and people around him is a gift; he does not even know he has it, but he manifests it in his concern for others. He does not take himself very seriously, and consequently he is free, not bound by a sense of his own self-importance. He is a natural follower to Stuart; both are driven by faith.

Quite clearly, Christ cannot be left behind in any clarification of the good. He provides the completest picture of the extent to which loving extension may go by his crucifixion. But because the picture itself has become an object of adoration, distracting attention from the actual task of loving, it needs to be broken up and reassembled. One could, of course, discard the picture altogether, but because the picture expresses more than the simple moral injunctions it enjoins, it awakens and moves the receptive spirit in an inexplicable way. Religion now takes on a role related to that of the greatest art; it moves and purifies through the beauty of its content. Religion, in order to make possible the complete moral experience, has to have an aesthetic component. Which is another way of saying that the beautiful is inseparable from the good; and also that we *love* the good and are led to it through experience of the beautiful.

Murdoch's reinterpretation of Christianity is related to the current hermeneutical process which constantly revises given texts and engages in re-enacting the past, not for the sake of knowing the past as past, but for clearer knowledge of oneself in the present. The interplay between the text and the interpreter leads to a truer recovery of the subject-matter. John Hogan in a recent article entitled 'Hermeneutics and the Logic of Question and Answer' mentions the implications of such dialectical inquiry for theology, and locates truth not in any one proposition or set of propositions, but in the question–answer complex.[25] He quotes Gadamer on 'the fundamental non-definitiveness of the horizon in which the understanding moves', and on 'the fact that after us others will understand in a different way'.[26] This has a direct bearing on Murdoch's approach. Her conscious destabilising of the myth in which 'truth' has been immured, her concurrent reappraisal of the chaff and retention of the grain, show that she sees dialectic as indispensable for proper understanding. Though a demythologised Christ is absolutely essential to her task, something of the myth, some residue, is retained for the purpose of awakening and stirring the consciousness. In an article entitled 'Ethics and the Imagination' she speaks of moral improvement as involving a progressive destruction of false images, but goes on to remark:

> Theology needs speculative imagination. A most important case: the word 'God' is less often used and means less. Should we let it dwindle and go, together with what it used to designate? Or should we, while allowing its sense to change, try to preserve and renew its ancient power?[27]

This is from a fairly recent article, but as early as 1956, in 'Vision and Choice in Morality', she indicated the need for simultaneous reinterpretation and retention of myth. She says:

> Certain parables or stories undoubtedly owe their power to the fact that they incarnate a moral truth which is infinitely suggestive and open to continual re-interpretation. . . . Such stories, precisely through their concreteness and consequent ambiguity have sources of moral inspiration which specific rules cannot give.[28]

As specific instances, she mentions the New Testament story of the woman with the alabaster box of precious ointment and the parable of the prodigal son. That the life of Christ itself has a similar ambiguity and moral power is suggested both by her reinterpretations of the Christ figure, and by the sentence following the remarks quoted above. She says:

> Consider too the adaptability which a religion may gain from having as its centre a person and not a set of rules.[29]

The implication is that a story concerning a central figure has a directing and regenerative power not available to a set of rules. Talking of certain obstinately unclear situations, she suggests that 'a fresh vision may be derived from a story', and that this represents an alternative 'mode of understanding'. A set of rules leaves the imagination unsatisfied. This explains why the Buddhist teaching, which is really a set of prescriptions, accrued to itself a set of stories which the Buddha himself would have set aside, or concerning which he would have maintained a noble silence.

In short, religion needs both myth and demystification of myth if it is to involve the believer in a total participation. Iris Murdoch's treatment of Christ illustrates the truth of this very vividly.

Murdoch has said that she has always been deeply interested in Buddhism because it stresses the need for a change in consciousness and deals with the efforts required to make such a change. Its emphasis on three dispositions of the mind, 'first, that of the will to be gentle and peaceful; second, that of prayer and meditation; finally, that of universal goodwill, *maitri*'[30] goes close to Murdoch's own moral–religious position clarified through her emphasis on love and prayer in *The Sovereignty of Good*. Moreover, there is no belief required here in a redeeming Saviour; only the self can redeem the self. The Christ who appears to Anne in *Nuns and Soldiers* utters an essentially Buddhist thought when he tells her she must do all the work herself.

Reading Dominique Dubarle's comments on Buddhist spirituality, one can readily see why this should appeal to Murdoch. Dubarle says:

> Buddhist spirituality seems to me the supremely convincing example of what man can reach existentially, by himself, without a religious faith in the proper sense of the word, without in any case making use or referring to what the word 'God' is taken to signify in the monotheistic religious tradition. . . .[31]

and a little later,

> one must admit that without explicitly confessing any God, man
> is able to pray, meditate, contemplate and lead an existence
> devoted to something quite other than the profanity of life.[32]

Buddhism, without revelation, without a Saviour, invites the
pilgrim to try out the way, even invites its own rejection but offers
a path. While it posits no personal God, it does assert the possibility
of transcendence to be experienced, once the Buddha-nature has
been awakened, through a life of purity, selflessness and loving-
kindness. Continuous control and effort must follow the awakening. The transcendent, unconditioned state, *nirvāna*, asserted by
Buddhism is not merely a psychological state of release which
comes with the quietening of the anxious consciousness; there is a
clear moral–ethical path leading to it, though it is itself a state of
goodness beyond the usual good–evil opposition.

Murdoch's stress on the importance of proper seeing as the
beginning of the way out ('There is a magnetic centre. But it is
easier to look at the converging edges than to look at the centre
itself . . . . I think there is a sense in trying to look': SG 100) is not
unlike the awakening of the Buddha-nature. In an article entitled
'A Christian Perspective of Buddhist Liberation', Roger Corless
suggests that the importance of proper seeing is related to the
wheel image so central to the Buddhist picture of causation
and human existence, and contrasts it with the Christian linear
explanation with its mythological *illud tempus*. Corless says
excellently:

> A wheel does not have a point at which it begins, only a point
> at which one starts to look at it.[33]

Murdoch likewise insists on attention as the starting point for
understanding the real, and corrected vision as the beginning of
that obedience to reality which is freedom. She says:

> the true half of (freedom) is simply a name of an aspect of virtue
> concerned especially with the clarification of vision and the
> domination of selfish impulse.   (SG 100)

This is similar to the Buddhist stress on accurate seeing, without the colour provided by falsifying mind, if one is to proceed from *avidya*, ignorance, to *vidya*, knowledge, to *asamskrta*, the unconditioned state.

Buddhism's coherence and rationality, and the place it makes for proper loving and true seeing, make clear why Murdoch is drawn to Buddhism. Is Murdoch really a Buddhist, first and last, in spite of the fact that only one novel out of the six considered here has a Buddhist at the centre?

There is no doubt that both Murdoch's method of realising Christ, as well as the content, the realised Christ, are really within the Eastern spiritual tradition. Her Christ comes to represent an interior state of mind identical with the rich silence and stillness of Hindu–Buddhist meditation. Christ is experienced within this tradition, and this affects both the method of attaining him and the 'thing' attained. Brendan's understanding of the need to destroy the person, both human and divine (HC 159), points to a Buddhist encounter with the ultimate. Such an encounter requires silence; such quiet sees the self dissolve, and of such a state one can say with equal accuracy that this is emptiness, or that it is a state filled with Christ.

A close look at the process set going by Brendan Craddock shows a movement, unencumbered by images, towards James Arrowby's sort of inner stillness. With Anne, Christ returns, but from now on, the realisation of that Christ is through patient waiting (William Eastcote); white inner light (Stuart Cuno); and peaceful, dissolving mental mist (Jenkin Riderhood). The white fog, white mist and white light used to suggest the inner centres of the two last-named figures, indicate meditative states of a positively charged blankness, what might be called a plenum void. This is *sunyata* or filled emptiness. If Stuart and Jenkin, working outward from such a source, are spoken of as if they are Christ, then clearly Christ is being gradually identified with such a state of consciousness. The link with Buddhism is inescapable.

Close affinity undoubtedly exists, but the presence of Christ and the whole weight and emotional colouring of the Christian tradition haunt Murdoch's imagination too closely for the Buddhist impression to dominate. She is a Western writer who, having trained Buddhism's clear, dry light upon Western thought, reinterprets the Western world more richly to itself.

To begin with, humility, essentially a Christian virtue, figures predominantly in her picture of the good. She says:

The good man is humble. . . . Humility is a rare virtue and an
unfashionable one and one which is often hard to discern. . . .
In fact, any other name for Good must be a partial name; but
names of virtues suggest directions of thought, and this direction
seems to me a better one than that suggested by more popular
concepts such as freedom and courage.   (SG 103)

This is unmistakably Christian. The Hindu–Buddhist tradition does
not give humility this degree of emphasis. The path to self-
realisation undertaken here by the self alone leads to a powered
release, not to loving surrender and endless humility as in the
Christian. To be sure, this is power over oneself. The truly
enlightened one will give up all kinds of usable power released by
control of the self, as discussed in a later chapter on James Arrowby.
But it is power, nevertheless, leading to an unconditioned state,
asamskrta, a state of boundless freedom.

To the Christian this is not the essential picture. His salvation
comes through a humble embrace of pain and willing submission
to it. Roger Corless says:

The Buddhist concentrates on the misery of the world only to
escape it himself and to help others to escape it. He does not
descend transformatively into the suffering as the Christian can
descend into the depths of the desolation of the dying God–Man
and make of that very desolation his *Te Deum Laudamus* with the
blessed in heaven.[34]

An embrace of suffering based on faith in its purifying power
differentiates the Christian from the Buddhist who steps aside
from the suffering through thought and self-control.

Finally, Murdoch's acceptance of mystery is ultimately Christian.
Her picture offers no complete and rational explanation of the
world's density, or of good's compelling power. She says:

A genuine mysteriousness attaches to the idea of goodness
and the Good. This is a mystery with several aspects. The
indefinability of Good is connected with the unsystematic and
inexhaustible variety of the world and the pointlessness of virtue
. . . Good is mysterious because of human frailty, because of the
immense distance which is involved. If there were angels they

might be able to define Good but we would not understand the definition.   (SG 99)

Such resting in mystery is Christian. The Buddhist does not ultimately rest in mystery; he rests in enlightenment. The ecstasy on the face of the Buddha in Buddhist art derives from mind, reason, intellect; it is a clarified, rational ecstasy. The most significant moment in the life of the Buddha is the moment of illumination under the Bodhi tree, whereas the most significant moment in the life of Christ is his surrender on the Cross: 'Into your hands I commend my spirit'. It may be noted here that in *Henry and Cato*, Brendan, on the eve of his departure for India, speaks of the temptation of thought, of the possibility of some great illumination, and says that when such illumination comes, it is bound to be an illusion. What would he have had to say of the Buddha's illumination?

While Murdoch wholly enters the Buddhist tradition and values and retains some of its key concepts, the dominant backdrop is Christianity. This is because, in the work of a Western writer writing about the Western world, allusions to the life of Christ carry denser and richer implications. Actually, she has it both ways. She applies the supreme validity of Eastern spiritual insights to the supremely beautiful life of Christ. Finally, then, in the world of disorder her novels evoke, if there is any kind of narrative pattern offered, it is that of the life of Christ. This does not bind or unify the whole novel; it is merely one strand among many, but the only one that shines. It strikes the attention not only because it is beautiful but because it makes an assertion of values in a wheeling world, and offers, in a subterranean way, a point of rest; and thereafter, a way, a path. The fact of transcendence is suggested by this one pattern, and her presentation of it makes a simultaneous vertical and horizontal movement in which the upward and outward extensions are dialectically united. There is no doubt, however, that the horizontal, outward extension, the placing of Christ unrecognised in the ordinary world, is the only way of bearing witness to the transcendent good. Christ stands as the source of other streams because he lived out this loving extension of himself with the greatest intensity and to the farthest limits. His existence, the historical fact of his life and suffering, are crucially important because goodness can have no meaning without being enmeshed here and being recognised, without loving and knowing pain. He is important as an example of pure suffering because he loved and suffered in such a way that he broke through the dark extremities, releasing light. Flashes from that great good figure – of which five of the six studied here are pale shadows – affirm a totality of light, of goodness that exists.

Christ, then, is Murdoch's great example in the novels under consideration in this present study. Different stages in the interpretation of this example have been traced, and the question must now be asked whether the handling has been just and convincing. I believe there can be no doubt about the acute understanding Murdoch has of the process needed to retrieve religious meaning. She moves gradually from a questioning of the orthodox view to a finely-tuned presentation of contemporary Christian faith by way of a thorough demythologising. Of Brendan Craddock, Anne Cavidge, William Eastcote, Stuart Cuno and Jenkin Riderhood, the first three good figures mark successive stages in a progressively clarified understanding of Christ, and the last two figures present the new clarified picture without any direct reference to Christianity, the good figures themselves standing in for Christ. The chapters that follow spell these out in some detail.

These last figures of good carry an unquestionably Christian message in their voluntaristic activity among and for others. Speculation (Brendan) gives way to simpler thought (Anne), which in turn yields to a quiet patient and recollected be-ing (William Eastcote). The next phase is a resolution to act and a beginning made (Stuart); and finally, an unconscious acting out of loving concern (Jenkin).

A question arises. Why has she not taken the final agony and abandonment head-on, as it were, subjecting her Christ figures to the final pain? Jenkin's accidental death may be not only a comment on the indifferent and levelling tendencies of the present time, but also a refusal to tread romantic ground. Possibly, she skirts the issue because the final dereliction and suffering lead to romantic drama, breeding, as Brendan says, beautiful images which distract attention from the moral centre. That is, while Christ's death is the extreme manifestation of the loving good, contemplation of it in art turns it into something else. It must be known, understood, imitated, but not talked about, brooded over, or *presented* by the artist. Christ as venerated object distracts attention from the task at hand. Murdoch's wholly good person combines Mary and Martha in himself. Stuart and Jenkin represent such a combination. Both have their secret, white places of interior light, yet go about the daily round, the common task.

Apart from the pattern shown by Christ and the Buddha, her novels provide no narrative unity in the light of which we can tell our own stories to ourselves. None of the settings-out, overcomings, exchanges and pairings in the later novels provide structural assurance. On the contrary, there is a disturbance at work undermining such structures. Henry and Colette in *Henry and Cato* are possibly the 'happiest' of the lot, but the possibility of an undercutting irony has already been mentioned. Gertrude and Tim in *Nuns and Soldiers*, despite the tenderness and understanding following the classic ordeal, posit a question-mark. If this is happiness, it has a touch of the tawdry. Charles Arrowby in *The Sea, the Sea* is left stripped and alone; the minor figures who pair off die in explosions or survive disaster somehow. Tom McAffrey marries Hattie in *The Philosopher's Pupil*, but after the prolonged revelation of horror, muddle, aridity and near-madness, they provide neither comfort nor hope. In *The Good Apprentice* Midge goes sadly back to her husband, and in *The Book and the Brotherhood*, all possibilities are thrown wide open, even as the partners settle down temporarily with each other. What makes the whole picture so unsettling is that Murdoch is writing black comedy; no tragic deaths affirm any value or stand. She makes deliberate ironic play with conclusions, calling all into doubt even as she closes. There is a deliberate rejection of closure; nothing makes the pattern intelligible.

This introductory chapter may come to a close with the observation that the deliberate ambivalence of Murdoch's assertions is inextricably mixed with her moral vision. Is she a teacher? Yes, but not in any simplistic sense. Her consideration of the inexhaustible variety of the world and the questioning that goes with it are supremely moral. The ambiguity is part of the morality, for truth resides in the coming together of contradictions, in the dialectic between them. This explains why the overall impression is disturbing; why her critics complain of incoherence. Coherence and form militate against the multiple nature of the world, its extreme untidiness.

In *A Fairly Honourable Defeat*, it comes as a surprise to see that Tallis lives in utter disorder and squalor. The description of his filthy kitchen is one of the most unforgettable things in Murdoch's work. Julius, on the other hand, is obsessively clean and tidy; he rolls up his sleeves, washes the milk-bottles, scrapes the surfaces, and tidies up. Tallis's mess is indicative of his letting people go free; Tallis's mess is a *moral state*; it has to do with proper loving. Julius's arrangement and order indicate his will to arrange and order people.

In *Henry and Cato*, the dismemberment of Brendan's flat is, as Conradi remarks, an indication of his spiritual readiness.[35] Rugs, velvet curtains, books, even the Spanish crucifix, must all be got out of the way to make way for complete dispossession and emptying.

Finally, in *The Book and the Brotherhood*, Jenkin in his neat, ordered room, is indicative of a farther stage, when loving, cleansing actions are no longer linked with manipulative moves. The good figure has at last earned the right to order.

But meanwhile, the Tallis-state, excluding nothing, is the only way of being close to the truth. Murdoch's novels project a related, non-excluding, non-simplifying picture of the world. They suggest a way out of the chaos, the path of selflessness and love, but they do not minimise the surging darkness around.

Ultimately, she is a novelist of faith, not because she subscribes to any set of beliefs, but because you cannot posit an ethics of love without faith. She sees the world outside, its rhythm and flow, its huge expanses and its million-pointed details. She knows what, in this darkness, the human being is – selfish, deluded, driven by anxiety, and subject to chance. But she also knows what he is not, yet; she knows what he can be. Here is a vision in the darkness. That clear, loving and attentive gaze turned on the world is an act of faith.

2

Brendan Craddock in *Henry and Cato*

Brendan Craddock, a Roman Catholic priest in *Henry and Cato* (1976), is the first of the six figures who form the subject of this study. It is appropriate that the exploratory process should begin with the most traditional of religious frameworks. The good to which Fr Brendan Craddock has openly dedicated his life is the old anthropomorphic God; he has a name and is a person. Brendan is a representative of the rich mystery in which religion generally shrouds its truth, but his exchanges with Cato, also a priest in the same order, indicate the beginnings of a progressive demystification. With each successive novel after this one, the governing idea of good is increasingly pared till it reaches a stage of unselfconsciousness and simplicity that would be hard to surpass.

I

Murdoch establishes a connection useful but not ultimately necessary, between God and good. She defines God as 'a single perfect transcendent, non-representable and necessarily real object of attention', (SG 55), and sees this as a source of good because attention properly directed to God as its object helps to check the mechanism of the ego. As explained in Chapter 1, Murdoch's idea of good involves a dying to self, a seeing of the world outside as clearly and accurately as possible without the ego's intervention. God, if properly regarded, is a vitally powerful source of good, since he draws the attention away from self and redirects it to the world outside the self. On the other hand, the image of God can easily degenerate in the unguarded believer's mind and lead to romantic self-absorption.

Murdoch is concerned, in the religious aspects of this novel, with both possibilities. One of the key words in her definition of God is 'transcendent'. At this stage in Murdoch's thought, good thought and action derive energy from some invulnerable, higher source beyond the empirical horizon.

The impingement of such a reality on the ordinary, everyday consciousness and the complexity inherent in interpreting it aright are both suggested symbolically in an unforgettable scene midway through the novel. Elizabeth Dipple has commented on this but it can bear closer scrutiny.[1] After his decision to leave the priesthood, even at the very moment of pressing his discarded cassock into the rubbish tip, Cato sees, hovering above the Mission, a kestrel. His rich friend, Henry, has seen it earlier on a visit to Cato at the Mission, and its association with Christ is lightly established early in the novel. It is worth remarking that Henry in that earlier scene, compares the waste land near the Mission to the end of the world. Henry speaks first:

> 'I came across a place like the end of the world. I saw a hawk there.'
>   'A hawk?'
>   'Yes, a kestrel.'
>   'Symbol of the Holy Ghost.'
>   'Your familiar.'
>   'One does occasionally see hawks in London.' . . .   (HC 71)

This exchange between Henry and Cato occurs after years of separation, and the kestrel and land references, suggesting between them a different order of reality, serve to establish the distance between the religious and secular domains. The kestrel near the desolate Mission suggests Christ, a recognition made explicit through Cato's reference to the Holy Ghost. Henry's reply, 'Your familiar', implies that Cato's being haunted by the Holy Spirit places him in another stripped world, which wealth-laden Henry simultaneously admires from afar and lightly mocks. Cato's remarks that one does occasionally see hawks in London only emphasises the fact that usually one does not, and indicates the extraordinary nature of religious experience.

The kestrel reappears at that interesting moment when Cato dumps his cassock into the rubbish tip. This time, Cato's sighting of the kestrel and his reaction to it underscore the inescapability and poignancy of Christ as *kerygma* or proclamation in a person's life. Here is the passage:

No one had seen him. He dusted off his hands against each

other and began to walk across the waste ground. Then he saw
the kestrel. The brown bird was hovering, a still portent, not
very high up, right in the centre of the waste, so intent yet so
aloof, its tail drawn down, its wings silently beating as in a cold
immobile passion. Cato stood looking up: There was no one else
around upon the desert space where already, after the rain,
upon the torn and lumpy ground, spring was making grass and
little plants to grow. The kestrel was perfectly still, an image of
contemplation; the warm blue afternoon spread out behind it,
vibrating with colour and light. Cato looked at it, aware suddenly
of nothing else. Then as he looked, holding his breath, the bird
swooped. It came down, with almost slow, casual ease, to the
ground, then rose again and flew away over Cato's head. As he
turned, shading his eyes, he could see the tiny, dark form in its
beak, the little doomed, trailing tail. 'My Lord and my God' said
Cato. Then he laughed and set off again . . .   (HC 205)

This passage is saying several things at once through metaphor
and allusion. The reference to Hopkins' kestrel in 'The Windhover'
is unmistakable. Cato watches the kestrel, holding his breath with
the same absorption as Hopkins ('My heart in hiding stirred for a
bird/The achieve of, the mastery of the thing'). His utterance 'My
Lord and my God' evokes the shades of St Thomas the Apostle
and St Augustine.

The religious association clearly established through these echoes
is undermined, however, by 'the tiny, dark form in its beak, the
little doomed trailing tail'. Coming after this, 'My Lord and my
God' takes on an entirely different meaning. It can now be an
exclamation of horror. If the kestrel is Christ (Hopkins' Windhover),
the tiny creature is – what? the doomed human being? Or is the
tiny, suffering creature Christ? The whole theodicy problem – how
to reconcile the terrible crimes and disasters of this creation with a
God who is both almighty and loving – is offered through the
deliberate confusion created by the kestrel.

The reader's instinctive reaction of horror to the tiny creature
and the doomed tail calls into question the interpretation of Christ
as hunter ('*Orion* of light' is Hopkins' phrase in *The Wreck of the
Deutschland*). If the kestrel is Christ, then the dismembering of the
surrendering believer is the supreme good. But there is no beauty
here; and the shock of the creature in the kestrel's claws indicates
that to accept the experience of being hunted and rent apart as the

greatest good is the most difficult thing in the world, a reality not to be endured for long. That at the level of contemplation it may be beautiful is indicated by Cato's spellbound gaze as the kestrel circles and swoops. But at the level of experience, it is sheer pain, provoking a 'My Lord and my God' expressive of horror. Did Hopkins and doubting Thomas and St Augustine choose *not* to see? If they had seen, would it still have been possible to speak of the sparks that fall then being a thousand times lovelier, as Hopkins does? May Thomas's utterance as he placed his hand in Christ's side be read as horror rather the acknowledgement of divinity? That Cato is aware of all this is indicated by his laughter as he walks away. The absurdity and falseness of religious rationalisation strike him at this point. The kestrel scene, with its multiplicity of meanings, simultaneously affirms and casts doubt on transcendent reality. There is ironic play on traditional religious interpretation, but concurrently, the scene suggests powerfully what is to happen to Cato, the extreme pain through which he has to relearn (if he ever does or can) what it is to accept Christ.

II

While Brendan is the crystalline realisation of the Christian under-standing of good, he can be fully appreciated and understood only in the light of Cato's conversion and subsequent loss of faith.

Cato is a priest who is mistaken in his apprehension of God and good, and the contrast between him and Brendan serves to clarify the dangers and opacity in an enclosure (the religious order) judged by the world to be automatically good or absolutely absurd.

The question, what exactly is meant by the religious experience, has to be asked, not only because this is an age 'without God', but also because religious experience needs endless reliving at the experiential level, and endless clarifying so that the theological terms do not remain at the level of mere words.

William James in *Varieties of Religious Experience* describes religious feeling as an enchantment not rationally or logically deducible from anything else, an 'absolute addition to the subject's range of life'.[2] There are some persons for whom religious ideas cannot mean anything whatsoever – good people, but incapable of imagining the invisible, or of surrendering to a certain kind of feeling. Emotion is the *sine qua non* of the religious experience (though not necessarily of the religiously regulated life). Not being accessible through the senses or through the reasoning intellect, an unseen reality can be real only at the level of feeling. The genuine religious experience requires a certain kind of imagination and susceptibility, and it generates a clearly higher joy in the presence of which other considerations pale.

John Forbes, Cato's father in *Henry and Cato*, is an example of the wholly rationalistic mind which dismisses the religious experience as madness or sickness. His astounded incredulity at his son's conversion and the degree of his incomprehension are pinpointed so as to emphasise the inwardness and non-explicability of such an event. He is an endearing figure, but the touch of comedy surrounding him makes the inadequacy of such rationalism quite clear. John Forbes has, for all his intelligence, missed out on something immensely significant.

The real nature of this immensely significant experience unfolds through the Brendan–Cato contrast and through what happens to Cato. How would Brendan have handled the crises that overtake Cato? Considering that question helps us to see the true nature of good within the Christian religious context. Religious conversion through which another, higher reality ingresses into the ordinary, requires thereafter a difficult process of unselfing. The examination of this difficulty through Cato's 'failures' is especially interesting because it occurs in a religious order which takes such unselfing as given, as an automatic process.

To the outsider such a choice and such a life seem touching, possibly admirable, but also absurd. Why absurd and why touching, and why is Cato the priest necessary to Beautiful Joe, Henry, and even Colette?

Absurd in the present context because God, as Vorgrimler says in 'Recent Critiques of Theism', is unnecessary as a hypothesis for explaining the world; he no longer occurs in the area of empirical experience, of this-worldly values and the utilisable;[3] but also touching because scientific rationalism, though it seems to have the last word, is dumb when confronted with the problem of human existence. Man finds even now, and often to his surprise, a hunger in himself to be more serious, the sort of impulse that drives the sceptical Larkin into churches just to look around. The inexplicability of the human personality haunts his mind. It is conceivable that psychology may uncover as many mysteries about the mind as the physical sciences have about the external natural world, and God may eventually become unnecessary to explain even this particular mystery, but he will continue to linger through the question of the *why* of human existence. Finally, Cato the priest is necessary because the celibate priest is, for the laity, even the unbelieving laity, a *sign* of important transcendent realities, of the possibility of holiness and purity; he is a guarantee that these exist somewhere, at least for others, if not for ourselves.[4]

Insufficiency or incompleteness makes man regard the world, at least sporadically, in a different light, and attempt a move towards the beyond, hoping for the possibility of completeness or satisfaction in some otherwhere, or in a transfigured *here*. Iris Murdoch, taking full account of such longing, shows through Cato how it may be mistaken and diverted, and through Brendan how it may be corrected and transformed so that it does not 'run after itself'.[5]

The role of emotion in the religious life is explored through the character of Cato to demonstrate both its indispensability and its dangerousness. Cato Forbes, carefully nurtured by his rationalist father, is subject to a striking and sudden conversion which comes with no warning whatsoever. He is not 'a sick soul'; in the middle of a golden summer vacation, relaxed by an animal happiness, and absorbed in his historical studies, Cato is struck as if by lightning. His healthy rationalism, his at-homeness in the world, and the excellent understanding he has with his father are carefully sketched, so as to stress the overwhelming nature of the experience. Without reason, he is invaded by Christ, and with a sense of tumult, melting and crisis, he passes from one order of reality to another.

The account of conversion in William James's *Varieties of Religious Experience* throws some light on what happens to Cato. Speaking of the mental fields which succeed one another in the consciousness, James says that the centre is determined by a person's set of interests. The margin, however, is indeterminate, and images stored in this hazy region may enter the central field and alter it altogether.[6] Why such a shift should occur is inexplicable. Cato's conversion experience fits in perfectly with such a description. The vivid nearness of the image of the Trinity, the loss of all worry, the certainty of perceiving truths not known before, the change the world appears to undergo, all point to Cato's 'assurance-state' to use James's terminology. Cato, as Brendan remarks later, falls in love with Christ.

What exactly is one to make of Cato's experience? The language used to describe it suggests that the author is inclined to believe that it has a kind of genuineness. Murdoch's account touches on the experience without irony and with delicate inwardness. The superiors in his order, while recognising that revelation can come to some, treat it with suspicion and detachment, warning him against excessively exalted states and his 'too devotional Christianity'. The point is: does this happen to Cato because he has, in James's terms, 'pronounced emotional sensibility', 'tendency to automations', and 'suggestibility of the passive type', and are these therefore wholly subjective, private, quasi-hallucinatory experiences? Or does 'God speak' to Cato through his aroused 'subliminal consciousness', and what does that mean?

There is no clear answer. The only answer given is 'maybe'. Brendan, most intellectual of beings, asks Cato to remember that *'something happened'* during his conversion. When emotional Cato says in despair, 'there is an intellectual conclusion, there must be', it is Brendan who asks 'why must there be?'. That is, the mystery is accepted by Brendan even while it is questioned, taken apart and thrown away by Cato who actually experienced it. The saintly Fr Milsom accepts Cato's experience when he writes to him:

> 'do not mistrust the revelation that led you to God. You saw him then in a clarity and with a gladness that is denied to many who are holy.'   (HC 178)

The deliberate ambivalence playing over the presentation reinforces the 'maybe' of the answer. The religious superiors were, as mentioned above, suspicious at first, but Fr Milsom's letter validates the experience later. The tenderness of the prose describing the actual conversion-experience is at odds with the novel's implicit warning against unreliable romantic emotion. The intellectual Brendan rests in the mystery; emotional Cato presses for a clear 'A or not-A' conclusion. The image at the close of the novel is of a Cato who has left the order, but is carrying a crucifix. Such ambivalence implies the need to locate truth in an in-between region, to shift back and forth and step outside so as to see more clearly. The watchfulness and discipline epitomised by Brendan seem almost inadequate in the face of Cato's blackness and the events through the novel constitute the severest critique of Brendan's affirmation. His authenticity is wrung out of the situation.

The disastrous direction that Cato's 'too devotional Christianity' will take is indicated in the text by the use of a simile involving the Platonic myth of the cave:

> He entered quite quietly into a sort of white joy, as if he had not only emerged from the cave, but was looking at the Sun and finding that it was easy to look at, and that all was white and pure and not dazzling, not extreme, but gentle and complete; and that everything was there kept safe and pulsating silently inside the circle of the Sun. And what was so strange too was that this new grasp of being came to him quite clearly identified as an experience of the Trinity. The Trinity was the Sun, so white and complete and when you looked straight at it so thrillingly alive and gentle.   (HC 29)

The danger signals are already there, a warning against too rapid an ascent out of the cave into the light of the sun. In Plato's myth (Book VII of *The Republic*) Socrates says that the prisoner liberated from the cave is distressed by the glare of the light from the sun – that is, the good:

> And if he is compelled to look straight at the light, will he not have a pain in his eyes which will make him turn away to take refuge in the objects of vision which he can see, and which he will conceive to be in reality clearer than the things which are now being shown to him?
>
> True, he said.
>
> And suppose once more that he is reluctantly dragged up a steep and rugged ascent, and held fast until he is forced into the presence of the sun himself, is he not likely to be pained and irritated? When he approaches the light his eyes will be dazzled and he will not be able to see anything at all of what are now called realities.
>
> Not all in a moment, he said.
>
> He will require to grow accustomed to the sight of the upper world. And first he will see the shadows, next the reflections of men and other objects in the water, and then the objects themselves; then he will gaze upon the light of the moon and the stars and the spangled heaven; and he will see the sky and the stars by night better than the sun by day?
>
> Certainly.

Last of all he will be able to see the sun, and not mere reflections of him in the water, but he will see him in his own proper place, and not in another; and he will contemplate him as he is.

Certainly.[7]

Plato's sun is the good; the point here is that the good can be seen only with effort and patience by those who have been accustomed to the firelight in the cave. Cato's experience points to the fact that what appears as dazzling truth, if not properly attended to, may turn out to be yet another shadow cast on the wall.

Murdoch's own stand, if such a word can be used of something that has frequently to shift in order to be true, can be guessed at through the remark about Cato's easy and happy gazing at the sun. In this case, either it is not the sun, or Cato is looking at it through the protecting glass of his romantic nature. His experience – which he does not dignify with the word mystical – is too closely related to the fluctuations of his emotional life. It must begin there but it cannot end there. It must be related to, but not dependent on the emotions. He learns through the bitterest experiences that the shield has to be smashed to smithereens before he can advance towards the sun.

After some years as a scholastic, and then as a fully ordained priest entirely at one with the rhythm of the church, Cato's faith vanishes as abruptly as it came. After several weeks of doubt that assail him like an illness, he wakes up one morning with the absolute conviction that he has been mistaken and that there is no God.

At the same time that the doubts about God's existence begin, something devastating happens to Cato, and he wonders whether these two things are somehow connected. He falls in love with one of his parishioners, a teenager named 'Beautiful Joe', a cheerful, lapsed hanger-on of the Mission in the slum where Cato works, a highly intelligent, irresistible boy living on the criminal fringe. Joe, who denounces private property and the evils of modern society and claims to be involved with shoplifters and petty larceny, has for Cato a respect and affection laced with sardonic amusement.

Cato never knows where exactly he is with Beautiful Joe, how much to believe and what to disbelieve. With quicksilver speed Joe flashes from one subject to another, and frequently tells Cato:

'you're the only one who understands me, you're the only one who can get through to me'.   (HC 42)

The personal equation begins to matter (more than it should) to Cato. There is a comment:

> What was extraordinary from the start was how easy he found it to talk to Joe . . . . He and Beautiful Joe chattered about the Resurrection, about the Trinity, about the Immaculate Conception, about transubstantiation, about papal infallibility, about Hitler, about Buddhism, about communism, about existentialism . . .   (HC 41)

Cato is happy and relaxed, but the interaction turns gradually into selfish pleasure. He is flattered and touched when Joe tells him that only he (Cato) understands him.

> 'You're the only one who has ever cared for me, Father, you're the only one who can really *see* me at all.' This was irresistible. If this is even half-true, Cato thought, I must stick to this boy through thick and thin.   (HC 42)

Cato makes half-hearted attempts to give up Beautiful Joe and to send him on to Fr Thomas. At one point he has a clear moment of truth:

> He put out the cigarette, thinking clearly for the first time, I cannot help this boy. Our relationship is a dangerous muddle and a nonsense. I must leave him absolutely and for good. I can do nothing for him, nothing. I must say goodbye to him tonight. This is the logical, the easiest moment to do it. It is, oh God, now. No need to make a drama. I must save myself. I must go away somewhere and think. I must go back to some more innocent place where I can see.   (HC 44)

He says so to Joe, but then buckles under pressure, and agrees to see him the next week.

Joe quickly senses Cato's emotional involvement with him and his own power over Cato. When their eyes meet, Cato is the first to look away. Joe now has a weakened Cato to play with. Cato is weakened by his emotional susceptibility and Joe's flattering 'dependence' on him. He will be the vehicle of Joe's salvation;

simultaneously he will love him and *own* him. Cato reiterates to himself the non-possessive nature of his love, but in fact it seeks to bind and hold. Extremely human and vulnerable, Cato's inability to control and check his feelings points to the dangerousness of emotional excess. He has become the victim of his emotions.

It is this, rather than the homosexual nature of the attachment (whatever the church's official teaching on the subject), that is the subject of critical examination. Brendan, Cato's superior, expresses neither shock nor disapproval, and when he tells Cato, 'Stop seeing that boy', he does so not out of prudery or moralistic rigidity but because Cato's loving is too self-involved. The conversation goes like this (Brendan speaks first):

'Stop seeing that boy.'
'I can't', said Cato. He gripped the edge of the door. 'I can't abandon him—'
'You mean you can't surrender this pleasure. Are you doing him good? Is he doing you good?'
'I'm the only person who can save him.'
'I doubt that. There is hope for him of which you do not dream, because you insist that you and only you must be the vehicle. Let someone else have a try. Give this to God. Make a hole in your world, you may see something through it.'
'I can't.'
'You talk about truth – but it seems to me you are being totally frivolous and self-indulgent. It's a dream, Cato, you are only saving him in a dream. In reality—'
'*Stop*', said Cato. He pushed out of the room, and without saying anything more went into his bedroom and shut the door.   (HC 160)

The nature of Joe's fatal attractiveness for Cato, who sees himself as both Joe's lover and saviour, emerges clearly from that conversation. It is a relationship of domination and ownership that Cato seeks, though this he cannot yet see.

The irony is that, through this narcissistic passion, he places himself in Joe's hands, and is dominated by him to an unbelievable degree. When he leaves the order (horrifying Joe who then rejects him with insults), he imagines he is walking into freedom and joy. He finds the opposite. Joe's kidnapping and imprisonment of Cato, his convincing Cato that he is acting for a murderous gang,

demanding first Henry's money, and then Cato's sister Colette –
all this incredible drama becomes possible only because Cato has
become *prey*. Joe's literal imprisonment of him comes only after
Cato has imprisoned himself.

There follows quick action. Cato writes at Joe's dictation to Henry
to bring a hundred thousand pounds, and then again to Colette
begging her to come if she wants him to live. Colette comes like
an arrow; Joe attempts to seduce her; Cato hears her screaming;
with all his might he breaks down the locked door of his room,
brings down a piece of bathroom pipe on Joe's head and kills him.
There is worse to follow. Not only has he killed the boy he loves;
he discovers that there is no gang. Joe was working alone. It
proved all to easy to trap, drug and imprison Cato. Cato was
simply not watchful and careful with himself.

He survives into a living death worse than anything he could
have imagined: there is no God; he has himself killed the boy he
longed to save; worst of all, self-esteem has gone and he is a poor,
ridiculous object of mockery. The punishment is very severe; the
sin was that of 'loving'.

The vision generated by the bare plot, quite apart from the
language, is bleakly existential. To the reader, as to Cato looking
into the darkness, there is indeed no God. Painfully, the learning
process begins after the demolition of the myth. The old anthropomorphic religious belief has to be reinterpreted for him and for us
by Brendan Craddock.

Cato loses his faith, but the kind of faith he held had to go, and
the meaning of faith had to be thrown wide open again. Faith
cannot be a matter of emotion or even intellect alone; it is
understanding and action, to be tested on the anvil of pain and
horror.

Cato's emotional faith turned into a self-feeding, and the *other*,
the real, the good, began to recede. Devotion to God or good
requires unselfing, and Cato did not, at the critical juncture, 'put
on Christ'.

The delicate balance in which emotion is to be weighed and held
suspended is thrown into relief by Cato's ecstatic joys and black
despair. The same consciousness that lovingly and joyfully felt the
reality of Christ's person looks into the blackness and feels with
certainty the absence of God. The point here is that emotion,
because it surges around a personal God, quickly substitutes
one image for another: Joe for Christ. After his first extended

conversation with Brendan, when he abruptly says 'stop' and leaves the room (see above), he sits on his bed, knowing that Brendan is praying for him, wondering why he cannot pray for himself. When he tries, the substitution of Joe for Christ takes place almost unnoticed.

> He did not kneel but closed his eyes and in the darkness called out silently as he had done when he was younger. And he gazed into the darkness and the darkness was not dead but terribly alive, seething and boiling with life. And in the midst of it all, he saw, smiling at him, the radiant face of Beautiful Joe.   (HC 160)

This passage indicates that the image of Christ was held by Cato in what Murdoch has elsewhere referred to as 'the warm, messy empirical psyche' (SG 81). The 'empirical psyche' counts separate images. The image of Christ had seemed to be the repository of truth, but now, when the image of Joe supplants it, 'truth' seems to shift and be relocated here; the earlier picture seems a fiction. When the radiant, smiling face of Joe forms in the darkness,

> everything to do with his belief and his faith seemed to him at that moment flimsy . . . he felt himself confronted with an ineluctable choice between an evident truth and a fable.   (HC 161)

Christ now seems not worth a straw compared with this new certainty. Cato's needs generate his images, as is the case with most of us. Is there a tiny, hard stone of 'the real' in the surge of emotion, and does Brendan show how this may be kept and not swept away again? A painful sense of loss starts to haunt Cato almost as soon as Joe's face supplants Christ's, a sense of lost good. Cato is no longer a believer; things have been settled; only the formalities of laicisation are left; but the pain does not disappear:

> What made him feel that he must be crazy was this: that he had given up the most precious privilege in the world and he could not determine when or exactly why he had decided to do it.
> It has all dissolved, all faded, he thought, trying to find some image of his loss of faith. Had it been some weak substance then, some mere reflecting picture? It has gone, hasn't it? he constantly asked himself. Yes, it had gone, that seemed clear.

But what had he lost? His livelihood, his friends, his mode of being, his identity. But what else, surely something else had gone, surely *the* thing had gone? But the thing is no thing, he thought, is that not the point? What is it that hurts me so, that pains me as if I had committed some awful crime or made some awful mistake? He thought, God is nothing, God the Father, that is just a story. But Christ. How can I have lost Christ, how can *that* not be true, how can it, how can it?   (HC 206)

It gets very much worse for Cato as his passion for Beautiful Joe licking him 'like a flame' leads him from one indignity to another till he kills Joe when he hears Colette screaming. After that ordeal he speaks, with striking clarity, to Henry out of his wretched state:

'All that so-called morality is simply smirking at yourself in a mirror and thinking how good you are. Morality is nothing but self-esteem, nothing else, simply affectations of virtue and spiritual charm. And when self-esteem is gone, there is nothing left but fury, fury of unbridled egoism.'   (HC 326)

There is a relentless logic here. It seems at this point that one can never know in what supreme ordeal the barriers will fall. One is lucky if, like Fr Milsom, one does not outlive the joy of one's faith.

But powerfully established as this point of view is, it is offset by the implication that Brendan (and Fr Milsom) would have handled it differently. Perhaps they, too, fell, rose again, and learned to walk carefully. So too, Cato may.

III

Fr Brendan Craddock is the measure by which all that happens in the novel may be weighed. He defines, with care, the notions of faith, security, freedom, and stands unmoved as witness for the mystery of God. If Cato's experiences point to the inescapability of the finite condition, Brendan points to the inescapability of the infinite condition, of the reality of Christ as a principle of change in human life.

Brendan Craddock incarnates, with devastating attractiveness, a role which declares openly to the world that it is dedicated entirely to good – the good named God. There are dangers built

into this role which militate against its very *raison-d'être*. The chief
of these is power, doubly dangerous because power in more overt
and worldly senses is abrogated in favour of a spiritual power over
the souls of men. Cato's relationship with Beautiful Joe has
an unmistakable strand of this woven in with the emotional
entanglement. An important part of Joe's appeal was to Cato's
sense of his own power to save. Taken beyond a point, it turns
into its opposite and Cato becomes prey or victim. It is instructive
to see how Brendan handles this.

Brendan is Cato's friend and superior in the order, and there
are indications that the relationship is a close one. In every crisis
Cato remembers Brendan even if he does not always take his
advice. When Cato discloses to Brendan that he has lost his faith,
Brendan deals with it without taking a feverish interest. This is
the moment to wield power, but Brendan is detached. The refusal
to expatiate except when absolutely necessary is beautifully brought
out by the apparent off-handedness:

> Brendan came on a flying visit. Cato said to him, 'Oh by the
> way, I've lost my faith.' 'Rubbish.' 'God is gone. There is
> no God, no Christ, nothing.' 'I expected this.' 'You expect
> everything.' 'That darkness comes to us all.' 'I knew you'd say
> that. But suppose the darkness is real, true.' 'Hold on.' Brendan
> went away, then wrote him a wonderful letter, but the darkness
> persisted.   (HC 38)

Later, when Cato's crisis has deepened, and Cato and Brendan
have had a long and purposeless conversation in Brendan's flat,
he tries ineffectively to stop Cato from leaving, acknowledging
openly that he may be mistaken, but pleading with him to stay.

> 'Don't go Cato, It's important that you shouldn't go. I said
> everything wrong. I was tired. I should have waited. Nothing I
> said matters, not the details I mean. May be I'm wrong about
> the boy. I don't know enough, may be everything I said was
> phoney. But don't go away from this. Wait, stay, rest. Forget
> about retreats. I won't say anything to anyone. Just stay
> here.'   (HC 161)

Brendan admits to his powerlessness even at the moment of his
appeal; furthermore, the appeal is made for the sake of something

larger than either Cato or Brendan. That Brendan is 'above' personal reasons in asking Cato to stay, that he does not ask Cato to stay in the order because he wants to hold on to him is evident from the fact that he gives him up at the proper moment. The last exchange between them at the close of the book indicates that the relationship with Cato is more important to Brendan than has yet appeared, and must therefore be renounced. This is a discipline, a way very different from Cato's. Brendan is about to leave for India. Cato speaks first:

> 'So I won't see you before you go?'
> 'No,'
> 'Shall I come and see you in Calcutta if I can raise the money from somewhere?'
> 'Well, better not.'
> There was silence for a moment.
> Cato put on his coat. 'So you're giving me up too.'
> 'I'm giving you up too.'
> They faced each other.
> 'I've always kept you as a last resource', said Cato.
> 'I know. But you mustn't have this sort of last resource. More conversations like this won't help you. What after all would they be about?'
> 'Oh hell' – said Cato.
> 'I'm going, as it happens, the way things fall out, and I probably won't be back, at any rate not for many years. All sorts of things will happen to you—'
> 'Will you write to me?'
> 'I doubt it.'
> 'Will you pray for me?'
> 'Everyday.'
> Cato stood in silence, not looking at his friend.
> 'It's raining' said Brendan.   (HC 374)

Though in the course of the conversation it is Cato who expresses need, Brendan's brief answers suggest something held in check, a disciplining of emotion; an enactment, at the affective level, of directions given by the intellect. Brendan's 'I'm giving you up too' suggests that this is something of a sacrifice. But he sees the danger inherent in playing saviour to Cato, and he steps aside at the right moment. He has done enough for Cato. The rest he leaves to

Christ, a fact clearly indicated by the gift of his beautiful Spanish crucifix to Cato. He had advised Cato to give the matter of Beautiful Joe to Christ; he applies that advice to himself now and acts on it. Disciplined in every sense, he acts, he helps, and though undoubtedly he feels, he does not allow this to interfere with his chosen path of renunciation. He does not make Cato's mistake.

The question whether, being temperamentally different, he is able better to ride the storm, is finally unanswerable. But there is enough textual evidence to show that Brendan too has felt the burden of personality and the trials it brings. He is unsurprised by Cato's confession of passion for Beautiful Joe. His reaction ('The angel with the hexagonal glasses? Don't worry, we all fall for lovely boys') suggests experience and patience with himself and with others. Later, when Cato again refers to his compulsive love for Joe, Brendan quietly replies, 'I understand that'.

Brendan's last and most serious temptation is the intellectual temptation. Addicted to speculation, he admits that he has begun to feel that if he can 'hang on just a little longer' he will receive 'some perfect illumination about everything' (HC 373). He realises that if it does come, it will be an illusion. His going to India is the visible sign of the shift in his understanding, of his recognition of the danger in 'understanding too much'. It may be read as escape, but I am inclined to read it as renunciation. By itself the move cannot prevent the intellectual temptation. Obviously he cannot, by going to India, stop thinking; equally obviously, there will be others there who can lead him on, draw him out along these same paths. But going away suggests the breaking of a circle that has grown too comfortable. The Indian scene implies a different kind of activity from the purely speculative. This is now a mission, a new milieu demanding a different sort of effort. There, Brendan will have to start afresh, will not be known as one of the best theologians in the order.

The last chapter of the novel opens with a scene of Brendan packing, preparatory to departure for India. Commenting on the statement 'The little flat was being dismembered' (HC 368), Conradi remarks that Brendan alone of all the figures in the novel has earned the right to renunciation.[8] Does he mean that Brendan's discipline brings him to voluntary and quiet dismemberment, where Cato had to be taken and torn? Perhaps Brendan himself has learned quietness, patience and loving renunciation through earlier, more violent rendings.

There remains the issue of God and good to whom and to which
Brendan is dedicated. What does Brendan Craddock believe?

Brendan's explanations of God are in line with the demythologising of the old personal God that began in the sixties with such
theologians as Rudolf Bultmann and Paul Tillich. The notion of a
personal God came to be seen as a 'reification and finitisation' and
consequently a reduction and falsification of the absolute which is
God. Bultmann, though refusing to speak of God as a person,
acknowledges that the Word of God calls man out of all man-made
security, and is at once a grace and a summons that cannot be
explained away. Tillich's programme meant the end of theism,
setting 'God above God', preventing him from becoming an object
in faith, or the object of religiosity or theology.

As a Catholic priest, Brendan is surrounded by structures and
images but, like a true priest, he sees beyond them to the reality
of which they are shadows. When Cato in the first conversation
stumbles over the dogma, Brendan replies:

> 'There are worlds and worlds beyond the dogma.'
> 'How far can Christianity go beyond the dogma and still
> remain a religion?'
> 'As far as the human soul extends.'   (HC 156)

Such an answer could come from a Catholic priest only after the
Second Vatican Council of the sixties when Catholic theologians
followed Protestant theologians in seeking a freer, less literal
interpretation of scripture. Brendan's answer to Cato implies that
God's reality is an answer addressed to the seeking human person,
simultaneously enclosing and transcending the personal acts of
man in a way he can *no longer understand*. It is the presence of
mystery, of inexplicable encounters and destinies that affirms a
reality larger than anything grasped by science.

What becomes now of the personal God? Brendan accommodates
and discards him at the same time. If he turns into a restrictive,
excluding force, he may be left behind and no harm done to the
religious soul. But if the believer, in his freedom, feels touched by
his grace, that is real too. When Cato asks him about his belief in
a personal God, Brendan is for a moment silent. Then he says:

> 'That's another picture. We deal in the idea of persons, we have

to. But God is unimaginable and incomprehensible and nameless. *Dyphrastos* and *thaumastos.'*   (HC 372)

This is a clear recognition of the need to leave images behind even in the midst of dealing with images (the Eucharist, the Cross, the Gospel narrative). *Thereafter*, surrender to a person, a name, does not diminish, once the recognition has passed through the screen of the name. Cato grows impatient, and there is an extremely interesting exchange which indicates that Brendan's having it both ways is the only way of approaching the truth.

'But Brendan, do you believe in God or not? I mean, I'm not accusing you of being a fake, you're real and because of you something else is real – but this doesn't add up to God. I mean even you can't invent Him. *Do* you believe in God?'

'It's impossible to answer a question truly unless you know what the question means to the questioner.'

'Oh do stop being subtle. If you don't know whether God is a person what happens to your Christology?'

'I let Christ look after my Christology.'

'You should have been a lawyer. I remember Fr. Bell saying that you were the best theologian we had.'   (HC 372)

Brendan's 'I let Christ look after my Christology' suggests that extreme demythologising, reducing God to a purely subjective, psychological experience, an inner event in the soul or a 'trans-psychological' event,[9] is also a limiting of the boundless and infinite. If he is not an anthropomorphic God Almighty 'out there', alien to man, neither is he only an event in the soul. He is both within and without; he is both nameless and named; contradictory attributes may be predicated of him; only so is the infinite and unlimited to be understood.

One way of expressing this unbounded reality is to say, as Hindu scripture does, *Neti, neti*: not this, not this, i.e. the reality is other than what we can know.

Another way (taken by Brendan here) is to say that he is all these things – and more. He is the resolution of all contradictions; so he is the un-imaged, but he is also Christ. When Cato says that most of religion is pure mumbo-jumbo, Brendan replies, 'Oh yes, of course. But Cato, never mind about reason and intelligence. Just hold on to Christ, the Christ that the Church cannot take away from you' (HC 373). When the point comes for Brendan where he can go no farther in understanding, and when he has gone as far as possible in the rejection of theism, at that point he surrenders to Christ. Only through such openness to all encounters can the human soul recognise the divine.

When Cato says that he cannot, as an intellectual being, believe in God the Father, Son, or Holy Spirit, Brendan asks why he insists on an intellectual conclusion. Cato replies that this is a matter of truth ('If Christ be not risen, then is our faith vain. I mean it's either A or not-A': HC 157). Brendan's counter to this is that Aristotelian damage has to be undone, that if Christ is indeed the stumbling block, then 'we all stumble'. This is the classic argument for the limitations of human reason and for the recognition *by the reason* of something greater than itself, i.e. we are rationally required to acknowledge the supra-rational.

That this is the overwhelming reality is Brendan's grounded belief. In a letter to Cato after that long, futile, earlier conversation, he writes:

> 'It's not so easy to get *out* of that net, my dear, and of course I don't mean the stupid old order or even, *sub specie temporis*, the odious old Church. Fishes move in the sea, birds in the air, and by rushing about, you do not escape from the love of God.' (HC 177)

What makes Brendan such a credible witness is that he does not make light of Cato's doubts. He recognises the impossibility of ever completely understanding, but equally the importance of keeping up the struggle. He continues in the same letter:

> 'I am not belittling your "intellectual crisis". We are intellectuals, we have to undergo these crises, in fact to undergo them is an essential part of our task. We have to suffer for God in the intellect, go on and on taking the strain. Of course we can never be altogether in the truth, given the distance between man and God how could we be? Our truth is at best a shadowy reflection, yet we must never stop trying to understand.' (HC 177)

He is a credible witness because he takes account of different kinds of wrestling, emotional, intellectual, spiritual, and still affirms the impossibility of ever getting out of 'that net'. Just as Cato the priest is important evidence of holiness as a sense datum to Joe, Henry, even Colette, so Brendan is evidence to Cato of something *other*. Cato says to Brendan, 'because of you something else is real'. When men as intelligent, as intellectual as Brendan affirm, in the teeth of analytical philosophy, the reality of a truth that cannot be formulated but must be thought about, the point comes over strongly. He remarks to Cato that thinking about these things is a way of keeping near the truth, even when, especially when, the truth cannot be formulated.

Through him is defined the nature of faith. For Brendan, as for Bultmann, faith in the Word of God means the abandonment of all human security; it thus brings victory over the despair which arises from the always vain search for security. When Cato tells Brendan that his version of faith sounds like despair, Brendan's reply is:

> 'The point is, one will never get to the end of it, never get to the bottom of it, never, never, never. And that never, never, never, is what you must take for your hope and your shield and your most glorious promise. Everything that we concoct about God is an illusion.'
> 'But God is not an illusion?'
> 'Whosoever he be of you who forsaketh not all that he hath, he cannot be my disciple.'   (HC 374)

Brendan's remarks here are closely related to Bultmann's desperate 'nevertheless' which acknowledges God despite the actual circumstances of life. Bultmann says:

> faith can become real only in its 'nevertheless' against the world. For in the world nothing of God and his action is visible or can be visible to men who seek security in the world. We may say that the word of God addresses man in his insecurity and calls him into freedom in his very yearning for security.[10]

Brendan's faith is akin to Bultmann's existential interpretation of God. Despair itself becomes the reason for hope and faith; the absence of God *is* the presence of God; that is, thus to feel his absence is to be in his presence. Brendan's 'never' is Bultmann's 'nevertheless'. The impossibility of finding meaning is an argument for faith, for to find ultimate meaning is to reduce, diminish and falsify.

Thus Brendan, from the heart of the most mythologising, image-buttressed of Christian sects, propounds a demythologising which denies every longing for security in the manner of Bultmann who says:

> He who abandons every form of security shall find the true security.[11]

Is Brendan dispensing altogether with theism? Though he dispenses with images one by one as he thinks his way through, he ends with an image and a name:

> 'I let Christ look after my Christology.'

With the emotional evocation of a name, colour comes flooding back, and Brendan's rich Catholic mystery once again takes over. At this stage in Murdoch's exploration, there is a critique of theism but no rejection. An irreducible theistic core remains.

The narrative closure of the text makes the religious implication inescapable. Having left the order, Cato at the end is a sign pointing to the unparaphrasable reality even more significantly than he was at the beginning, robed in a cassock, set on saving Beautiful Joe from himself by throwing his gun into the Thames. Cato has none of the old belief left, but the regular banging at his knee of the Spanish crucifix given him by Brendan is a reminder that he is, albeit unwillingly, a christopher – a carrier of Christ. Brendan has made the mystery intelligible, even inevitable.

So much for the apprehension of a magnetic good, called here Christ, modifying the human personality in a deep way, from a 'beyond' which cannot be grasped through the intellect or senses. The *implications* of such a modification in the here and now are spelt out by Brendan in his first extended conversation with Cato:

> 'Christ isn't a sort of once-and-for-all pill that you take. He's a principle of change in human life—And a human life takes a good deal of changing. "Not I but Christ". Your complaints seem to be all I and no Christ.'   (HC 158)

One may ask *why* Christ is seen as a principle of change in human life. He need not necessarily be so. It is, after all, possible to contemplate the idea of good as a concept without being changed. Murdoch sees this as unnatural, unusual. Only such a singular and exceptionally strong figure as Julius King in *A Fairly Honourable Defeat* can know about good and resist its transforming power.[12] Such untransformed, resisting knowledge seems to go against human nature, is seen as diabolic and exceptional. Despite the blackness of her dark world, Murdoch's view of human nature is not, at bottom, wholly pessimistic. If only men can be awakened, made aware; if only they can allow that awareness to work on and change the given mechanism, there is no option but to be good. Sin is a matter of selfish ignorance; a terrible drag, but not insuperable.

Brendan's articulation of Christ as a principle of change raises moral-ethical questions which have always been linked with religion. If good has been perceived through an encounter with God, it somehow follows that it must affect, or even more, *alter* one's life. Good action follows from apprehension of the good; it is taken for granted that such an apprehension involves transformation.

Change consists of unselfing, the death of the ego. Clearly, Murdoch sees the selfish self as the repository of all that goes wrong in a life. Easy enough to take in as a concept, unselfing is extraordinarily difficult and complicated. The self enters in subtle, unrecognised ways to assert itself over and over again till the moment of death. To work forever, without respite against one's own interests is a formidable and frightening task. Brendan says:

'the ego in you is appalled. It's like a death sentence. It *is* a death sentence. Not pain, not mortification, but death. That's what chills you. That's what you experience when you say there is no one there. Up till now you have seen Christ as a reflection of yourself—It has been a comfortable arrangement.'

'Really—!'

'You are in a dream state. Ordinary human consciousness is a tissue of illusion. Our chief illusion is our conception of ourselves, of our importance which must not be violated, our dignity which must not be mocked. All our resentment flows from this illusion; all our desire to do violence, to avenge insults, to assert ourselves. We are all mocked, Christ was mocked, nothing can be more important than that. We are absurdities, comic characters in the drama of life, and this is true even if we die in a concentration

camp, even if we die upon the cross. But in reality there are no
insults because there is nobody to be insulted. And when you
say "there is no one there", perhaps you are upon the brink of
an important truth.'

'I don't understand', said Cato.

'You say there is no one there but the point to be grasped is
there is no one here. You say the person is gone. But is not the
removal of the person just what your own discipline as a priest
has always been aiming at?'

'Well – the human person—'

'And if the human person is the image of the divine?'

'This is philosophy.'

'It's theology, my dear fellow . . .'   (HC 158).

This dense and difficult exchange, necessary for an understanding
of Murdoch's religious position, tempts one to agree with Conradi's
remark, made to me in conversation, that Brendan is really a closet
Buddhist. What he says here is derived unmistakably from Zen
Buddhism, and is not unlike the spirituality of J. Krishnamurti,
both of which stress the blocking nature of the ego. From this self-
importance or 'status' arises the need to be fed with praise and
protected from mockery. All hurt and resentment, all desire, all
plans for change and 'liberation', flow from this assertive and
important ego. If the death-sentence is passed on this ego, then it
does not matter whether we are mocked or glorified. As Brendan
says, there are no insults because there is nobody to be insulted.
It is to that self that Christ died; so his humiliation on the cross
and his glorification make no difference since the self that would
have experienced those things was destroyed. Such an interpretation has nothing to do with traditional Christianity; the Christ of
this dying and this silence comes from the Eastern religions which
state that what seems real is a tissue of illusion or *māya*.

Not his assumption of role as redeemer but the annihilation of
the ego, then, is the meaning of Christ's death upon the cross.
This is a frightening prospect; we may well ask, *what then*? If the
self dies and nothing that mattered to that self matters any more,
where do we go from that point? Murdoch does not push the
argument further here, but the pointers indicate *nirvāna*, total
release, unimaginable freedom. The slaying of the self upon the
cross – supremely illustrated through Christ – brings freedom.
Released from self-centred conditioning, consciousness is freed.

Cato, chained down by his need for Beautiful Joe, is far from even knowing about this freedom. He sees his choice of leaving the order and going away with Joe as an exercise of freedom. He tells Joe,

> 'I've made myself free of everything else so that I can be with you . . . Surely you want to be free and happy?'   (HC 212)

Instead, he is bound, literally imprisoned by Joe in a dark basement, and his understanding of freedom turns out to be self-defeating. Bultmann says of freedom:

> Genuine freedom is not subjective arbitrariness. It is freedom in obedience. The freedom of subjective arbitrariness is a delusion, for it delivers a man up to his drives, to do in any moment what lust and passion direct . . . *Genuine freedom* is freedom from the motivation of the moment; it is freedom which withstands the clamour and pressure of momentary motivation.[13]

That erotic love contains very large narcissistic elements is a point Murdoch makes over and over again.[14] Cato's case is of special interest because it begins as filial or charitable love, is invaded by the erotic, and is unable to transform itself once again into non-erotic loving. Brendan, by contrast, appears capable of transforming and purifying emotion of its self-regarding aspects. In this process the vocabulary of negative theology is relevant; dark experiences orientate the soul to the cross, and a consequent emptying follows. Brendan tells Cato that he 'fell in love' with God, and then continues:

> 'Falling in love is egoism, it's being obssessed by images and being consoled by them, images of the beloved, images of oneself. It's the greatest pain and the greatest paradox of all that personal love has to break at some point, the ego has to break, something absolutely natural and seemingly good, seemingly perhaps the only good, has to be given up. After that there's darkness and silence and space. And God is there. Remember St. John of the Cross.'   (HC 370)

Cato, we are then to understand, failed to clarify the nature of love. In what sense then is this God, who dwells in love, who *is* love, radical transforming love, to be understood, and what exactly is Cato's failure? Murdoch clearly distinguishes between pathological love and love which is concern or compassion without reference back to the self (SG 75). Cato, unlike Brendan, is unable to keep the boundaries clear. He confuses what *seems* to be the supreme and only good with the supreme good itself. Robert Johann, as noted in the notes to Chapter 1, distinguishes between love as an emotion and love as a task, and remarks that 'love as an emotion or a felt attraction for some particular good is an insufficient guide for the total orientation of our lives.'[15]

The blanket word 'love' is used in English to cover quite different affective extensions, and it is possible that the linguistic factor is partly responsible for the confused response. Sanskrit, by contrast, has different words for the different responses: *Shringāra, Vātsalya, Snēha* connote desire, loving-kindness, affection. The different words may themselves generate distinct responses which are distinctly recognisable. The word 'love', on the other hand, promotes the overflow of feeling from one category into another, so that the experience itself remains richly shadowed and unclear. When we are commanded to 'love' our neighbour, it is not at once clear that we must do so in a strictly practical, helpful way. The love mentioned in connection with the disciple whom Jesus 'loved', for instance, suggests only an intensification of the emotion mentioned in the commandment to love our neighbour. The glorious inclusiveness of the word may be at the root of Cato's troubles, making it difficult for him to see and label clearly exactly what it is he feels.

However, it is the infusion of *love* into the notion of duty, or practical help for one's neighbour that characterises the Christian response, and it is exactly this warm feeling that makes it simultaneously beautiful and potentially dangerous. The egotistical element here has to be carefully separated.

Brendan's arguments circle round the crucial issue of the ego. He tells Cato that his guilt and unhappiness after his killing of Joe are further manifestations of the hard ego:

> 'Your guilt is vanity, it's to do with that self-esteem you were talking about, which you haven't really lost at all, it's only wounded. Repent, and let these things pass from you.' (HC 371)

It is at this nadir that Cato's real experience of God can begin. God is a *deus absconditus*, and his actions do not appear to be identical with our notions of the providential, or with visible events, but Cato's suffering can lead to renewal and greater purity than he has yet been capable of. When Cato says bitterly, 'I feel damned. I loved that boy and I led him astray and I killed him', Brendan replies, 'We live by redemptive death. Anyone can stand in for Christ.' That is, the pain of this experience may lead Cato towards greater authenticity, and by effecting this, Beautiful Joe now dead, can play a redemptive role.

All this can be read as colossal rationalisation, an attempt to keep man from raging at the universe. Good is located in the non-raging, the quiet, clear-eyed and loving acceptance of things as they are and as they happen, and above all in selflessness and 'invisibility'.

Invisibility is the condition to be aimed at. Brendan, when asked by Cato how he came to God and religion, replies that he had the advantage of growing up with a saint, his mother. 'She was the sort of saint no one ever notices or sees, she was almost invisible.' Invisibility, or near-invisibility, is the criterion because that alone proclaims the death of self. Rather, it *manifests* the death of self, for invisibility and proclamation mutually exclude one another. True humility proclaims nothing; it is merely itself and must go, as far as possible, unnoticed. Brendan, though he is clearly a figure of good, is far from unnoticeable. On the contrary, he is strikingly noticeable, but by refusing to nourish the self, he has started out along the path. At this stage, with these friends, the only way to be invisible is literally, physically, to remove himself from their sight. He knows, through the memory of his mother, the kind of discipline required, and his willed removal from his centre is his recognition of the need for effacement. In another milieu – India – he may be less in control of situations and people, or such will be the case at the start, at any rate; and with watchfulness he can prevent his self-importance from growing.

Brendan's mother is the type of the saint – one so quietly unselfish that no one sees. Perhaps only Brendan saw; the fact that he seeks to emulate her is an indication of the visibility of the almost-invisible. Unnoticed by the world, she has still passed as an example. Iris Murdoch says in *The Sovereignty of Good* that unselfish mothers of larger families are likely to be those in whom most good resides (SG 53). There is less opportunity for the self here to wish or desire; all must go into furthering the well-being of others. For a religious missionary like Brendan the path is more tortuous. The chances of intellectual battening and of social role-playing are greater. The very fact of priesthood, being set apart, bestows a sense of the special which may be inimical to humility. As Murdoch turns these issues over in successive novels, she points increasingly towards invisibility and unselfconscious devotion to good. Jenkin, the last in this series, is the nearest to the type she envisages. Brendan, the first in this study, is wonderful, perhaps too wonderful; a beautiful figure, the epitome of moral and spiritual charm. The emphasis grows gradually more puritan as the trappings fall away, the anchorite carries his cell into the actual world, and eventually gives up even the idea of a cell. Brendan is at the head of this process of denudation.

However, though he is an expounder of the *via negativa*, he needs his images. It is these that feed the soul and help it to turn to the good. God, in a sense, is an image of the good. At the level of day-to-day life, within this religious structure, prayer is the means of turning away from self. As *attention* to a source outside (petitionary prayer being a childish stage to be quickly passed through), it purifies the ego. Brendan says to Cato: 'prayer is the most essential of all human activities; it should be like breathing'.

Brendan stays within the structure even while being fully alive to its odiousness because it provides a design, a pattern which acts as pointer and example. The figure of Christ exercises a power over him which he cannot explain. Even as he practises dying to himself, he freely acknowledges loving attachment to this force outside himself called Christ.

3

James Arrowby in *The Sea, the Sea*

The novel that followed *Henry and Cato*, while dealing with the same middle-class section of the same Western world, explores it from a different angle, through the perspective of a religious tradition alien to the Western mind. Iris Murdoch in *The Sea, the Sea* has turned to the Buddhist explanation of reality and explored the meaning of good there. Good in this context seems related to a particular state of consciousness, one which has freed itself from attachments of all kinds; learned to let go what the thrusting ego seeks to grasp; sees accurately; is then free of pain, and ready to enter compassionately the world outside itself. The self-abnegation leads not merely to a psychological state of liberation but has moral–ethical dimensions as well since the path to that liberation lies through moral codes. In setting James and Charles Arrowby in a Buddhist frame of reference, this chapter will regretfully have to leave out a great deal of the novel's richness – its superb characterisation, its sharp stylistic control and much else – but it may serve to emphasise Murdoch's inwardness with Buddhist thought. The actual references to this in the novel are confined to the fact that James Arrowby is a Buddhist, to a few remarks about *nirvāna* and the wheel of rebirth, and some mention of Buddhist relics in James's flat. The extent of Murdoch's projection of Buddhism becomes startlingly clear only when one realises that Charles's journal (which comprises the novel) is itself an example of the delusion recognised by the Buddha and out of which he showed a path. The entire work is a brilliant and extraordinarily sustained account of *samsāra*, the manifested, contingent world as it presents itself to the agitated consciousness. Charles Arrowby's journal is a striking illustration of the falsification of unawakened mind reacting to the world of phenomena.

I

James Arrowby, though seen through the distorting glass of
Charles's journal, is an example of one whose Buddha-nature has
been awakened, one far advanced in the long journey from
unreality to reality and clear vision. James's significance can stand
out only if placed against Charles's unawareness. If there were no
ignorance there would be no enlightenment, according to the
Buddha. Elizabeth Dipple persuasively argues that James is as
much, or even more, of a tragic failure than Charles.[1] While it is
true that James's use of magical power and Tibetan brand of
Buddhism indicate a movement away from the stringent simplicity
of Buddhist teaching, I propose that James be seen as the *opposite*
of Charles, as the example of the 'realised' soul, one of the most
striking figures of good that Murdoch has created. He may lapse
momentarily, but to have shown a perfected James would have
brought him dangerously close to the delusions of the unenlightened mind. To think that one is enlightened when one is not is a
sign of *avidya* or ignorance. It is enough that James is shown as a
guide, a pilgrim, an example.

Both Upanishadic and Buddhist thought maintain that there is
in every human consciousness, and in all that lives, an element by
which the soul may enter into an immedate relationship with the
Absolute. If it does not do so it is because, resting in a state of
ignorance, *avidya*, it mistakenly concentrates on the individual self-
centred self. This is the root of all delusion and evil for the
Buddhist. Proper seeing is prevented by selfishness; and that
which is uncompounded, whole, one, is seen as composite,
multiple, fragmented – *samsāra*. More sustainedly than any other
character in the Murdoch canon, Charles Arrowby displays a
demented, often unconsciously hilarious preoccupation with his
own needs, desires and compulsions – *his* success, *his* women, *his*
pain, *his* house, *his* tower. To be thus attached is to be bound to
samsāra, the manifested world of experiences, to be reborn again
and again, immersed in *samsāra-sāgara*, the ocean of existence, or
samsāra samudra, the sea of existence.

The title of Murdoch's novel, *The Sea the Sea*, has an added
significance in the light of this Sanskrit phrase. Dipple has commented illuminatingly on the title taken from Valéry's *Le cimitière marin*.
Another reading of the symbolism of the sea suggests unconfined,
unordered experience; all that lies outside and presents itself to

the perceiving consciousness; the whole, random, contingent
world. The Indian mind has instinctively spoken of that through
the metaphor of the sea – hence *samsāra sāgara*, or *samsāra samudra*
(*sāgara* is ocean and *samudra* is sea). The sea's endless change-
lessness, its very great beauty and its dreadfulness, its unvarying
indifference to beings who view it from the shore, and the way it
remains itself through its infinite changes – these things make it a
natural symbol of the inexhaustibility of life. *Sāgara* is really a great
sea, an ocean, a connotation released by the repetition in the title,
suggestive of huge expanse and limitlessness.

While the phrase *samsāra sāgara* has passed into common speech
in the Indian languages, it is worth noting the reference in the
Buddhist *Itivuttaka* to *samsāra* or life as 'this ocean with its sharks,
demons and fearsome waves'. Again, a verse in the *Samyutta
Nikaya* describes the ocean as life thus:

> whosoever conquers the impulses arising from the data peculiar
> to each of the six senses, has crossed over the ocean with its
> waves, and whirlpools, its sharks and demons.[2]

Demons and whirlpools figure in *The Sea, the Sea* in a crucial
way, and are seen to be the products of restless *manas* or mind,
most specifically Charles's mind. His fall into the whirlpool, Minn's
Cauldron, and his rescue by James, take on distinct symbolic
significance. Charles reflects later:

> that fall into the sea did damage me after all, not with body
> damage, but with some sort of soul damage . . . (SS 496).

James, in his first exchange with Charles says, 'The sea, the sea,
yes'. While the repetition suggests awe, the 'yes' at the end of the
phrase modifies Valéry's 'La mer, la mer, toujours recommencée',
and introduces a note of understanding, even of control, not mere
unmitigated wonder. James, far advanced on his own spiritual
voyage, is fully aware of what is involved. He comes close to the
ideal described by the Buddha in the *Dhammapada*:[3]

> For whom there exists neither the hither
> nor the farther shore,
> nor both the hither and the farther shore,

who is undistressed and unbound –
him I call a *brāhmana*.   (Dh. 26:3)

Titus, who also utters the phrase, 'the sea, the sea', drowns in it. This is suggestive of the indifference of the sea of life to those who cross it or contemplate it, who sink or swim. Crossing the sea comes with understanding and control; with the heightening of these, the hither and the farther shores vanish, there is no crossing to be done, no whirlpools or demons – only the undistressed, unbound consciousness, an unconditioned state, *asamskrta*.

Such a freeing is the ideal. More ordinarily, the individual self reacts to *samsāra* by attaching itself to objects within that sea. In doing so, it becomes discriminating, separating mind. This is *vijñana*, or the notion of separateness. This is a fetter to be cast aside in the soul's long journey from the dark state of *avidya* to the light. The Buddhist doctrine of *vijñanavada*, or Mind-Only, asserts that all phenomena are falsely taken to be real by discriminating mind. The first verse of the *Dhammapada* says:

Mind precedes all unwholesome states
and is their chief; they are all mind-wrought.   (Dh. 1:1)

The relevance of such an explanation to *The Sea, the Sea* becomes clear when Charles's journal is seen as revealing the workings of his frenzied mind. Charles emerges from his journal as an impossible man; possessive, mistaken, hugely egotistical. He sees things in his own special light; and the reader, uncertain at first, soon learns how unreliable he is as observer. The reinterpretation the reader has continuously to make of Charles's account relentlessly underlines his distorting perspective.

The crisis in *The Sea, the Sea*, Charles's abduction of Hartley, is precipitated by his mind, and his speculations concerning various figures and events show its busy activity as it passes from one point to another. The interior monologue in stream-of-consciousness novels is usually intelligibly related to things in the outside world; but not here. In this novel, the discrepancy between the record in the journal and the truth grows gradually clear to the reader, and Charles's interpretation of things illustrates sharply the Buddhistic notion of the mind's falsifying tendency. It is difficult to demonstrate this through quotation since the whole work exhibits the process. A summary of the book, however, must serve to suggest the frantic disturbance within Charles Arrowby.

The novel consists of Charles Arrowby's journal presented as a first-person narration without authorial comment. From this we learn that he is a famous theatre director, who, having announced his retirement from the theatre, comes to Shruff End, a house by the sea. Through his journal we learn about his obsessive attachment to a childhood sweetheart Hartley, his accidental rediscovery of her, now an old woman, in this seaside village, and his attempt to abduct her and live happily ever after in the never-never land of a recaptured golden time. He tells us of his innocent childhood in a protected, loving milieu threatened only by the black cloud of his cousin James, richer, cleverer than himself, seen as eternal rival in a jealous competition for the world. Jealousy of James blackens Charles's sky. It is worth noting that Hartley is the one thing he did not share with James in a childhood of shared holidays and humiliating comparisons. Is that a reason for her being such a fixation in his life?

Charles discovers with a shock that the 'old creeping bag' of a woman seen in the village is indeed his first love, now ordinary Mary Hartley Fitch living with her husband in a pretty house named Nibletts. Ignoring the passage of the past forty years, he frantically schemes and plots to tug her out of her marriage, and hold her to himself. As he works out his plans in his house by the sea, men and women from his past begin to appear; Rosina, whose marriage to Peregrine he wrecked; Lizzie, who loved him with tenderness; Gilbert, who would have liked to be his lover; Peregrine, whom he hurt; finally, James. In not a single one of these relationships has Charles seen the freedom and value of the other. No more now does he respect the ageing, stout Hartley as he pesters her to come to him with a maddening, infantile persistence. Complications are introduced with the appearance on the scene of Titus, her adopted runaway son rejected by her husband because he wrongly suspects him to have been fathered by Charles. As Titus comes seeking Charles to find out if he is indeed his father, Charles puts out his tentacles and draws him into the situation, using him as a decoy to lure Hartley to his house. He holds Hartley captive in his house for a few days. Titus drowns in the dangerous sea against which Charles, vainly not wanting to be thought timid and old, has not warned him. Ben and Mary Hartley Fitch emigrate to Australia, Rosina remarries Peregrine, Lizzie re-establishes her peaceful sexless menage with Gilbert, James quietly dies after pulling Charles out of a whirlpool in the sea, and Charles is left alone.

No retelling can capture the impression of Charles's violently agitated mind, jumping like a monkey from branch to branch, wholly self-centred as it records the minutiae of its jealous fantasies and plots. He himself says: 'as for self-centred, of course I am pursuing my own interests here and not just altruistically hers' (SS 206). He suspects everyone and everything, buzzing from thought to thought like an infuriated bee. On no evidence whatsoever, he concludes that Ben Fitch has pushed him into the whirlpool when Ben was not even present on the scene.

Because the reader is made to stand outside and see through the web of Charles's deceiving imagination, the journal brings triumphantly into being a wholly mind-created, falsified world. The Buddha remarks:

> Because of this ignorance people . . . become attached to a whole body of delusions . . . A single picture is capable of an infinite variety of details. So the human mind fills in the surroundings of its life. There is nothing in the world that is not mind-created.[4]

A tiny illustration of specific delusion from this novel which projects a whole pattern of delusion is Charles's misapprehension of Freddie Arkwright, 'a chauffeur whom I once had when I was a grandee and who regarded me with rancorous hatred'. He turns away uneasily from his memory, a fact referred to more than twice. When the man finally appears at the end of the novel, the truth turns out to be the opposite of Charles's imagined fears. Far from being a hated demon in Freddie Arkwright's mind, he has unknowingly been a beneficent angel all these years. The man thanks him because his association with the famous Charles Arrowby has helped him to an acting career in the theatre (SS 457). Charles's apprehensiveness, entirely without foundation, is evidence of the shrinking, self-protecting ego living in a cloud of pain.

The delusion in this instance is relatively unimportant and soon dispelled; it is small enough for the encounter to re-enter Charles's life and be seen for what it is. In all his other relationships, most of all those with Hartley and James, he does not emerge till the end from the state of *avidya* because his mind's selfish preoccupations darken the horizon of his seeing. Despite Hartley's rejection of him, Ben's rudeness to him, and the strong structure of their long-tested marriage, Charles still thinks in terms of *rescuing* Hartley.

> There was a kind of dreadful violent leaping ahead in this thought, as if I were being powerfully jerked by something which already existed in the far-off future. Hatred, jealousy, fear and fierce yearning love raged together in my mind. Oh my poor girl, oh my poor dear girl. I felt an agony of protective, possessive love, and such a deep pain to think how I had failed to defend her from a lifetime of unhappiness. How I would cherish her, how console and perfectly love her now if only . . . (SS 158).

In moments he seems aware of the wrongness of his action in confining Hartley to a locked room.

> What was I doing, or rather what was happening to me? I held my head in my hands. I was totally vulnerable and helpless. I had lost control of my life and of the lives with which I was meddling. I felt a dreadful and a terrible fatalism; and a bitter grief, grief such as I had never felt in my life since Hartley had left me so many years ago   (SS 310).

But this momentary awareness is not enough to break the darkening machine of his self-regard, and the next morning he is as adamant and blinded as ever. Even at the very end, when the light of truth shines a little more continuously, he lapses into mistaken and crazy speculations that James has not really died but gone underground as an intelligence agent.

Shocking and maddening as it is, Charles Arrowby's threshing consciousness is sufficiently similar to the daydreaming ego to be recognised as universally present. Charles is devastatingly credible; this is everyman's consciousness exposed without mitigation so that the *avidya* in which it exists may be thrown into sharp relief, and the falsifying tendency of the uncontrolled mind clearly recognised. What he is, we all are, except the saints.

It might be added that he has a highly cultivated mind. He loves Shakespeare and describes at length his discovery of Shakespeare, his love of Shakespearian women, his Prospero-like part near the sea. This love of Shakespeare seems at first to sit curiously and uneasily on his frantic view of things. Shakespeare has not really modified Charles himself; all that beauty and insight have been

taken in by the expert director but have not altered the essential
Charles Arrowby. The whole issue of Charles and Shakespeare
illustrates again the self's obstructing nature even in the presence
of the greatest art. Charles's absorption of Shakespeare is not
superficial; it seems rather to be one of the deepest things in his
life; to judge him as unresponsive to the best is to underestimate
Charles's devotion both to the theatre and Shakespeare. But the
ego determining his devotion separates and falsifies, so that his
great productions of Shakespeare are, as he himself says, his way
of shouting back at the world and unproductive of moral lessons.
Shakespeare cannot teach Charles because Charles does not want
to learn.

Murdoch suggests through this the great difficulty of shifting the
ego that crouches on its haunches in the human consciousness.
Nothing but extremity works here. Would Charles have learned
anything even from James if Titus had not drowned, Hartley
gone away, and James himself died? It is only when faced with
irrecoverable failure, when all possibilities of consoling fantasy have
been closed, that Charles begins to see. After these events have
chastened him, Charles can respond to Shakespeare differently.
The point to be stressed here is that the *state* of the consumer of
art has to be purified and prepared for the total and proper
receiving of art's great messages, and such a preparation demands
humility. Charles is humbled and disciplined by events; thereafter,
Shakespeare's magic turns to illumination (SS 482). But in the
interim he mistakenly assumes a god-like role even while he allows
possessive yearning to sweep over him.

> I wanted, in the time that was left to us, to console her as a god
> consoles. But I also wanted increasingly, and with a violence
> which almost burnt the tenderness away, to own her, to possess
> her body and soul   (SS 186).

Avidya or ignorance prevents the individualising self from knowing
that the object of our desire can never be possessed in any
real way. The consequence is suffering. For the darkened, ignorant
mind, all is suffering. *Sabbe sankhāra dukkha*. The Buddha says:

> Birth is suffering, decay is suffering, disease is suffering, death is
> suffering, association with the unpleasing is suffering, separation

from the pleasing is suffering, not to get what one wants is suffering.[5]

Dukkha, suffering, takes in discord of various kinds, feelings of incompleteness and discontent, and pain of all sorts. Charles's journal is a self-absorbed threnody of pain for what he has not had. He speaks of the powerful pain-sources and says 'the image of Hartley changed in my mind from fiery pain to sadness but never became quite blank'. He is tormented by figures who resemble her a little, and by the thought of her dead. Before he comes upon her in the village he remembers her thus:

> A little while ago the thought came to me that she was dead. That strange pallor, those dilated pupils: perhaps these were presages of disease, of some quiet killer biding its time? Perhaps really she died long ago when I was still young? In a way I would be glad to know that she was dead. What would my love do for her then? Would it peacefully die too or be transformed into something selfless and innocent? Would jealousy, the jealousy which has burned even in these pages, leave me at last, and the smell of fire and brimstone fade away?
>
> Even now I shake and tremble as I write. Memory is too terrible a name for this terrible evocation   (SS 86).

In his interaction with others in the course of the book, Charles either suffers himself (as with Hartley or Ben), or makes others suffer (as with Lizzie or Peregrine). It is an extended scene of tension and unease, of *dukkha* of all kinds.

Of course, Charles has moments of pleasure or exultation, but they occur against a background of anxiety and knowledge of change. The factors that compose them pass away rapidly, reinstating *dukkha* as the dominating backdrop. His selfish moments of 'joy' are either momentary (his fantastic and fastidious delight in food), or exclusive and separative, turning quickly to pain. For instance, after his meeting with Hartley in the church, he places his hands on the pew where hers had been and asks himself anxiously what he is going to do, how he will manage himself for the rest of his life now that he has found Hartley again. Moments of unselfish joy – the sublimity of the starry night, for instance – are truly joyful and always available, but Charles's selfish anxiety prevents him from rejoicing often and long in things outside himself. The very next morning his never-resting thoughts about Hartley had taken over, and he unrealistically looks for a letter from her. When he tries to remember his feeling as he looked at the stars, he finds the memory already fading. By ten o'clock he is once more outside Nibletts where Hartley lives.

Dukkha or pain, then, is omnipresent because of the ignorance in which the ego, dominated by falsifying mind, attaches itself to people, power, fame, money, whatever, and suffers with their passing away.

Dukkha is caused by craving or selfish desire, *tanha*. If Charles could let Hartley go, if he did not crave to possess her, he would not suffer pain. His hatred, anger, and malice are only aspects of his desire, his desire for the disappearance of displeasing objects or creatures. The pain-clouded anxiety through which we see what happens in *The Sea, the Sea* is the direct outcome of his attachments. Hartley is the central attachment and therefore the greatest pain-source; but all his other entanglements are sources of pain. Whether he thinks of Lizzie, Rosina, Clement, Doris, Jeanne, Gilbert, Peregrine, even his beloved dead father, he feels pain. Charles is clearly prey to *tanha*. This *tanha* has, as its direct cause, sensation or *vedana*, and as its direct consequence, appropriation or *upādana*. From these are born the various forms of suffering, disappointment, regret and torment. Charles provides an accurate illustration of precisely this state. His sensation leads to desire, which leads predictably to his *appropriation* of Hartley. He cannot rest till he has bodily appropriated her and kept her against her will.

The force of such attachment and Charles's utter inability to accept the truth reach a climax at the end. Hartley has been returned to her husband, they have bought tickets to emigrate to Australia, and have a dog whose quarantine period is a subject of comfortable worry. They invite Charles to tea, tell him their plans, offer him cucumber sandwiches and cake, but he cannot accept this indestructible, cosy domesticity. Even as the door is being shut on him he tells her she cannot go to Australia; he will not let her go, and so on. Obdurately, amazingly, the mind persists in not seeing what is clearly there and creating instead an imaginary picture. For days after this tea-party he still hopes she will return, to the extent that when he has to leave the house for short periods, he leaves a note, *Wait. Back very soon*, in case she comes to him. The effect is simultaneously comic and sad. Only the incontrovertible evidence of her empty house, the neighbour's pitying gaze, and the news that Hartley has sent her a picture postcard from Sydney convinces him she has indeed gone and will never return; indeed had never intended to return.

Through bitter lessons he will have to learn the nature of the truth and the good. Characteristically and mistakenly, he identifies Hartley with the good. In a mockery of the Beatrician vision of Dante's mind, forever haunted by the good glimpsed in childhood, Charles's thoughts circle around Hartley.

> We would have become one and the holiness of marriage would have been our safety and our home forever. She was a part, an evidence of some pure, uncracked, unfissured confidence in the good which was never there for me again   (SS 84).

Not his love for Hartley, but his grasping desire to have and to hold generates torment. The passage quoted above may be fruitfully placed beside the teaching of the Buddha on precisely this point:

> Birds settle on a tree for a while, and then go their separate ways again. The meeting of all living beings must likewise inevitably end in their parting. Clouds meet and then fly apart again, and in the same light, I see the union of living beings and their parting. This world passes away and disappoints all hope of everlasting attachment . . . It is therefore unwise to have a sense of ownership for people who are united with us as in a dream – for a short while only and not in fact. The colouring of their leaves is connate to trees, and yet they must let it go; how much more must this apply to the separation of disparate things.[6]

The impermanence of all things, of even the obsessed conscious-ness, is called *anicca*, a concept related to the Heraclitean flux. Everything is in a state of change, constantly being built up, torn down, and renewed in an endless process. Charles's folly in pursuing a phantom Helen takes on a fresh dimension when towards the close, she begins to recede. The *idée fixe* of a lost Hartley who must be recovered starts to fade like the memory of the night of stars. Things are not as sharp and clear as they once were; when he asks himself what he has really been after, he cannot remember because the mad emotions have passed away. This is what he thinks at the end:

I cannot now remember the exact sequence of events in those prehistoric years. That we cannot remember such things, that our memory, which is our self, is tiny, limited and fallible, is one of the important things about us, like our inwardness and our reason. . . . Now my brave faith which said, 'Whatever she is like, it is her that I love', has failed and gone, and all has faded into triviality and self-regarding indifference; and I know that quietly I belittle her, as almost every human being intentionally belittles every other . . .   (SS 492)

Because of his long and stubborn refusal to recognise mutability, Charles's coming round to such a view of things illustrates *anicca* or impermanence very sharply.

Images of *anicca* or impermanence have been beautifully and explicitly articulated by Charles himself as he writes of the life of the theatre:

one lives out in a more vivid way the cyclical patterns of the ordinary world. The thrill of a new play, the shock of a flop, the weariness of a long run, the homeless feeling when it ends: perpetual construction followed by perpetual destruction. It is to do with endings, with partings, with packings-up and dismantlings and the disbanding of family groups.   (SS 36)

This is beautifully and self-consciously written. The difference between knowing these things with the cognitive and aesthetic faculties, and actually letting them colour one's deepest self is born out by the whole novel. He speaks of perpetual constructions and perpetual destructions, but he cannot let go of the psychical structure in which he keeps Hartley till it is smashed and broken utterly.

II

It is against such a background of the darkened, unrealised self that James Arrowby's significance as a figure of good emerges. Charles and James, taken together, present the Buddhist world-picture. James throws light on the nature of *saṃsāra* and points the way. André Bareau describes the Buddha's understanding:

the Buddha was aware . . . of the non-convergence of ideas of the world and things in it, which are very different to what they seem to be when presented to our senses and to our mind, especially in the case of matter which the mind believes and grasps at, which is then shown to be no more than an illusion resulting from our imperfect means of cognition. The objects of human desire (which condition most of our activities) are therefore no more than shadows, and not solid and lasting creatures such as we think them to be; this difference between reality and appearance is one of the main causes of distress and suffering because of the deceptions it evokes.[7]

This throws light on the James–Charles contrast, and our first encounter with James serves to lighten a little the stifling effect of Charles's journal. He is quiet and reasonable, and his remarks are immediately recognisable as good and true. As a Buddhist, James recognises that the world of phenomenal things – things that have become: *yathā-bhūtham* – is not to be mistaken for the real, which is one and which is without attributes. He knows that personality or *ātma-bhāva* is but one of the manifestations of the world of becoming; it must be seen for what it is and not given more than its due. When Charles tells James in their first exchange that he has met Hartley, that she has been and is his only love despite the numerous women in between, that he will rescue her and make her happy, James introduces notes of reason and good sense:

'. . . you may be deluding yourself that you have really loved this woman all these years. Where's the proof? And what is love anyway? . . . I cannot attach much importance to your idea of such a long-lasting love for someone you lost sight of so long ago. Perhaps it's something you've invented now . . . your rescue idea is pure imagination, pure fiction. I feel you cannot be serious. Do you really know what her marriage is like? You say she's unhappy, most people are. A long marriage is very unifying, even if it's not ideal, and those old structures must be respected. You may not think much of her husband, but he may suit her, however impressed she is by meeting you again. Has she said she wants to be rescued?'   (SS 178)

Such a tone and words, recorded verbatim by an angry Charles, come as a relief after the nerve-jangling pressure of Charles's presence. One instantly recognises the reasoned, reasoning voice of the good.

James's relatively cleansed mind and his break with selfish concern is indicated, as critics have noticed, by his openness to the world outside and his love for the particularities of nature. This in Murdoch is always a sign of virtue. The contrast between such an outward-looking habit and Charles's turned-in gaze is brought out in the following exchange. James speaks first:

> '. . . I must come and see your seaside house and your birds. Are there gannets?'
> 'I don't know what gannets look like'.
> James was silent, shocked.   (SS 175)

There are other comments on shags, choughs, curlews, and oyster-catchers, again contrasted with Charles's ignorance – he confuses shags with cormorants. Ignorance at this level nicely suggests the general *avidya* in which his consciousness lives. An interest in anything outside the self is a path to virtue. James has already traversed these stages along the road.

The *quality* of such interest introduces or bars the entry of virtue. Charles certainly knows about Shakespeare, but James's knowledge of birds is more restful and non-obsessive. The birds he observes are not swallowed up by his consciousness; they remain outside. Whereas Shakespeare (except at the very end) is absorbed and used by Charles to aggrandise his own importance. Or even when not directly so used, his preoccupation is narcissistic, as when he declares himself to be in love with Shakespeare's heroines.

James, through his words and actions, shows how one may learn to free oneself from delusion through proper attention and control. Charles's state mirrored *dukkha*, pain caused by craving. Freedom from pain is won by eliminating selfish desire, and this in turn can be done by following the noble eightfold path, the *āriya attānghika magga*. The points of the path fall into three main categories: (1) morality or *sila*, (2) mental discipline or *samādhi*, and (3) wisdom or *panna*. Morality includes right speech, right action and right livelihood. Mental discipline includes right effort, right mindfulness and right concentration. Wisdom includes right thoughts and right understanding.

In the course of examining James as a follower of the eightfold path (nowhere mentioned in the novel) it is important to remember that it is an integrated path; one aspect is not taken up first to the exclusion of others; and while James may falter in one or other area, striving in the many prescribed directions sets him once again on the path. He has more trouble with the mental discipline aspect of it than with anything else, and even here, it is a little uncertain whether he 'fails' because he uses 'magical' powers, or whether he simply proceeds afterward to a high level of understanding where he sees psychical processes as hindrances and then discards them.

It seems probable that there is no serious regression; instead, an evolution and growth upward.

At the moral–ethical level (*sila*) James clearly has little difficulty. He is sufficiently developed and controlled, in marked contrast with the others, with Peregrine, for example, or Rosina, certainly with Charles. The rightness of his speech has already been mentioned. It has a naturalness and reasonableness which are unmistakable. As for right action, he shows how firm he is here when he persuades Charles to release Hartley, organises the expedition, and personally escorts Hartley back to her husband. Right livelihood in James's case has been a career in the army. When James turns professional soldier, his parents, who had hoped for great things from him, are disappointed, but Charles feels 'obscurely cheered' because he senses that James has taken a 'wrong' turning, and almost immediately afterwards goes on to speak of his own 'will to power' in the theatre and his dazzling success there (SS 64). Without making too much of it, army life with its emphasis on discipline and obedience may be seen as a preparation for the self-control and inner freedom that James seeks.

In the matter of ethics, *sila*, then, James has done well. The other five points, spanning the mental discipline (*samādhi*) and wisdom (*panna*) categories, have to do with the more evolved aspect of personality. To consider him in the light of these five aspects of the eightfold path it is necessary to recall what Charles records of his past and his conduct in the present.

Charles draws a clear picture of James's childhood: comfort, privilege, joy, a happy home and adoring parents. Yet he takes what the world sees as a 'wrong' turn and is lost from view for years in India. The renunciation of privileges for which his early life has been a preparation, and the going away to India play out, very remotely, the classic renunciation of worldly pleasure and the disappearance from view for several years of Gautama the Buddha.

He left the palace as Prince Siddartha; he returns as the Buddha or enlightened one.

Murdoch can hardly have been unconscious of the parallel when she introduces James into the novel as one who is enlightened about the nature of good. In a shadowy way, James is a buddha of sorts himself, as indeed anyone may be. What we get here, however, is Murdoch's critical understanding of the Buddhist ideal and the dangers besetting the pilgrim on that road.

The chief of these dangers, as noted by Elizabeth Dipple and Peter Conradi, is the assumption of power by a mind grown powerful through self-control, so powerful that it can use magic for its (good) purposes. Murdoch probably portrays James as a Tibetan Buddhist because Tibetan Buddhism, of all the schools, is the one most closely bound up with magic and sorcery, having absorbed elements from the magical practices of the indigenous Bonpas as well as from Hindu Tantric practices. It is a shock to read of the relics in James's flat, bits of feather and stone stuck together and the like. These magical practices have little to do with the stringent austerity of Theravada Buddhism. James is clearly no superstitious follower of ritual. On the contrary, he is an enlightened figure, so far advanced in the control of mind, that he can use it in a remarkable way, and is tempted so to use it. Knowledge is power, and while there is no prohibition in Buddhist thought to eat of the Tree of Knowledge, there is a clear recognition that the power that comes with control and knowledge must be carefully watched. A verse in the *Dhammapada* says:

> A blade of *kusa* grass wrongly handled
> cuts the hand; asceticism wrongly practised
> leads downward, to hell.   (Dh. 22:311)

This is what James means when he tells Charles, 'White magic is black magic'. The power for good that comes through self-control and understanding can easily be used to feed the self's needs, to manipulate people and situations.

The fact of James's being a Tibetan Buddhist (initially puzzling to the Indian reader) makes sense in the light of Murdoch's remarks (in an interview on BBC Radio's *Kaleidoscope* in 1978) that the novel is about the dangerousness of the road to goodness. The magical practices of Tibetan Buddhism are the strongest, most concrete way of representing the dangerousness of powers acquired by the mind through meditation. Buddhagosha in 'The Path to Purity' speaks of the five miraculous powers that come through meditation; becoming invisible, knowing the thoughts of others, diving into the earth, floating like a bird on the wing, and walking on water. When Charles at one point asks James whether he is meditating, James replies that if he were, he would be invisible. Also, he seems to know other people's thoughts. When Charles goes on and on about his being sure that Ben must have pushed him into the whirlpool, James very quietly and firmly says that it was not:

'I *know*. I know it wasn't Ben.'

The intensity of James's tone, his eyes and his fierce face carrying conviction are recorded by Charles's resisting mind, but he cannot help wondering, 'How could he *know* this?' James's power is illustrated seconds later by his simply saying 'Peregrine', at which point Peregrine confesses that it was he who pushed Charles in. The most striking instance is, of course, James's walking on water when he rescues Charles from Minn's Cauldron, the whirlpool into which he has fallen. Buddhagosha's account of this power got through meditation says:

He walks on water without sinking into it. This is done with the help of the earth device which begins with a contemplation of a disk of clay, and which allows him to transform into hard earth as much of the water as he has marked off.[8]

Charles finds that his note, written in weariness on the night of his rescue, records just such a feat:

I must write this down quickly as evidence, since I am beginning to forget it even as I write. James saved me. He somehow came right into the water. He put his hands under my armpits, and I felt myself coming up as if I were in a lift . . . But he was not standing on anything. One moment he was against the rock as if he were clinging on to it like a bat. Then he was simply standing on the water.   (SS 468)

Add to this James's strange hold over Titus who, meeting him for the first time, feels he has seen him somewhere, perhaps in a dream.

All this makes it very clear that James's practice of magic is deliberately being underscored to emphasise the power of asceticism. It should perhaps be stated at this point that the demonology which haunts *The Sea, the Sea* is again a way of illustrating the power of mind, both unenlightened and enlightened. The sea-serpent that Charles sees and the mysterious breakages in his house are related to Charles's own agitated and falsifying mind. Similarly, James's miracles are to be seen as the power of purified, enlightened mind.

Ascetic practice liberates immense power and the question here is whether it can be legitimately used. Elizabeth Dipple's conviction is that this is an abuse and corruption,[9] and James's own admission in his last exchange with Charles bears this out. Charles's uncomprehending Western reactions set off perfectly the deep seriousness of James's realisations. He explains that religion is power; that true ascetic religious practice can bring about change in oneself, can destroy the self, but that this power is a great temptation. He is referring indirectly to himself. He has himself yielded to the temptation of using his power to 'restore' Titus to his grieving mother and to 'save' Charles from death. The question is whether this exercise of power has been 'properly' done, quite apart from whether it should have been done at all.

This brings us to the last five stages of the Buddhist eightfold path.

It is in the second category of mental discipline, comprising right attentiveness, right concentration and right effort that James falters. In the quagmire of the personality it is extremely difficult to separate the pure from the surrounding morass.

To take the matter of right attentiveness first. When Charles speaks to him at their first meeting of Hartley's adopted son who has disappeared without trace from home, he is properly attentive and responds with the right attitude, of compassion: 'Lost – that must be sad for them' (SS 177). But he is not absolutely in the clear here. He 'brings' Titus to Shruff End – for what purpose? To restore him to his parents, doubtless, but also to feed his own sense of power as he organises the scene and arranges the reconciliations, much more of a Prospero than the blundering Charles? He indicates awareness of this when, in his last exchange with Charles, he says, 'Goodness is giving up power and acting upon the world negatively' (SS 445).

In the matter of right concentration James unquestionably lapses.

The failure here is a failure of technique with disastrous practical consequences, similar to the incident earlier in his life with a young Nepalese sherpa who died of cold in the mountain pass because James's concentration could not generate enough body-warmth. In the instance here, he is so exhausted by the physical and mental effort spent in rescuing Charles that he stops thinking about Titus. His dejected sitting down on the road while the others bring in the body, his mumbling, 'I should have held on', indicate that he might have prevented the accident if he had only held Titus in his thoughts lovingly and attentively enough. While he fails at this point, he continues to make an effort, and with right thoughts and understanding, is able at the close to undertake right concentration or *samma samādhi* at a much higher level.

There remains the question of right effort. Should James have, at this stage, when Charles is drowning in the whirlpool, made the effort to abjure his 'magical' powers? Such power is released through psychical processes generated by concentrated meditation and patiently-exercised, disciplined control over body and mind. The practice of *yoga* begins with exercises for the control of the body, and moves towards control of the mind which then brings the disciplined body under its control. I am not arguing for levitation or walking on water, but merely affirming an age-old tradition, still practised on the Indian sub-continent, of mastery over physical and mental processes. James himself dismisses these as *tricks*, 'nothing to do with anything important, like goodness or anything like that'. He does not over-value their significance, but he *uses* them to save Charles, perhaps also to bring Titus to Charles. James knows afterwards that he has not withstood the final temptation. He says to Charles:

'The last achievement is the absolute surrender of magic itself.'   (SS 445)

The point is: should he have saved Charles from the whirlpool through his powers; should he have assumed the role of saviour? The moral dilemma is a real one. Buddhism does not advocate passive watchfulness while the neighbour drowns. The *Metta Suta* and the *Itivuttaka* speak of the overwhelming importance of love and compassion.[10] James in such a crisis does not hesitate to use his 'good' power.

I suggest that with right understanding and right thoughts (the wisdom category of the eightfold path) James's mind is further cleansed. He continues to make small efforts in the direction of right. An instance is his confession to Charles of his wholly innocent but secret friendship with Lizzie. This little incident is not intrinsic to either plot or characterisation, and is explicable only in the light of James's path to self-perfection. It has been a perfectly innocent relationship, but it must be acknowledged now, despite the certain prospect of Charles's rage:

> 'I should have told you earlier', he repeated; 'it should not have happened at all. Any lie is morally dangerous. . . . It has been a barrier. And a—and a . . . a flaw . . . Secrets are almost always a mistake and a source of corruption.'   (SS 407)

Predictably this sets off a jealous fury in Charles's breast. He angrily forces Lizzie's hand into James's and commands them both to leave his house. James leaves.

But there is more effort, more thought and more understanding required. Perhaps James sees now that the physical 'seizing' of Charles, rescuing him from Minn's Cauldron, points to other subtler temptations to effect salvation for others. A passage from the *Diamond Sutra* on the Buddha as saviour makes the position on this clear (Tathāgatha is the Buddha or perfected one).

> What do you think, Subhuti, does it occur to a Tathāgatha that he has set beings free? Not so should one see it, Subhuti. *And why?* There is not any being whom the Tathāgatha has set free. For if there had been anything to be set free by the Tathāgatha, then surely there would have been on the part of the Tathāgatha, a seizing on a self, a being, a soul, a person. One speaks of a 'seizing on a self', but as a no-seizing, Subhuti, has that been taught by the Tathāgatha.[11]

This kind of understanding has come to James; such understanding and such thoughts bring him to the wisdom of the eightfold path. He needs now, before he dies, to let go of Charles, to let this last attachment go without bitterness, anger, or (on his part) longing between them. Conradi argues convincingly that James loves Charles,[12] and must learn to renounce that love, or at least to put it in its proper place. There is a last conversation between them. James knows that they will not meet again; Charles does not. But

James needs to purify the relationship of its traces of self so that
he is no longer bound to *Samsāracakra* – the wheel of *samsāra*.
James's last visit to Charles and the right understanding he shows
there of the *dharma*, the samsaric wheel, and the liberation thence
indicate a further stage in his evolution. While his lapses point to
the immense difficulty of sustained improvement, he shows a true
understaking of *karma*, the law of spiritual causality which governs
the present out of the past, and the whole future from the present.
While the *karma* doctrine explains the present as determined by
the actions of the past, it also brings the future entirely into one's
hands. One is wholly accountable and responsible for oneself.
Every thought, word and deed in the present determines the future
and the distance from *nirvāna* or liberation. One must work out
one's salvation with diligence, for there is no saviour, no
redemptive salvation. For this reason, every moment is important
for James.

I suggest that James with his renewed effort and clarified
understanding is in a better state, a more evolved state, than at
the beginning. All the different aspects of the path coalesce at the
close to make his last meditation the right kind of concentration.
The sort of concentration used earlier for other purposes has
dropped away.

The fifth-century commentator Buddhagosha speaks in the
Visuddhimagga, or path of purification, of a stage of comprehension
when such powers are seen to be hindrances and discarded.

> Thus, as the grosser darkness which enveloped truth disappears
> in him, his mind no longer takes to any of the psychical processes
> at all . . . Whatever serves as the occasion for psychical processes,
> whatever activates them – all that appears to him as hindrance.[13]

James is ready for *samma samādhi*, a state of meditation so profound
that it brings on a perfect stillness. Such samadhi leads to *nirvāna*
or the extinction of the self.

The Indian doctor's account of James's death points to *samma
samādhi*, down to the detail of James dying seated in a chair (those
who die in a state of *samādhi* are usually buried in a sitting position).
On his face there is a smile, clearly indicative of peace attained,
perhaps even beatitude. The doctor (with the curious name of
Tsang) writes thus to Charles:

I want also to tell something to you alone. Mr. Arrowby died in much quietness. He telephoned me to come to him, and was already dead when I arrived, and he had left the door open. He was sitting in his chair, smiling. I must tell you this . . . There are some who can freely choose their moment of death and without violence to the body can by simple will power die. It was so with him . . . He has gone quietly and by the force of his own thought was consciousness extinguished. Thus it is good to go. Believe me, Sir, he was an enlightened one.   (SS 472)

Even if one were to interpret the doctor's letter as uncritical Eastern reverence for spirtually advanced souls, the smile (earlier seen by the uncomprehending Charles as James's 'inane grin') shows that James is at peace. The attendant demons that confront the soul in the *bardo* regions have receded, and it looks as if James recognised and comprehended the clear light of reality which, according to the Tibetan Book of the Dead,[14] flashes upon the soul as it leaves the body. The overwhelming majority are shocked into terror by the illumination, miss the moment of salvation, and are reborn again. But the composed soul that comprehends it aright is freed of the *samsāric* wheel and is no more reborn. This is *nirvāna*. James speaks of this to Charles, and the extracts from the Tibetan Book of the Dead in Edward Conze's edition of the Buddhist scriptures elaborate and clarify James's half-uttered hints.

How are we to understand the *nirvāna* that James speaks of? *Nirvāna* means extinction, snuffing out. It may be understood either as the cessation of rebirth into *samsāra*, or, more intelligible to the Western mind, as the extinction of the egotistical self as it merges with the universal Absolute. Buddhagosha quotes the Buddha:

There is, ye monks, an unborn (ajātam), unbecome (abhūtam), unmade (akātam), uncompounded (asankhatam). If, ye monks, this unborn, unbecome, unmade, uncompounded, were not, an escape from the born, become, made, compounded, would not be discernible. But because, ye monks, there is an unborn, unbecome, unmade, uncompounded, therefore an escape from the born, become, made, compounded is discernible.[15]

This does not rule out the possibility of 'escape' or liberation in this life. Satkari Mookerjee, who cites the above passage in his *The*

Buddhist Philosophy of Universal Flux, goes on to say that we can legitimately infer that Buddhaghosha refuses to believe *nirvāna* to be an absolute ceasing of existence, but sees it instead as the ceasing of suffering, lust, hate and delusion.[16] From this point of view physical death is not necessary for attaining *nirvāna*, as some of the Mahayana schools of Buddhism contend. James's death may merely coincide with the death in him of *moha* (error), *lobha* (greed) and *dosa* (hatred), the fires that fuel the ego. With the extinction in him of these, James is freed. The smile on his face at the moment of death becomes comprehensible only in this light.

Though involved through compassion in the emotions of others, though involved momentarily in the muddle of his own emotions, he returns from these to *upekha* or equanimity, a restoration of the mind's impersonal serenity, *not* a selfish indifference to the welfare of others.

James's detachment from selfish desire is not, it must be repeated, bland neutrality. Ordinary indifference which is a feeling like any other – happiness or hurt or anger – is not the Buddhist's goal. Contrary to the popular notion that passivity is the natural outcome of detachment, James is neither passive nor indifferent. Rather, he is, most of the time, contained, low-keyed, and controlled. Buddhist detachment is the refusal to refer feelings to the self, and is marked by equanimity, not stoical calm. Hence James's smile.

James Arrowby, as much a figure of good as Brendan Craddock, is clearly an examplar showing the way. His occasional failures make him credible; more, they make the path he takes a distinct possibility for everyman. His failures, seen by Dipple to be tragic, seem to me essential to his growth as a spiritual being. The fact that James is not perfect, besides being part of Murdoch's overall picture of the impossibility of finding perfection or being perfect, can be accommodated within the notion of the *Arhat* or Perfected One. At a famous council in Pataliputra, the issue whether the *Arhat* can lapse was discussed at length.[17] Against the Theravada insistence on the absolute perfection of the *Arhat*, Mahadeva argued that the *Arhat* could be subject to minor flaws without ceasing to be an *Arhat*. In fact, the notion of incompleteness is necessary if the *Arhat* is not to fall into the delusion of believing that he has accomplished more than he has. A perfected *Arhat* would be spiritually arrogant, and therefore inferior.

James may not be an *Arhat* or Perfected one, but he is a *sotapathi*, a 'stream-winner', the first rough version of a saint who has detached himself from worldly existence and followed the path to goodness. The *Anguttara Sutta* discusses three types of persons. The first is the *arukūpamacitta*, or one with a mind like an open sore that festers at the slightest stimulation. Charles is such a person. The second type is *vijjūpamacitta*, one with a mind like lightning, capable of seeing things as they are (*yathābhutam pajanati*). James fits this description. The third type of person is *vajirūpamacitta*, one with a mind like a diamond, who has destroyed the enemies of mental good.[18] James is not far from this category.

The doubleness of effect at the end concerning James is characteristic of Murdoch's refusal to make a simple affirmation. Through the thoughts of the chastened Charles, different reasons and explanations are offered for his final 'casting-off'. A verse in the *Dhammapada* says:

> Whoso, having cut off all fetters, trembles
> no more, he who has overcome all
> attachments and is emancipated – him
> do I call a Brāhmana.   (Dh. 25:397)

James fits this account on the whole, But Charles's wondering whether there was, in the end, a dangerous failure ('disgust because he had had to use his "power" to save my life') subverts slightly the reverence of the Indian doctor ('Believe me, Sir, he was an enlightened one'). But there is, on the whole, a bias in favour of the latter. Charles's ruminations about James's possible liberation or failure themselves indicate his recognition of 'a different pattern of being, some quite other history of spiritual adventure or misadventure'   (SS 474).

There is a sub-textual sense of James as free and at peace. At the level of overt discourse, the text offers the possibility of James as an aching shadow in *bardo* haunted by his mind's demons, but Charles's own prayerful mood suggests a calm elsewhere. The following passage talks of both, but the rhythm of the two antithetical sentences has a quietening effect, evocative of an overarching peace:

> Would he meet *one* there, in the shape of some persistent horror, a foul phantom of me, the creation of his mind? If so, I prayed that when he achieved his liberation he might not forget me but

come in pity and in compassion to know the truth. Whatever
that might mean.   (SS 475)

The uncertainty and ambivalence expressed here are only at the
level of sense or understanding; washing below that is a slowed-
down, gentle tide of peacefulness communicated through the rise
and fall of the sentences. The paragraph that follows describes the
soft slap of the sea, Charles's sad, strange thoughts, and the night
sky thick with stars:

And far, far away in that ocean of gold, stars were silently
shooting and falling and finding their fates, among those billions
and billions of merging golden lights.   (SS 475)

Such lines, following thoughts of James's death, suggest very
beautifully the course of blest souls finding their fates. The silence
and merging of gold with gold point to calm, light, expansion, and
joyous, peaceful dissolution. Underlining such positive affirmation,
Charles notes that he slept to hear the sound of singing in his
sleep. A beneficent loving-kindness absorbs James, Charles, and
the reader into its fold, and in the morning there are four playful
seals, 'beneficent beings' come to visit and bless Charles.

The important point is that James, in this last phase, has an
effect on Charles. The section that follows, entitled Postscript,
mockingly undercuts this vision of beauty and peace, but while
the diary reveals a Charles back in the machine of his old suspicious
habits, it indicates a slightly altered mind, a mind a little more in
touch with the truth of things. Charles's remarks on the impossibility of making any final summing-up or affirmation are very
characteristic of Murdoch's refusal to console. The Postscript does
not altogether invalidate the affirmation of the preceding vision,
but it shows the inevitable and constant breaking-in of disorder,
selfishness and ordinariness. Life's untidiness allows peak experiences, but flows back and over and around them again. The human
mind cannot bear very much of anything except ordinariness; these
moments occur, but they fade. What can they really do after all?
Provide a light to live by? Perhaps. The rest of the journal records
both the difficulty of change and the fact that it can occur. Such
people as James can bring about small changes in others.

III

Through the Postscript, Charles 'limps on' in his usual manner, wondering about this and that, noting the course of his own reputation and commenting on the lives of his friends, but there is an indisputable if slight difference. Remarks such as 'the worthlessness of what we have long pursued and will so soon return to pursuing', and 'irretrievable moral failure' are more frequent. There is a new awareness, almost a humility: 'I eat and drink and gossip just as if I were an ordinary person. Well, am I not one?' (SS 482). He finds room for pity when he hears of Peregrine's death in a Londonderry bomb-blast ('Poor Perry. He was a brave man'), but is honest enough to realise that he grieves not so much for Perry's death as his own. There are many such small signs of marshalling and effort in the ego's usual morass recorded by the journal.

He is not at ease in James's flat but refuses to live elsewhere. There is a significant passage where, playing with the stone he had given James seems to him like touching his hand. There are two immediate modifications. One is in brackets: '(What sentimental nonsense)', and is the typical Charles reaction. But the next lines are:

> I hold the stone and play with a kind of emotion which I keep
> at bay. Loving people, isn't that an attachment? I do not want
> to suffer fruitlessly.   (SS 496)

There are two important changes in Charles to be noted here. One is that he loves the cousin whom alive he feared and resented. The other is his recognition that suffering is caused by attachment, and that detachment from selfish loving is one of the steps to be taken. Considering the kind of person Charles is – very like ourselves if we become aware of our inner fantasising life – this is an immense step forward. He may fall back again, of course, but light has dawned.

There is another step on the next page where Charles examines his 'Hartley obsession' in the light of something suggested to him by James. With more honesty than usual, he admits that he might indeed, in their early relationship, have been too dominating, too bossy, as Hartley had put it, and that she left him for that reason. With even more pain he admits that Ben might have effected in her a sexual awakening which he himself had been unable to do. He breaks off abruptly from such hurtful speculation, but the process of self-examination has begun. The next page retracts these honest admissions in his usual manner, but looks forward to a quieter acceptance of things as they were and are.

> She was not able to be my Beatrice, nor was I able to be saved by her, but the idea was not senseless or unworthy. My pity for her need not be a device or an impertinence, it can survive after all as a blank, ignorant, quiet unpossessive souvenir, not now a major part of my life, but a persisting one. The past buries the past and must end in silence, but it can be a conscious silence that rests open-eyed.   (SS 500)

This reluctance to use his pity as a device contrasts strongly with the casual summoning of Lizzie at the opening of the novel and the imperious use of everyone and everything in sight to win Hartley. However, he is himself mindful of his 'new' state and does not presume too much:

> Can one change oneself? I doubt it. Or if there is any change, it must be measured as the millionth part of a millimetre. When the poor ghosts have gone, what remains are ordinary obligations and ordinary interests. One can live quietly and try to do tiny good things and harm no one. I cannot think of any tiny good thing to do this moment, but perhaps I shall think of one tomorrow.   (SS 501)

These excerpts, illustrating nicely the calming of his restless mind, show Charles looking away from himself to the world outside and learning to see it as in itself it really is.

The casket that falls, releasing whatever demon was inside it, mentioned in the very last entry in his journal, serves to show that Charles is now aware of the mind's demons. Open to possibilities, he is ready to wait with reasonable patience and more acceptance then he was capable of at the beginning:

> Upon the demon-ridden pilgrimage of human life, what next I wonder?

The book finishes on that wry, humorous question, not making too solemn an issue of anything, allowing all alternatives to be present in delicate balance. There is no doubt that this is a modified Charles taking his first, faltering steps on the path.

Against Elizabeth Dipple's conclusion that both James and Charles Arrowby have failed, I suggest that both have (in a limited sense, because we are limited, finite beings) succeeded at their different stages in the struggle out of the darkness of *avidya*. James may have resorted to magic but that is not a fatal failure. He reasserts control, puts the magic in its place, and cleanses his heart and mind over and over again. No one life, not even many lives, may be enough to bring the seeker to the goal. That James is a pilgrim far advanced in the spiritual journey is enough; he has shown the way. He has, perhaps, even reached the goal. And through his struggle he has taught others; that is the most he can do; to take on more is antithetical to the goodness he seeks – the extinction of selfish self.

Charles is left to sort matters out alone. A verse in the *Dhammapada* says:

> One indeed is one's own saviour.
> One is the refuge of oneself.   (Dh. 25:380)

Charles alone in James's flat is an appropriate imaging of the aloneness in which the psyche must wage war on itself, and from which it learns to move out of its existential limits. Charles is at last completely alone.

> I felt an odd new sensation which I had never known before and which it took me a little time to recognise as loneliness. Without James I was at last alone. How very much I had relied upon his presence in the world, almost as if he had been my twin-brother and not my cousin.   (SS 473)

He recognises that this state of aloneness, while desolating, is necessary.

> I feel now as if something of me went with James's death, like part of a bridge carried away in a flood.   (SS 497)

The image of the flood (*ōgha*) is even more important in the water-symbolism of Buddhist literature than the sea. The floods of sensuality (*kāmōgha*), will-to-be (*bhāvōgha*), views (*dittōgha*) and ignorance (*avijjōgha*)[19] threaten to submerge and overflow the confines of mind. The Buddha teaches the way to cross the floods, but he is not a saviour, only a shower of the way.

The dying of the self that begins for Charles with James's actual death and the demolition of the bridge that James might have been are both necessary for Charles's liberation. His loving thoughts of his cousin after his death hint that he might have clung to the bridge or raft.

Reliance on none other than the self – the opposite of selfish concern with self – is basic to the Buddhist creed. The self on which one must rely is the free, unimpeded self, responding accurately to things and people; through such clear seeing the individual self is purified and is the *Self*. Here freedom is to be found. In the *Mahā-Parinirvāna Sutta* the Buddha says:

> O Ānanda, take the Self as a lamp, take the Self as a refuge. Betake yourselves to no external refuge. Look not for refuge to anyone beside yourselves. Work out your own salvation with diligence.[20]

The extinction of the smaller, selfish self brings an emptiness, *sūnyata*. Such a dying or emptying leads to expansion and fullness. This comes with effort.

Charles Arrowby is far from such states but a process has begun. His veering in the Postscript from thought to thought, the uncertainty surrounding his aperçus, and his awareness of uncertainty, suggest that questioning of empirical existence and compounded reality which is a prelude to an understanding of their illusory nature. This is hard, and dying to self is very hard; something of the floundering it causes is suggested by the jumpy waverings in the Postscript. Charles's state at this stage is accurately described by a verse in the *Dhammapada*:

> Just as a fish pulled out of its water
> resort and cast on land quivers and
> quivers, even so the mind while leaving
> the realms of *Mara*.   (Dh. 3:34)

The realms of *Mara* are the nets of delusion in which the individual soul is caught. Leaving them is a kind of death, and

Charles's quivering state is like that of the quivering fish pulled out of the sea of *samsāra* which is its element. This annihilation must take place and the 'the bitter nothingness' of existence be painfully recognised. It is this pain, so different from the frantic agitation of the sections in the novel called Pre-history and History, that colours the section entitled Postscript. Though there is much of the ego left, the earlier madness is dying down, and a quieter, less self-assertive Charles can be seen in the making.

4

Anne Cavidge in *Nuns and Soldiers*

The Buddhist emphasis on the need to control and purify consciousness through willed effort is carried over into *Nuns and Soldiers* and placed in a Christian context. In this novel, Anne Cavidge, a former nun, struggling to understand the nature of Christ, finds that he is identical with her own capacity to love without thought of self.

It looks as if, by this time, goodness for Murdoch has to be a cancellation of itself in its articulated sense. When Anne joins the convent, 'holiness' or 'goodness' is her goal.

> The idea of holiness, of becoming good in some more positive sense, naturally gained power in her mind in the earlier years in the convent.   (NS 56)

But after some years she discovers that this 'path' somehow leads backwards, and can perhaps be found only if abandoned. 'A kind of negative humility which did not aspire to the name of goodness', a simplicity or innocence, seems to be the only proper objective. But nothing is clear and Anne is filled with strange doubts.

There is a glance at Cato in the hint at an involvement of some kind within the convent, but nothing to indicate that it carried her along on an emotional tide. Anne is not at the mercy of her emotions as Cato was, and her reasons for leaving the convent arise from a growing conviction that the convent is not the right place for her as seeker.

It is no easier in the world outside the convent. She falls in love with Peter, but is required not only to love him without hope of ever being with him, but to love *differently*, i.e. selflessly, and to recognise that this different loving is the presence of Christ.

Christ appears to Anne and, in the course of reinterpreting what and who he is, rejects the role of saviour which has been placed upon him, and underscores, instead, the need to do all the work oneself. This is similar to the Buddha's advice to take only the self as a refuge. It was noted in the chapter on Brendan that his interpretation of Christ has a distinct Buddhist emphasis in its insistence on the elimination of the person and the tissue of illusion which is human consciousness. This elimination of 'the person', or the grasping self, involves an elimination of divine images also. Brendan knows this, but after all has been eliminated he lets 'Christ look after his Christology'. Anne would like to do the same but her Christ gently refuses. She must do all the work herself.

One could speak of this in terms of the Protestant view of salvation by works, and there is no doubt that there is a gradual and growing puritanism at work through the entire canon. It would, however, be a mistake to mark her work as sectarian. Her main purpose, as noted in the introductory chapter, is to clear away much of the religious lumber so that the supreme good is identified with the capacity and will to love properly. The meaning of Christ is selfless love; every other encrustation must be set aside so that this truth is understood. Christ undertakes the task of educating Anne in this matter. He existed once, yes, but the only sense in which he is real now is in the human capacity to see and love others without selfish interest.

This capacity to love is a miracle, and not just a mere response to a rule. Hence the name Christ is retained, the beauty of his presence made to shed its light over the encounter, and the power of this mystery acknowledged. Murdoch's account of Christ's visitation is derived directly, as has been generally recognised, from Julian of Norwich, the fourteenth-century English mystic. I have concentrated on the relationship between Murdoch and Julian of Norwich to show how Murdoch modifies Julian in ways essential to her purpose while retaining the central emphasis on love. Elizabeth Dipple, in an illuminating chapter, speaks of the ironic connection of Anne's 'unredemptive vision' to Julian's *Revelations*. She says:

> In every way opposite to Anne's showing, Julian reflects a community of shared belief and an utter certainty of divine reality through the images of Christianity.[1]

I suggest that Murdoch modifies, but does not relate *ironically* to Julian's message of love. That remains the central message to be reinterpreted for Anne. Gadamer's description of 'the fundamental non-definitiveness of the horizon in which the understanding moves' and his recognition of 'the fact that after us others will understand in a different way', referred to in the introductory chapter, are relevant here. Anne understands in a different way; she comes after Julian; and after Anne, another will understand differently. Anne's is not 'an unredemptive vision' as Dipple would have it; there *is* salvation (NS 291) and redemption, but no redeemer *outside*. Dipple grants this when she observes that Anne 'alone is responsible, as is every human being in Murdoch's work, for whatever shall be well in the world'[2] and rightly emphasises moral discipline and virtue. But she plays down the miracle that this is. Love is a miracle, and it is for this reason that Murdoch makes *Christ* step into the novel. Only such an extreme measure can evoke the wonder, the sheer astonishment at the existence of love.

Julian's famous 'All shall be well' refrain occurs in almost every Murdoch novel in varying contexts. The link between *Nuns and Soldiers* and Julian's *Revelations*, however, goes well beyond the usual quotation. The first section of this chapter examines general assumptions shared by Iris Murdoch and Julian of Norwich. The second section deals with the Christ–Anne encounter and relates it to Christ's appearances to Julian as recorded in her *Revelations of Divine Love*. The third section comments on Anne's difficulties in the ordinary world, and her 'new' understanding of love. The fourth section indicates that a background of mysticism is necessary for the assertion of love.

I

Murdoch says in *The Sovereignty of Good*:

> If I attend properly I will have no choice and this is the ultimate condition to be aimed at.   (SG 40)

This stand is related to the neo-platonic vision in which all creation is seen as concentric circles placed in ever-widening rings around the central light, and also to the Augustinian view of evil as simply the deprivation of good. Good and evil here are not equally strong, see-sawing forces, but rather states farther from, or closer to, the light. At the centre, evil simply vanishes, ceases to exist. To be absorbed into that still centre is the object of the good characters in Murdoch's fiction. The fact that they inhabit worlds which are abundantly alive with the flawed and wicked shows her refusal to see this as an easy solution. Though from one point of view it seems simple, the way to the still point is fraught with backslidings.

Julian of Norwich expresses such a view in Christian terms. Christ, who appeared to her in sixteen showings, is the centre of a trinity of 'All-might, All-wisdom, and All-love'. He *is*, and by his being makes sin irrelevant. Because he is, all manner of things shall be made well. But why, asks Julian, are things not well *now*, how might all be well 'for the great hurt that is come by sin to the creature?' The answer to this is:

> But for failing of love on our part, therefore is all our tra-
> vail.   (RDL 76)

Proper loving leads to stillness and good; the failure of love leads to troubled unhappiness and to bad. Evil is extreme wretchedness arising from a sinful failure to love.

The visions of Christ's bleeding figure to Julian reinforce the fact and power of his presence, of the sovereignty of good. Christ merely looks at Julian, and through her, at the world. His seeing is his action. He is not moved to anger, neither does he condemn. We judge and condemn ourselves. Julian says:

> I saw soothfastly that our Lord was never wroth, nor ever shall
> be. For He is God: Good, Life, Truth, Love, Peace. His clarity
> and unity suffereth Him not to be wroth. For I saw truly that it
> is against the property of His might to be wroth, and against
> the property of His wisdom, and against the property of his
> goodness. God is the Goodness that may not be wroth, for He
> is not other but goodness.   (RDL 97)

Julian goes on to say that the loving goodness which is her Christ is directed towards quietening *us*, lessening our wrath:

> it behoved me needs to grant that the mercy of God and the
> forgiveness is to slacken and waste *our* wrath.   (RDL 102)

For Julian, awareness of the perfection which is Christ diminishes, if only momentarily, our passionate, warring impulses.

Murdoch also emphasises the quiet, non-warring state of consciousness produced by understanding the nature of good. She says that the ideal situation is a kind of necessity in which a patient, loving regard is directed upon a person, a thing, a situation, and which presents 'the will not as unimpeded movement, but as something very much more like obedience' (SG 40).

Both Julian and Murdoch assert the magnetic pull of a transcendent force. Seeing is the dominant metaphor. In Julian, Christ looks at us; in Murdoch, we are directed to look *there* patiently and accurately. Choices have to be made elsewhere, i.e. *here* in the world where the selfish, muddled heart fails to see and love properly. The opposition set up by both writers is between a still centre and a moving, conflict-ridden periphery.

In *The Sovereignty of Good* Murdoch speaks repeatedly of the importance of accurate vision as the beginning of moral growth; true seeing occasions right conduct:

> It is in the capacity to love, that is to *see*, that the liberation of the soul from fantasy consists. . . . What I have called fantasy, the proliferation of blinding self-centred aims and images, is itself a powerful system of energy, and most of what is called 'will' or 'willing' belongs to this system.   (SG 66)

Such an attitude is closely related to Julian's parable of the Lord and his Servant in Chapter 56 of the *Revelations*. The servant, running in haste to do his Lord's will, falls, is in great distress, unable to see his Lord, unable to rise:

> But himself was letted and blinded from the knowing of his will; and this is to him great sorrow and grievous distress: for neither does he see clearly his loving Lord . . . nor doth he see truly what himself is in the sight of his loving Lord . . .   (RDL 111)

Julian and Murdoch are both advising correction of the distortions that the frantic, self-seeking will imposes on the real.

Murdoch's saintly characters see more clearly than those surrounding them. Their perceptive awareness guards them from violent, willed impulse though they live in regions of confusion and wickedness.

Evil is not ignored or wished away; its pestiferous multiplication and vitality in the natural world emerges from the thickly-layered plots and the extraordinary shifts in human relations. Murders, suicides, incest, maniacal, possessive lunges – the worst that can happen usually does in a Murdoch novel. All the characters, and even, on occasion, the enlightened few, are shown as deluded, erring, unhappy, caught. They mistake the nature of the world in which they live and the nature of others around them no less than their own nature. So while, in one sense, evil disappears in the light of good, in another, it flourishes abundantly, a powerful ingredient in the mixture.

Julian, likewise, recognises the mixed nature of things outside the enlightened consciousness. She speaks of this medley in us of good and bad, of being so broken by various sins 'in which we are made dark, that scarcely we can take any comfort' (RDL 123).

Recognising the great effort needed for clear vision, both writers warn against a kind of false seeing which is doubly dangerous because it masquerades as real perception. Murdoch speaks of dangerous introspection which merely strengthens the mechanism (SG 67). Morgan's self-examination in *A Fairly Honourable Defeat* for instance, leads her to a credo of 'free' selfish love. Charles Arrowby in *The Sea, the Sea* holds an endless dialogue with himself which only imprisons him further in the net of compulsions. Cato in *Henry and Cato*, thinking of the whole disastrous chain of events, hates himself to the point of despair.

Julian also speaks out against excessive, unhealthy self-accusation: Christ says to her:

> Accuse not thyself overdone much, dreaming that thy tribulation and thy woe is all for thy fault; for I will not that thou be heavy or sorrowful indiscreetly.   (RDL 188)

There is a fine line to be drawn between self-awareness and self-obsession, and while both Julian and Murdoch say similar things about the need to be in touch with one's experience, both warn against becoming its prey. Murdoch points to that process in the mind where something like willed thought goes on, helping the moral endeavour. This is desirable and good. But against too much dramatisation and self-pity one may fortify oneself by looking at things outside oneself, learning a language, for instance, or taking an interest in plants (SG 89), or, like William Eastcote in *The Philosopher's Pupil*, surrendering the muddle to 'the healing goodness of God'.

Julian says something quite similar:

> willeth He that we see our wretchedness and meekly be aware

of it. But He willeth not that we abide thus, nor He willeth not that we busy us greatly about our accusing, nor He willeth not that we be wretched over our self; but He willeth that we hastily turn ourselves unto Him.   (RDL 193)

These two stages correspond to the two stages mentioned by Murdoch, first of self-awareness and then of non-obsessive thought or activity.

The there and not-there presence of the still point of light around which teeming confusion revolves is of the essence in Murdoch's world. Whoever said it was going to be different? the author seems to be asking. Julian, her spiritual ancestor, also speaks of the endlessness of the process:

He said not: *Thou shalt not be tempested; thou shalt not be travailed; thou shalt not be afflicted;* but He said *Thou shalt not be overcome.*

II

For Julian of Norwich Christ is uncorrupted good. Against his presence, travail and affliction are played out, and in his presence they dwindle. Taking her cue from this, Murdoch writes a scene in which Christ actually appears to Anne. The scene is set apart from the surrounding swirl and is not linked in any way with the complicated events of the narrative. Since it is not, strictly speaking, necessary to the action, its isolation gives it an extra significance. All that goes on in the novel must be seen in the light of this visitation, more especially because there is no connection. The apparent irrelevance indicates quietly the general forgetting of the most important 'truth'.

Murdoch's highly condensed account is based directly on Julian's experience.

To begin with, there are words which, common nouns though they be, are associated with Julian. 'Showing' and 'Revelation' are the words used to describe Christ's appearance to Julian. Her book, *Revelations of Divine Love*, was recently issued in a Modern English version under the title *Showings*. In *Nuns and Soldiers* when Anne and the Abbess are discussing Anne's spiritual state and decision to leave the convent, Anne concludes 'there was no great positive

"showing" here, no revelation of a new task' (NS 61). 'Anchoress
is another word used in connection with Julian. She is described
as 'anchoress at Norwich'. In Murdoch's novel, the Abbess presses
her to retain a connection with them, to be an 'anchoress' in
the world (NS 61). Much later Anne uses the word of herself
wondering whether she can really be an anchoress (NS 498). The
'All shall be well' refrain occurs (NS 228), as it does in almost every
Murdoch novel. Then comes the visitation of Christ; the encounter
as will be illustrated below, is based very firmly on Julian of
Norwich.

Care is taken to establish the fact that this is not a dream. What
leads up to it *is* a dream. The statues of the two beautiful angels
stepping off their pedestals in an eighteenth-century rose-garden
leading the way, then disappearing, leaving Anne alone listening
to the crunch of footsteps she somehow knows to be those of
Christ – all this is a dream from which she wakes to find herself in
her own bedroom. But in this moment of waking she knows that
there is somebody standing in her kitchen in the bright light of
the early summer morning. She knows that that person is Christ.

Establishing the actuality of the revelation corresponds to Julian's
difficulty in establishing the truth of what she has seen. Julian
herself wonders whether this is delirium (she is sick) or dream.

> Then came a Religious person to me and asked how I fared.
> said I had raved today.   (RDL 165)

But in the sixteenth and final revelation Christ says to Julian:

> Wit it now well that it was no raving that thou sawest
> today.   (RDL 169)

Julian thereafter goes over these words several times, contrite for
having thought she had raved. Repeatedly Christ's words come
back to her and Julian is reassured that this has been no dream.

In *Nuns and Soldiers* the novelist says:

> Jesus Christ came to Anne Cavidge in a vision. The visitation
> began in a dream, but then gained a very undreamlike real
> ity.   (NS 288)

Her hand raw, as if burnt, where it had brushed Christ's sleeve vill not heal; and she has left with her a small grey elliptical stone Christ put down on the table, though she is not sure that it is not one of the stones she had brought back from Cumbria. Later, meditating on her visitor, Anne is convinced of the genuiness of he visitation; she is certain 'she had not been dreaming or having some kind of chemically induced hallucination' (NS 312).

Next, Julian refers repeatedly to the 'marvellous *homeliness* of Christ' (RDL 17). Murdoch elaborates this homeliness considerably. n Anne's vision, Jesus is thin, of moderate height, wears shapeless, yellowish-white trousers, a shirt open at the neck and rolled-up sleeves, and plimsolls on his feet with no socks (NS 290). His appearance and speech are distinctly non-awful, but at the same ime piercingly beautiful. The mouth is tender and thoughtful, the eyes luminous, his words direct and simple. Julian's phrase marvellous homeliness' accurately conveys the impression Murdoch carefully builds up. The entire revelation is a triumph of tone; at no place is there a false step in the evocation of Christ. He is wholly contemporary, yet entirely other and himself. While part of the impression of infinite love and purity is communicated by the dense allusiveness of the word Christ, Murdoch creates, in addition, a figure of immense charm. This Jesus laughs, appreciates wit, and is simultaneously loving and humorous. His words are serious but not solemn.

Julian's Christ too is a joyful one; his countenance has cheer and mirth; he speaks mirthfully (RDL 52).

Describing his physical appearance, Julian stresses the effect of suffering on the flesh, particularly the skin. In the eighth revelation, she tells of the effect of wind and weather on the dying body of Christ, its discoloration, dryness and shrunkenness as if 'he had been seven night dead' (RDL 37). She dwells at length on the wounds, the garlands of thorns about the head; then returns to the 'small-rimpled' skin, 'tanned like a dry board when it is aged' (RDL 39).

Murdoch condenses Julian's long account into a single paragraph:

He had a strangely elongated head and a strange pallor, the pallor of something which had been long deprived of light, a shadowed leaf, a deep sea fish, a grub inside a fruit.   (NS 290)

Julian's entire page on the wounded head, thorn-encrusted hair, blood, tender torn flesh, has been reduced to

He had a strangely elongated head.

That is, Murdoch mentions the effect of such wounding rather than the wounds themselves.

There are other allusions to Julian which must be noted before the differences are discussed. The implied reference to St Veronica in *Nuns and Soldiers* is an example. St Veronica gave her handkerchief to Christ as he laboured under the cross and when she received it again from him his face was imprinted on it. Julian refers to this in her *Revelations* (RDL 23). Murdoch glances at this indirectly when Christ says to Anne:

> Of course the way to Jerusalem was not a state progress. Only the women didn't run; they loved me for myself.   (NS 291)

Of much greater importance is the direct allusion by Murdoch to Julian's first revelation. Christ shows Julian something like a hazelnut as a sign of all that is made:

> Also in this He shewed me a little thing, the quantity of an hazel-nut, in the palm of my hand and it was as round as a ball. I looked thereupon with eye of my understanding and thought: *What may this thing be*? And it was answered generally thus: It is all that is made. I marvelled how it might last for methought it might suddenly have fallen to naught for littleness. And I was answered in my understanding: It lasteth, and ever shall *last for that God loveth it*. And so All-thing hath Being by the love of God.   (RDL 10)

Julian explains that the properties of this hazel-nut-like thing which stands for all creation are that God made, loves and keeps it, and that though she cannot tell the nature of Maker, Lover, Keeper till she is 'one-d' to him, it is only in that final submergence that she will find rest. This Augustinian strain runs through Julian's revelations. In the last chapter of the book she comes round to the affirmation that the meaning of the revelations was not to underscore the longing of the separated soul for the distant other, but to show that the other is really nothing other than love. She asks repeatedly what the meaning of the revelations might be, and is made to understand 'that Love was our Lord's meaning'. She is answered thus:

Wouldst thou learn thy Lord's meaning in this thing? Learn it well. Love was His meaning. Who shewed it thee? Love. What shewed He thee? Love. Wherefore shewed it He? For love. Hold thee therein and thou shalt learn and know more in the same. But thou shalt never know nor learn therein other thing without end. Thus was I learned that Love was our Lord's meaning. (RDL 202)

Murdoch has telescoped Julian's first 'hazel-nut' revelation, and her final understanding ('Love was our Lord's meaning') fifteen years later, separated in Julian by nearly 200 printed pages, into half a page. We are meant to remember Julian throughout.

When Christ asks Anne, 'What am I holding in my hand?' her reply is *'A hazel-nut, Sir'*. But he says no and puts down on the table an elliptical grey stone. The exchange goes like this:

Anne stared at the stone. Then she said slowly,

'Is it *so small?*'

'Yes, Anne.'

'Everything that is, so little—'

'Yes.'

'But, Sir – how can it not perish, how can it be, if all this—'

'Ah, my dear child, you want some wonderful answer, don't you?'

'Yes, thought Anne, I do.

'Have you not been shown enough?'

'No, no, I want more', said Anne, 'more, more. Tell me— what are you—where are you—'

'Where do I live? I live nowhere. Have you not heard it said that birds have nests and foxes have holes but I have no home?'

'Oh, Sir, you have a home', said Anne.

'You mean—'

'Love is my meaning', said Anne.

He laughed. 'You are witty, my child. *You* have given the wonderful answer. Is *that* not enough?'

'No, not without you', she said, 'not without you.'

'You are spoiling your gift, already.'

'But what am I to believe', said Anne, 'you are so real, you are here, you are the most real, most undoubtable of all things – you are the *proof*, there is no other.'

'I prove nothing, Anne. You have answered your own question. What more do you want? A miracle?'

'Yes', she said.

'You must be the miracle-worker, little one. You must be the proof. The work is yours.'   (NS 293)

This conversation, clearly rooted in Julian, offers very interesting departures from the original. Murdoch's separation from her source surprises the reader into perceiving the stripped core and a new emphasis. To begin with, Murdoch has eschewed the emotional outpouring that fills Julian's book. She makes no place here for such words as Julian's Christ speaks to the contrite soul:

My darling I am glad thou art come to me: in all thy woe I have ever been with thee; and now seest thou my loving and we be oned in bliss.   (RDL 82)

When Anne is swept by longing for Christ (a longing sanctioned by the Gospel image of Christ as bridegroom), she is briskly told what she must do and is not allowed to surrender to feeling. Here is Murdoch's version:

She thought he is here, *he* is here; and she was suddenly shaken with a great shock of love so that she quaked and had to hold on to the edge of the table to stop herself from falling. She was filled with urgent desire almost as if she would seduce him. She wanted to touch him. She said, 'Do not go away from me, how could I live without you now that you have come. If you are going to leave me, let me die now.'

'Come, come, Anne, you will die soon enough.' He spoke briskly. 'As for salvation, anything you can think about it is as imaginary as my wounds. I am not a magician. I never was. You know what to do. Do right, refrain from wrong.'   (NS 292)

With such an exchange Murdoch shows how the emotions have their part but are not wholly reliable. Clearly the visitation of Christ to Anne must have some root in emotion, but emotion is only a starting-point, not to be lingered over. Love which remains as mere feeling is not an essential part of the structure of morality.

The remarks about suffering in the course of this visitation (coming before the elliptical stone passage) establish much the same point. Julian of Norwich broods over the passion in elaborate detail as those in religious orders are sometimes encouraged to do – the blood, its drying, the scourging, the tender flesh, the 'sweet skin' rent in many places. Julian's response is in line with orthodox Christian practice. Colledge and Walsh, in the introduction to their critical edition of Julian's revelations *Showings*, remark that she departs from her usual moderation in describing the physical details of the passion.[3] Julian invites us to behold Christ's blood overflowing all the earth, ready to wash all creatures of sin (RDL 30).

In Murdoch's version, when Anne mentions his suffering, Christ shrugs it off with,

'I have no wounds. My wounds are imaginary.'   (NS 290)

It is important to see the precise nature of the distinction Murdoch is making here. She does not underestimate the significance of the suffering Christ, but she understands the ease with which it can fall into consoling reverie.

The Judaeo-Christian mystique clearly recognises that the prophetic mission entails suffering because that mission runs counter to the larger structure present everywhere. From Jeremiah through Isaiah to Christ, it is taken for granted that suffering is an essential ingredient in the process of purification, for leading the authentic life.

Murdoch's attitude does not negate this. What she does decry, both here, in *Nuns and Soldiers*, and in *The Sovereignty of Good*, is an easy acceptance of the atonement, and the sentimentalisation of the image of the suffering Christ.

Suffering can be transformed into a spectacle so absorbing that it holds back the viewer. Brendan Craddock, the priest in *Henry and Cato*, observes that Christianity distracts the attention from death because its emphasis on suffering breeds the most beautiful images of all (HC 371). The dying Guy in *Nuns and Soldiers* tells Anne that Christianity is soft, sentimental, magical; it denies death; it changes death into an interesting kind of suffering. In *The Sovereignty of Good* Murdoch says:

It is very difficult to concentrate attention upon suffering and sin, in others or in oneself, without falsifying the picture in some way while making it bearable . . .   (SG 73)

Remarking that moral improvement involves suffering, she

reminds us that suffering must be the by-product of a new orientation and not an end in itself.

This is the attitude informing the Christ–Anne exchange. When Anne mentions the piercing and laceration on which Julian allows herself to dwell, Christ shows her his unscarred wrists. He affirms the crucifixion but refuses to emphasise the pain ('Yes, pain is a scandal and a task, but it is a shadow that passes': NS 291). He says to Anne:

'You do not need to see my wounds. If there were wounds they have healed. If there was suffering it has gone and is nothing.' (NS 291)

When Anne hesitatingly asks if the pain is not the point, he replies lightly:

'The point? No, though it has proved so interesting to you all' (NS 291)

Christ's redemptive suffering then is not the point. *Love* is the point; such love as Christ incarnates must be nurtured in the human heart. No room here for romantic indulgence or even passive faith. A practical, ethical Christianity divested of all its supremely beautiful consolatory imagery is offered. When Anne sheds blinding tears, Christ says to her:

'Don't cry. Are you really so sentimental? Art thou well-paid that *ever suffered I passion for thee? If I could have suffered more, I would have suffered more.* (NS 293)

This is a direct echo from Julian's ninth revelation:

Then said Jesus our kind Lord: *If thou art pleased, I am pleased: it is a joy, a bliss, an endless satisfying to me, that ever suffered I passion for thee; and if I might suffer more, I would suffer more.'* (RDL 47)

It is interesting to see how Murdoch has modified this. Heir to the modern tradition of empirical psychology, she underlines the danger of concentrating too much on suffering, both Christ's and Anne's own, with:

'Don't cry. Are you really so sentimental?'

But suffering as a part of the apostolic mission, as a means of coming to terms with one's limitations, as the in-breaking of an other-where on the consciousness, she sees as valuable, perhaps indispensable. The association of Christ with concentration camps made in the later novel *The Good Apprentice* is foreshadowed here when Anne says:

'But indeed you were wounded, Sir', said Anne, raising her eyes. 'Indeed you were. They pierced your hands and feet with nails and your side with a spear. They shot your kneecaps off, they drove a red-hot needle into your liver, they blinded you with ammonia and gave you electric shocks—'
    'You are getting mixed-up, Anne.'   (NS 288)

This indicates Murdoch's growing perception of Christ as pure good made to suffer pointlessly in the world, but mysteriously undegraded, an *idea* generating proper loving and true seeing.

Exactly what must our relationship be to this awful suffering?[4] Why does Christ shrug it off in *Nuns and Soldiers*? Murdoch's objection is to the self-indulgence to which such a direction of the imagination is all too susceptible. Emotional outpouring may parade as expiation, or *prevent* expiation. St Augustine speaks of art's dangerous capacity to cut one off from real things. Remembering his insensitivity to his own sins, he cries out: 'Yet all these I wept not, I who wept for Dido slain'. Murdoch likewise points to the fact that compellingly beautiful images may arrest the soul and hinder its progress beyond them. It is easy to mistake this for the true religious experience. But for Murdoch, no religious experience by itself is enough. Nothing can be the end and only such awareness as helps to shift the attention away from self is healthy.

Second, suffering may not only hold the soul rapt in complacent contemplation, it can tame and beautify death till it becomes 'painful and exhilarating, or at worst, charming and sweetly tearful' (SG 82). This is undeniable of much Christian art. The touching and beautiful *Stabat Mater* has precisely this effect; perhaps even the Pietà.

For this reason, Anne, unlike Julian, turns away from the recollected memory of the Passion, recoiling in horror as the romanticising haze clears away. Murdoch describes Anne's reaction thus:

> She was amazed to find her imagination flinching from his sufferings upon the cross as from an abominable, hardly conceivable torture. It was now like something she had read about in the newspapers, terrible things which gangsters or terrorists did to their victims . . . How there were no angels, no Father, only a man hanging up in an unspeakable anguish, of which for the first time she was able to grasp the details. She felt appalled and sick . . .   (NS 355)

This reaction comes much after the visitation. Christ had stressed death, not suffering:

> Suffering is a task. Death is a showing (NS 355).

Here Anne realises that suffering must be not a spectacle but a task, a continuous never-ending dying to self which one must be engaged in. Death must be the spectacle or the showing; the contemplation of death will persuade that the only thing of worth is the cultivation of virtue. Such suffering as this cultivation involves is welcome. Simone Weil, one of Murdoch's acknowledged influences, sees loving submission to pain as an active choice in the soul's ascent. Christ is the greatest example of such fine obedience. The giving up of the self, of which the great symbol is the Cross, makes for a new life qualitatively different from the old. Degrees of suffering (the dying of the grain) are involved in the discarding of selfishness. This kind of suffering as active task is central to Murdoch's moral–spiritual outlook.

One must note here that Julian too passes beyond the suffering Christ to the endless love which he is. Julian knows that pain is in time, but love outside it. She says:

> For the pains was a noble, worshipful deed done in a time by the working of love; but Love was without beginning, is, and shall be without ending.   (RDL 48)

Julian does not herself fall into the trap set by romantic adoration, but the tradition within which she writes can easily degenerate and miss the point. Murdoch's version shows that her reading of Julian has been extremely accurate, for it plucks out the essence of the *Revelations* and presents the core.

When it comes to the atonement, Murdoch takes a stand quite different from Julian's. In the fourth revelation Julian has a showing of Christ's copious bleeding, and she says clearly that this blood 'is ready to wash all creatures of sin'; it bursts the bands of hell, 'overfloweth all Earth', ascends to heaven and ensures the salvation of mankind. For Murdoch, the atonement seen as propitiatory offering poses an obstructing danger in the active regeneration of the self. The traditional concept of the salvific death of Christ which automatically ransoms the fallen soul is one with which she has little sympathy.

Her Anne cannot be thus cleansed and saved, though she cries out for it ('Help me. I want to be made good . . . I want to be made innocent, I want to be washed whiter than snow'). This Christ cannot help her ('Oh I'm afraid that's impossible', he said, looking at her sadly. NS 293). He tells her to try out the action of washing her hands if that is what she desires, and she does, only to find that it is no use at all. Murdoch means here that no force from outside can finish the regenerative process. It must start within the human heart. Christ, when Anne asks if there is salvation, replies 'Oh yes', but he says it almost carelessly. Then he adds, 'you must do it all yourself, you know.'

Murdoch's description of Christ's answer as 'said carelessly' reinforces his refusal to make a portentous, external process out of the matter of salvation. He says 'Oh yes' carelessly because he is no magician, no dramatic figure promising anything. This is in sharp contrast to the opening of Chapter 36 in *Revelations of Divine Love* in which Julian says:

> Our Lord God shewed that a deed shall be done, and Himself shall do it, and I shall do nothing but sin, and my sin shall not hinder His goodness working.   (RDL 72)

Anne's Christ merely affirms the fact of salvation – that is, the sovereignty of good – but nothing outside Anne can help her. She must help herself. He says to her:

> 'You must be the proof. The work is yours.'   (NS 293)

Murdoch's theology here has little in common with mainline Christian doctrine where perfect goodness and power are projected on to a divine imaginary being who has the double function of reducing man to an impotent creature and simultaneously providing him with a security outside himself. Orthodox Christianity has been criticised, by Feuerbach for example, for reducing man and alienating him from himself:

> Man projects his being into objectivity and then makes himself an object to this projected image of himself thus converted into a subject. . . . Man is separated from all that is good in him which is projected into a new being, and his own imperfection and nothingness remain his basic identity.[5]

Such a sense of imperfection and the perception of a contrast between the perfect and imperfect send Anne into the convent in the first place.

This earlier Anne has to be kept clearly in mind if we are to measure the distance she has travelled since her sojourn in the convent. Entering the convent after her conversion, she had surrendered fervently to a personal God, a personal saviour (NS 56). He was inextricably mixed up with her own unhappiness in the world and her flight from it. Her hope of redemption then lay with this being outside herself. This is the state of the earlier Anne, the Anne before the novel begins. Gradually the concept of a personal God falls away; she continues in the convent though she mourns loss of faith ('How did it all come, oh so gradually, to change': NS 57). Eventually, sensing a change inside like the symptom of a serious illness, she realises that it is her duty to move out of the convent, to abandon what had been achieved, and to start all over again.

She gives up the security of the religious life and returns to the world, a failed nun. Looking after her bereaved friend Gertrude of whom she is possessively fond, falling silently in love with Peter, who in turn is in love with Gertrude, Anne is drawn into a whirlpool of confused, possessive and jealous relationships. She emerges from this morass after the visitation with a clearer sense of herself and her religion. The old formula no longer holds; there is no God. But apparently *something* holds; otherwise there would be no visitation. Murdoch through the visitation is offering another concept of 'God'.

God is now found not above or outside the 'believer' but within the mind and heart. Acceptance of self, the world as it is, things

as they are, people as they are – this is the meaning of love. Anne
says to Christ, 'Love is my meaning', whereas Julian in the last
chapter of the *Revelations* says, 'Thus was I learned that Love was
our Lord's meaning' (RDL 202). The modification implies that the
separation of self from the 'other' and the transference of the self's
finest intellectual and affective capacities to a being outside no
longer hold. A unified self is given back to Anne. This is not to
say that Murdoch advocates a purely secular self-possession. An
enriched reabsorption and unification seem possible only after
painful alienation. For Anne, Christ was first external, and only
thereafter internalised and actualised.

Christ remains; it is Christ who awakens Anne, but he is no
miraculous being. He is simply the loving human heart. The birth
of love within the muddled selfish heart is the only miracle there
is ('You must be the miracle-worker, little one', says Christ to
Anne). The birth of love cannot be entirely explained away; hence
Murdoch presents it as a visitation, skirting the regions of the
mystical. However, such an experience is only a prelude to clearer
seeing and purer loving. It is as if the human psyche can generate
a vision of itself perfected, understand that it is none other than
itself, and live by the light of that vision. This is deity humanised
and internalised, a process altering the quality of consciousness.
As the self discovers the greatest good within itself and in the
created world, its fragmented torn pieces come together again,
making a loving whole and, thus restored, it moves towards the
still point of light.

How exactly is this good discovered and the spirit thereby
purified and healed? How does the discovery of the good within
the self necessarily improve the heart morally and spiritually? The
implication is that one can discover within, the strength to love
good and do right, the good within responding to the good
without. This brings peace. It needs no self-abasement, only
confidence in one's power to *be* good, to do right and refrain from
doing wrong. Christ's answer to Anne is as simple as the answer
in the gospel.

To do all the work by looking within is neither to triumph in
one's will-power, nor to punish oneself through contempt of self
and the world. Instead, virtue rises from proper loving, both of
the self and the world outside; it springs from a benevolent egoism
which simultaneously loves the self and sees the outside world as
love-worthy and independent. The difficulty of this is illustrated

through Anne's struggle in the world outside the convent.

III

Of all the good figures forming the subject of this study, Anne is the most flawed; the only one seen in the actual process of struggle. She is also the only woman; emotional forces that militate against control are spread out and displayed through her. In every personal interaction, from the moment she re-enters the world, there is a knot that needs to be untied through willed effort.

To begin with, Gertrude. Anne's old friendship with Gertrude, revived when she leaves the convent and seeks her out, has clear streaks of the possessive and quasi-erotic. She goes to Gertrude's flat only as a temporary refuge but readily stays when asked to. The extraordinary scene in which she plunges naked into the sea to be rescued thence by a panic-striken Gertrude (NS 109–13) has undercurrents of sexuality and emotional dependence that prepare the reader for the oblique hint at an earlier involvement with a 'beloved one' in the convent (NS 305). Daisy picks up the latent possibility with an unerring and ferocious promptness when Anne goes to 'interrogate' her:

> 'So you're an old friend of Gertrude's, I *see*. Now I've got it. The intrusive old girl friend. You're in love with Gertrude! That's why you're so filled with spite and envy, coming round here and insinuating things and asking questions! Tell bloody Gertrude to ask her own bloody questions! Get out! Jesus bloody Christ, as if I hadn't enough trouble without being persecuted by jealous nuns suffering from sexual deprivation! Oh *get out!*'   (NS 325)

When Anne, coming upon the last seconds of an encounter between Peter and Gertrude, realises that he is in love with her friend, she is disturbed. The comment that follows her immediate reaction ('how odd, how improper!' NS 120) is this: 'Anne felt suddenly sad.'

When she is shown the anonymous letter with the message: *Gertrude is having a love-affair with Tim Reede*, she feels 'a shock like a blow, then a hot flame and flash of emotion' (NS 239), and thinking of it later she frowns and turns away:

Her majestic Gertrude and that petty man? *No.*   (NS 240)

The point here is not the lesbian undercurrent but the impulse to possess and dominate Gertrude, to take charge of her life. When Gertrude sets that at naught by falling in love with Tim Reede, Anne experiences the pain of exclusion.

Her attitude to Tim is snobbish and judging; instinctively he is afraid of her, and sees her as cold and censorious.

The muddle gets much worse when Anne falls hopelessly in love with Peter (who is in love with Gertrude, who is in love with Tim, who was, once, in love with Daisy).

The whole point of such a circular pursuit is to indicate the unreliability of erotic love. The 'imperative of Eros', referred to more than once, is a shortlived imperative, and one can guess that the combinations will have changed in another five years. Anne's task is to step, once again, out of the world's muddle, and find her way alone. There is one point in the novel towards the end, after Anne's quiet preparation to give up her love for Peter (NS 378), when she, Gertrude and Peter in the South of France are surprised by a prodigal Tim who, having nearly drowned in the canal, turns up to fall into Gertrude's waiting arms. At that moment, a fierce self-centred joy rises up in Anne's heart; there is the prospect of Peter now free for her; she pulls him out of the house towards the two waiting bicycles, even puts his hands on the handlebars, and with a 'Come on, Peter, you're mine now', which he is too upset to hear, actually takes him away from France to England, laughing with joy ('a strange distant sound . . . Anne Cavidge laughing': NS 428). However, as Brendan had noted in *Henry and Cato*, this absolutely natural human good has to be given up by Anne. She sees that Peter and Gertrude want freedom to be 'reserved' for one another, even while Gertrude rests warmly in the nest of her marriage to Tim. There is a love-pact between them, and Anne understands that she must not even seek to break it; *their* freedom must be cherished by *her*. Love, finally, is letting others live; not asserting oneself; experiencing 'the solitude of the heart'. Love must exist without hope of return or union, and must not seek its own.

As mentioned in the introductory chapter, a properly loving regard sees the autonomy and freedom of other objects and persons, but given the strength of selfish attachments, this perspective, while simple enough to understand, is immensely difficult to achieve. Murdoch says in *The Sovereignty of Good*:

> The love which brings the right answer is an exercise of justice
> and realism and really *looking*. The difficulty is to keep the
> attention upon the real situation and to prevent it from returning
> surreptitiously to the self with consolations of self-pity,
> resentment, fantasy and despair. (SG 91)

That Anne finds this extraordinarily difficult is brought out by her
sullenness and her unbearable headaches. Her possessive longing
for Peter ('the terrible love-yearning, the *I want him, I want him, I
shall die without him* which kept returning and rising up in her
heart': NS 497) has to be opposed, controlled and redirected with
great pain. The love that Anne realises is her meaning lies
precisely in seeing Peter as another free, separate creature attached
elsewhere. Such accurate vision is proper loving and it entails the
renunciation of the other kind of loving. Thus Anne, after the
visitation, learns to understand the hardness of her task. Its
immense complexity dawns on her when she sees that even
planning the defeat of her own interests may be self-centred high-
mindedness. Everything in the situation has to be scrupulously
examined. She realises that in going to find out about Tim and
Daisy (the truth of which will mean the end of the Tim–Gertrude
marriage and so clear the way for Gertrude's happiness with Peter
with whom Anne herself is in love), she has been honourably
organising the defeat of her own hopes without thinking carefully
enough about the entire situation. In her egotistical assumption of
virtue she has not *seen* Daisy. She realises afterwards the imperfection innate in her own failure to feel, 'when she should have felt
it, pity. . .' (NS 496). She sees now that the mess of human
relationships has to be seen and thought through with infinite
care. Such accurate vision purifies the heart and reduces anxious
selfish concern.

Anne's answer to Christ, 'Love is my meaning', is heavy with
significance in the light of the intricate relationships that cross and
recross one another through the pattern of the novel. The word
'love' is applicable to most of them, but Anne, in that encounter
with Christ, sees suddenly and clearly the only kind of love which
has any meaning, the love which Christ incarnated, and which
must now be her own. What it amounts to, in terms of the novel,
is giving up Peter, Gertrude, and the warm comfortable ambience

of their world, by dying to her own needs.

One can understand that the explication of such a lesson comes best from the figure of Christ. Only then can the force of Anne's 'new' understanding be communicated. Hence the vision in which Christ appears to Anne.

IV

One last issue remains. The visitation described in *Nuns and Soldiers* is not a mystical experience of the kind described in *Revelations of Divine Love*. The Christ–Anne exchange is distinctly lacking in rapture. There is nowhere a sense of the invasion of the whole being and the world by something else, or the blotting-out and disappearance of the ordinary. For the true mystic *that* is real; for Murdoch the real is here and *this*. Julian's mystical rapture is unmistakable, but Murdoch's Anne, struggling almost sullenly ('Why does Anne have to say these dreadful, clear, definite things? Why does she always judge?': NS 248), is a creature engaged in a moral struggle, not capable of surrender.

However, excitement of a certain kind is certainly generated by the successful imaginative reconstruction of a concept. She uses the device of vision to clarify the understanding of good, and places the required emphasis on the altering of consciousness. This Christ, instead of picking up the burdens we lay at his feet as he is traditionally meant to do, directs the task of change back to Anne. Not the mystical evocation of vision, but the projection of an idea is Murdoch's intention here. It is this clarification that generates what Keats would have called 'an irritable reaching after reason and fact' and 'a giving up of the mystery'.

Her primary concern is with morality, and the Christ–Anne exchange is descriptive of 'a kind of moral psychology' rather than the mystical state.

If Christ gives Anne *all* the work to be done, does it mean that God or transcendent good, now understood as a reflection of human essence, is unnecessary? If so, moral philosophy needs no help from any outside source.

Murdoch treads a very honestly, minutely examined path here. She has herself raised the question in *The Sovereignty of Good*:

But now it may be asked: are you speaking of a transcendent authority or of a psychological device?   (SG 58)

She goes on to say that the idea of the transcendent in some form or the other belongs to morality. In the dialogue on religion in *Acastos*, Acastos says:

'I think it means that we've drawn to the idea of a sort of central – good – something very real – after all morality *feels* more like discovering something than just inventing it – and we want to sort of, assert this central thing.'   (*Acastos*, 85)

Christ may then be seen as a moving embodiment of a set of *a priori* moral imperatives to which assent is given. At one level he stands for the idealistic philosophers' acknowledgement of a magnetic pull from somewhere working on the soul and directing it towards itself. But she needs more than just the pure, naked concept; she needs a colour and evocation that cannot be entirely explained away in rational terms. To suggest that part of the soul which is free of mechanistic determinism she uses the image of Christ, and more especially a Christ associated with mystical experience, since mysticism can be neither wholly dismissed nor wholly explained.

Mysticism provides the background for moral activity. She says in *The Sovereignty of Good*:

Morality has always been connected with religion and religion with mysticism. The disappearance of the middle term leaves morality in a situation which is certainly more difficult but essentially the same. The background to morals is properly some sort of mysticism, if by this is meant a non-dogmatic, essentially unformulated faith in the reality of the Good.   (SG 74)

Clearly, some ireducible significance-investing faith cannot be given up, and this residual core seems to be love. There is no rational explanation for love. This is why Julian's mystical experience is an exquisitely appropriate background for Murdoch's purpose of clarifying the state of the soul caught in a moment of moral endeavour, seeing love as a task.

Anne's wounded hand refusing to heal and the little stone on the kitchen table where Christ placed it can be explained away by saying that Anne has developed a malignant condition, and that the stone is merely one of many she herself brought back from Cumbria. The fact that Anne has a *dream* of the angels and Christ's footsteps and then *wakes* up to find Christ standing in the kitchen can be explained by saying that Anne dreamed that she had dreamt and then awoke. But Anne's acts of renunciation cannot be explained away. Murdoch has left the door open for naturalistic explanation, but her use of Julian of Norwich here clearly indicates the connection she sees between morals and mysticism. The visitation begins with a dream in a rose-garden, an allusion surely meant to remind the reader of T. S. Eliot's mystical spot of time in the rose-garden of 'Burnt Norton'.

The entire exchange is handled with such reverence, tact and love, that it leaves the reader feeling that something extraordinary has happened. What Murdoch is saying may not be startling or new to liberal theologians today, for there have been radical changes in the interpretation of Christ over the last twenty-five years. She glances at this early in the novel when the dying Guy says to Anne that she need not have left the convent because she had lost faith in a personal God ('Maybe you should have hung on. Christian theology is changing so fast these days. The relieving troops would have arrived. You would have heard the sound of bagpipes' NS 65). But it makes a startling impact when fictionalised. The ingress of the spiritual into the temporal alters the quality of what is largely a realistic novel about the English upper-middle class.

The Christ of *Nuns and Soldiers* has immense charm, tenderness, humour. One cannot help quaking with love for him even as Anne does. However consciously Murdoch may be using language and image to project a certain idea, she appears to love her Christ figure. She cannot shed her ideas, true, but neither can she shed some inner conviction about the validity of mystical experience. This explains the 'in-between' effect of the Christ–Anne exchange, neither rising to rapture, nor entirely reducible to conceptual terms.

The conclusion is that the middle term – religion – may have disappeared in our time, but the first (the transcendent good there) and the last (moral effort here) are the same. Anne may not be Julian, but Christ is eternally himself, a light from a source beyond, playing over the sad muddle of the world till it is answered by a light from here.

5

William Eastcote in *The Philosopher's Pupil*

One way of considering Murdoch's development of simpler notions of the good is to see it as a movement towards an extremely Protestant notion of goodness. Different kinds of genuine spirituality as embodied in different religious traditions are carefully examined, the valuable in them lovingly offset against the surrounding charlatanism, and then a movement made to a further position inward. Denudation is an inextricable part of the exploration. I do not suggest that she ultimately asserts a Protestant version of truth, for it is very clear that she allies herself with no one version. But the movement itself, even when she has discarded the explicitly Protestant stand (as she does after *The Philosopher's Pupil*), is essentially a puritan expression; an attempt to purify and simplify.

The Philosopher's Pupil is, in a very obvious sense, Murdoch's most Protestant novel because the figure representing good here is a Quaker and the setting is a town largely dominated by Quakers. At the simplest level, such details as the Meeting House and the mention of 'good works' and 'blank Quaker rites' differentiate the religious tradition from that in *Henry and Cato* where the mystery of the Mass, the beauty of ritual and the weight of tradition were given their due.

The details do not merely provide local colour and define a milieu, though of course they do that as well, but they form an appropriate background for William Eastcote, a marginal character in this huge crowded canvas, the criterion by which all the rest may judge themselves, or the standard against which they are defined.

Of all the figures dealt with in this study, William Eastcote is the slightest in terms of the novelistic space he occupies. In a novel of 576 pages he himself appears directly only four times. On the fourth occasion he is dead. On the other three occasions he holds the attention for two pages at a time. There are about fifteen scattered references to him in the novel showing him present in the thoughts of other people, and two pages describing his funeral. The rest of the novel is given over to an enormous cast of people, a whole township, in which the philosopher Rozanov and his pupil George McAffrey provide two points of reference. It may be helpful to see William Eastcote as the hub of a huge circling wheel that churns up the mire as it turns, releasing disturbing energy in different directions but affecting not at all the still point at the centre. His virtual invisibility is highly significant, but because he says little and acts hardly at all, his significance has to be drawn out through contrasting major characters even more than with the other figures of this study.

This chapter deals first with the Quaker tradition which has produced William Eastcote; then with the man himself; thereafter, with four others who are very different; and finally, with his effect on those others.

I

Quakerism is the honed and refined end-product of the Reformation. Calvin went beyond Luther in defining the absolute importance as well as isolation of the individual's personal relationship with God, making Christian asceticism the daily affair of every believing Christian. Max Weber speaks of the deliberate and systematic elimination of magic from the religious life sought by the Protestant sects.[1] No visible church, no sacraments, priests or rituals could save the soul. Grace alone, manifesting itself in a moment-to-moment penetration of conduct in the ordinary world, could ensure salvation. The intentions of the believer and his efforts availed nothing. On the other hand, his good works were an indication of grace working within him. The whole Catholic cycle of sin, repentance, atonement followed by renewed sin, the endless chances awaiting the lapsed soul, were set aside.[2] Even those sects which did not adhere to the Calvinist doctrine of the elect insisted on the life of total consecration for everyman. He was to dedicate every single minute, thought, intention and act to God; his entire life was to illustrate his calling. As a result, every Christian had a calling and was a monk.

Of the various Protestant sects preaching the new morality, the Quakers went the farthest in the process of simplification. The individual was left alone with his conscience. He waited silently to be illumined by the Holy Spirit, and acted on the basis of this interior illumination. Silence was the source of spiritual spontaneity. The Meeting House of the Quakers contains nothing whatsoever, not even a Cross, nothing external to which the believer may relate. Christ has been wholly internalised.

At the spiritual level, this involves an absolute surrender of the will, an openness to the Holy Spirit, a profound inwardness, and self-examination leading to an amendment of life. At the ethical level it insists on an unremitting purity of motive and act proceeding directly from intercourse with God.

The Philosopher's Pupil was the novel that followed *Nuns and Soldiers* and William Eastcote here may be seen as the outcome of Anne's realisation in the earlier novel. In reply to her appeal to be cleansed, washed whiter than snow, Christ tells her to wash her own hands. She sadly realises that appeal to an outside redeemer is futile and she must do all the work herself. This stage in Murdoch's internalisation of good points towards William Eastcote. Quaker morality sees no opposition between the human and the divine, and affirms the divinising of the human through an indwelling Christ, a concept beautifully and accurately projected by the character of William Eastcote. The Quaker leader Barclay says in his *Apology* in 1678:

> The essence of the sacrament is inner washing, nurture, and Christ's real presence in worship; outward water, bread and wine are needless. Ministry and even prayer must wait for a result from divine leading.[3]

As Anne sheds tears over the futility of washing her hands, William Eastcote is already in the making.

With William Eastcote, to use Weberian terminology, Christian asceticism 'slams the door of the monastery'[4] (or convent) behind it, and strides into the marketplace, penetrating the daily routine of life, fashioning it into a life in the world, but neither of, nor for, the world. Eastcote retires early from a successful career at the bar to devote himself to good works. He comes of a wealthy family originally in trade. The connection between the spirit of modern economic life and the rational ethics of ascetic Protestantism is glanced at in those details. Twice Eastcote is referred to as 'a pillar of the Meeting House', an indication of his essential but unobtrusive presence in the world. He is also a highly respected citizen. Anne in *Nuns and Soldiers* leaves the convent, but will forever be an anchoress, carrying her cell with her through the world. In the *Philosopher's Pupil* that lingering trace of the recluse has disappeared. William Eastcote is the ascetic without a cell.

II

That he is indeed an ascetic, as the others surrounding him are not, becomes clearer as the novel unfolds. He is marked out from the beginning as being the one to whom the luminous flying-saucer over Ennistone has been clearly visible; the two or three others who see it have more dubious sightings (PP 28). In the blanket of rumour and superstition that envelops the town, it is agreed that if Bill the Lizard (William Eastcote) has seen it, there must be some truth in it.

The nature of Eastcote's rationality and truthfulness, the greater likelihood of his being in touch with good spirit than anyone else, grows gradually out of such remarks. Rozanov classes most Ennistonians as rotten swine, but makes an exception of Bill the Lizard. Nesta Wiggins is particularly attached to him. Emma Scarlett Taylor, a stranger in Ennistone, comes along to the Meeting House 'because of Mr. Eastcote'. The casual testimony of an outsider is significant; so too is his comment on what he liked most at the Meeting: 'The silence, the little dog. What Mr. Eastcote said.' These three things in combination are the locus of good.[5] Tom's rejoinder to Emma's reply is:

Yes – he makes one feel purified, washed clean, whiter than snow   (PP 210).

These are Anne's words to Christ in *Nuns and Soldiers*, and go back to Psalm 51.

Murdoch begins her account of Eastcote's address at the Meeting with a paragraph about Fr Bernard leading the faithful in prayer in the Anglican Church of St Olaf's. The beautiful phrases from Cranmer's Prayer book provide an effective foil for the silence that reigns at that very moment in the Friend's Meeting House. The blankness of Quakerism is seen to be rich in introspection as Murdoch takes the reader through the course of the Sunday morning there. There is nothing in the room but three benches, a table, and sunlight streaming in through 'wind-handled trees' outside. Silence reigns. No one need speak; anyone may.

As usual, Murdoch enters completely into the spirit of the tradition she is looking at. The simplicity and directness of Quaker worship are not only evoked with marvellous accuracy, they are posited as a kind of supreme excellence. Such silence and waiting for the Spirit of God to descend and illumine the consciousness has exactly the right blend of humility and purified emotion seen as desirable in *The Sovereignty of Good*. The beautiful is nowhere in sight to distract and charm; the good has been separated from the surrounding mesh and held up in its transparency against the light. Worship is nothing other than silent waiting upon God. 'Christ reborn in us', or 'the Seed' or 'the light' are the phrases Quakers use to describe the surrender in the silence, the transformation of the person into a better, kinder, simpler, more loving being. Each person wages, alone, the crucial inner war against human pride and corrupt desire. In the interior light, all of life becomes sacramental, grace abounds, and the consciousness is altered (but never once and for all) in the direction of good. There is no ministry; all true disciples are channels through whom grace may flow to others. William Eastcote is not, therefore, an avowed leader; all members have equal responsibility to be 'Good stewards of God's manifold grace'.[6] Yet in the Ennistone Meeting House everyone recognises that Eastcote is a freer, purer being than most:

No one at Meeting ever spoke after William Eastcote had spoken.   (PP 203)

He is singled out and centred in another way as well. Before his address the thoughts of some of the others are made known to the reader. Then he rises to his feet and speaks. Thereafter the silence rings with the sounds of what he has said as each member undertakes an amendment of life in the light of what he has heard.

At one level merely the words of an Evangelical preacher, they stand out with startling luminosity against the dark confusion in the hearts and minds of the people in the township, offering innocence as a real possibility. Similar sounds of innocence have been heard earlier in the two letters written by the invisible Fr Milsom to Cato in *Henry and Cato*, but there is a very precisely defined shade of difference. Fr Milsom's innocence was rooted in the knowledge and loving acceptance of all that can go wrong, and was expressive of a perpetually renewed offer of fresh starts. William Eastcote's words are innocent in a different way. They ask for an alert, intelligent conscience that can make the path simple and clear. Quakerism offers a practical mysticism, a directing of purified emotional fervour to *conduct* in the world. William Eastcote incarnates the poised equilibrium between reason and feeling that comes closest to that contemplative state of loving attention mentioned in the introductory chapter. He is not shown acting; that is left for the figures of good in the next two novels, but his capacity for right action is glanced at in the way the others miss his guidance after his death.

At the Meeting he clearly defines the norm that hovers over the disorders everywhere in the novel:

My dear friends, we live in an age of marvels. Men among us can send machines far out into space. Our homes are full of devices which would amaze our forebears. At the same time our beloved planet is ravaged by suffering and threatened by dooms. Experts and wise men give us vast counsel suited to vast ills. I want only to say something about simple things which are as it were close to us, within our reach, part still of our world. Let us love the close things, the close clear good things, and hope that in their light other goods may be added. Let us prize innocence. The child is innocent, the man is not. Let us prolong and cherish the innocence of childhood, as we find it in the child and as we discover it later within ourselves. Repentance, renewal of life, such as is the task and possibility of every man, is a recovery of innocence. Let us see it thus, a return to a certain simplicity, something which is not hard to understand, not a remote good but very near. Let us then seek aid in pure things, turning our mind to good people, to our best work, to beautiful and noble art, to the pure words of Christ in the Gospel, and to the works of God obedient to him in nature. Help is always near if we will only turn. Conversion is turning about, and it can happen not only every day but every moment. Shun the cynicism which says that our world is so terrible that we may as well cease to care and cease to strive, the notion of a cosmic crisis where ordinary duties cease to be and moral fastidiousness is out of place. At any time there are many many small things we can do for other people which will refresh us and them with new hope. . . . Above all, do not despair, either for the planet or in the deep inwardness of the heart. Recognise one's own evil, mend what can be mended, and for what cannot be undone, place it in love and faith in the clear light of the healing goodness of God.   (PP 204–5)

This address captures perfectly the essence of the practical mysticism mentioned earlier. The words, sentence-construction and rhythms evoke a particular kind of purified resoluteness which is simple, but far from facile or simplistic. There is a preponderance of compound sentences, with 'ands' and 'buts' holding the observations together. The balance of a compound sentence draws the attention equally to the different parts of the sentence, so that the overall impression is one of clarity and transparency. Subordinate clauses introducing qualifications and complexity are relatively few, surprisingly few for an address of this length. In addition, there are numerous parallel phrases. For instance:

Let us then seek aid in pure things, turning our minds to good people, to our best work, to beautiful and noble art, to the pure words of Christ in the Gospel and to the works of God obedient to Him in nature.

Parallel phrases also distribute the attention equally over the sentence, reinforcing the impression of unimpeded clear movement and just, fair attentiveness. The language accurately projects the nearness, directness and lucidity of the good he sees.

By contrast, Fr Bernard's worship comes mostly through the grandeur and majesty of the Prayer Book, with its circling suspended clauses and the cumulative sweep of sentence structures strewn with synonyms and rich images. At the close of the novel, when Fr Bernard has moved from a clouded and spurious religiosity into a crazed but clearer light, he writes to the narrator N about the simplicity he finally understands. But he cannot shed his rhetoric; the sentence-construction reveals that the longed-for innocence is still far to seek. Consider, for example, this from his letter to N:

Nothing else but *true religion* can save mankind from a lightless and irredeemable materialism, from a technocratic nightmare where determinism *becomes true* for all except an *unimaginably depraved* few who are themselves the mystified slaves of a conspiracy of machines.   (PP 570)

The length of this complex sentence, the attention-drawing italicised phrases, the many adjectives, the qualifying subordinate clauses, all contribute to an overall impression of emotional and spiritual tortuousness. If William Eastcote's words have the limpidity of a clear piece of water, Fr Bernard's suggest a churning flow. In the balance and rationality of William Eastcote's sentences there was no need for emphasis, for everything was equally important and plain. Language has been used by Murdoch not only to evoke a vivid impression but to suggest a theological–spiritual differentiation as well.

William Eastcote is himself surprised by his own address. As he sits down with beating heart and trembling hands he wonders silently to himself whatever possessed him to utter all those words, and where they might have come from. Even this much rhetoric seems to him 'high-flown'; it is as if absolute purity lies in silence alone. His address, while taking in the malaise of contemporary life – its cynicism, promiscuity and hopelessness – suggests that even this huge confusion may be saved by a resolute and willed return to innocence. While it has the moral earnestness characteristic of Baptist sects, it is not grim; the asceticism is softened by his implication that the beautiful as well as the good may alter and improve the quality of our consciousness. He calls not for an impulsive and spontaneous response, but for a disciplined, meditated ordering of thought and feeling.

The difference between an exhortation of this kind and discussion of morality as a concept is underlined by Eastcote's quiet ducking out of Rozanov's invitation to talk philosophy with him (PP 95). Instead he asks Rozanov whether he would like to go to Meeting:

'Will you come to Meeting with me on Sunday?'
   'I love your Quakerish meetings and your Quakerish ways, but it would be false.'
   'You mean it would seem false.'
   'You should have been a philosopher.'   (PP 96)

Each withdraws from the centre of the other's activity. Rozanov's remark later to Fr Bernard: 'Morality makes mincemeat of metaphysics by the simplicity of its claim . . . so a quiet life and no guilt'

(PP 188), defines the parameters of complexity and simplicity within which the human being moves. Rozanov's and Fr Bernard's 'interesting' conversations are far removed from Eastcote's address but that address is the moral centre of the book.

In the aftermath immediately following his speech, 'each person present promised himself some amendment of life'. Very significantly, 'an increase of being' is whimsically attributed to the tiny dog Zed because 'his nature was composed almost entirely of love'. Zed's immediate 'recognition' of Eastcote as identical with himself, another being composed of love, is the most explicit sign that the writer's moral standpoint is here.

Much later in the novel, N the narrator, speaking of the universal willingness of almost everyone to indulge in spiteful gossip, remarks that, because of his virtuous austerity, William Eastcote was someone who was never idly gossiped to – 'but in this respect as in others he was exceptional' (PP 425). That could be easily missed as just one observation among many, but in fact it pinpoints his singularity and value.

Is he, after all this, yet another insufferably self-righteous Puritan? Or if not self-righteous, too perfect and too good to be convincing? Of all the characters who form the subject of this study, he is the most tranquil; we see less of his struggle. But Murdoch manages to keep him beautifully balanced on the tightrope to saintliness, tenderly humanising him with frailties on occasion. Speaking of social snobbery among the best families in Ennistone and noting its absence in the younger generation, the narrator remarks on the presence of some grain of irrational superiority in the mind of William Eastcote. He is thus lovingly placed in his generation (his niece Anthea has not a trace of it), and shown as one moulded by the social structure that has produced him. Another touch of human weakness is shown in the Baths where Eastcote stands on the edge of the pool and watches young Tom McAffrey dive elegantly and unerringly into the water. Conscious of his age and his illness, he experiences stabs of envy as he takes in Tom's careless, strong grace. He thinks:

I would have enjoyed the snow and seeing Tom standing there and dive. Only now I can't. And I am envious of Tom, I am envious because he is young and strong and will live, and I am not, and will not . . .   (PP 292)

There follows a moment of doubt while he wonders whether to tell Rozanov that he knows death is imminent. It seems to him at this point that death is the greatest failure that there is. This is the only time we are allowed to see a little of his struggle. The quiet awareness with which he honestly faces himself is in sharp contrast with the confused struggles of other, more important characters in the novel, and is clearly seen by Murdoch to be an indispensable ingredient in the composition of good.

III

That William Eastcote's goodness is achieved through struggle and purification is an impression that grows not so much from detailed elaboration as from implicit contrasts with other characters who have not put themselves through the refining fire.

Gabriel McAffrey, for instance, wife of Brian and sister-in-law of George McAffrey, is drawn with much sympathy but is carefully distinguished from the cleanness and transparency which define William Eastcote. Gabriel is full of a welling sorrowful love for all unprotected vulnerable things, everything that suffers. It comes pouring out of her, almost as if there is too much milk in her breasts. The narrator uses the word 'invisible' in connection with her, a word Murdoch usually reserves for 'good' people.[7]

Invisibility implies quietness, and humility, and freedom from compulsive needs to draw attention to the self. So when the narrator says about Gabriel, 'She made her home her fortress where she was secure and content to be invisible' (PP 55), we are led to think she might be a possible moral centre.

In addition, she gives love copiously. She thinks of 'woodlice which had to be tenderly liberated into the garden, spiders which were to be respected in their corners'. She weeps for the unfortunate Stella; and for the poor fish which she redeems from the boys for two pounds and releases into the sea; and for the lonely Indian at the Ennistone Baths whom she fails to befriend in time and goes running after in vain. Her love reaches out ineffectually to George as well, and the lake of protective pity in her heart overflows at her eyes again and again. Her capacity to suffer with those that suffer is the mark of an innocent and admiring soul.

Why then does Gabriel seem slightly absurd? The answer may be found in the fact that her surging love is an expression of her

own need to give and perhaps not intimately enough related to
the object of her regard. The creatures she interacts with, animal
as well as human, are seen through the haze of her sentimentalising
sorrow. She allows pain and vulnerability to overwhelm her to the
point where they become a source of satisfaction, feeding a need
to feel. Tears rise to her eyes as she remembers that she had
refused to buy a cracked jug Adam had wanted. The section where
Adam whimsically personifies the jug and insists on its forlornness
and abandonment (PP 200) reveals the precise nature of the
'tortured sensibility' she is handing on to her son.

Gabriel's emotionalism, good in moderation, becomes a self-
regarding attention to things outside, a way of looking which is
not calm and objective as well as loving.[8] She is imprisoned by her
subjectivity and written off as weak. As she rushes out impulsively
to find the lonely Indian, her mother-in-law Alex McAffrey sarcasti-
cally comments on her distraught appearance, 'My daughter-in-
law is so quaint . . . we all love her' (PP 298). Alex has little
affection for Gabriel and few people in Ennistone have much
respect for her; whereas, when Eastcote dies, even hardboiled Alex
recognises the source of comfort and strength he had been.

Clearly William Eastcote manifests a different kind of love,
strong, quiet and reliable. For love to have these attributes, the
pain of self-denial has necessarily to be endured. Gabriel's pain is
too much an indulgence of her emotional needs. Eastcote thinks
of his dead wife Rose (PP 203), talks to the child Adam (PP 292),
smiles at Gabriel McAffrey (PP 199) – but all emotional responses,
while genuine, are low-keyed.

Gabriel has a moment of self-awareness at the Meeting House:

> Gabriel felt nothing but pain . . . . Her feelings . . . were part
> of her silliness, part of the stupid feeble sensibility which made
> her encourage Adam's funny soft porous attitude to the world,
> and be hurt by it at the same time . . . it was all to do with her
> feeling so sorry for everything.   (PP 200)

However, she is unable to check and modify the feeling; it
remains a weakness. Loving-kindness is one of the ingredients of
good, but it is not by itself enough. It needs to be linked with
other qualities of the mind and spirit to evolve into goodness.
Good contains all the virtues within itself, is made up of a number
of different qualities. Gabriel, lacking some of these, is as much a

contrast to the still point at the centre as Rozanov and George McAffrey, though less obviously so.

If Gabriel falls short of goodness because mind does not enter sufficiently into her response, John Robert Rozanov, the philosopher of the title, has let it enter too much, to the exclusion of other essential components. Or such was the case before the beginning of the novel. Now, at the point the novelist has chosen for depiction, his starved, uncultivated heart rages in reaction. Rozanov is famous, Ennistone's most famous son, brilliant exponent of the analytical approach so characteristic of British philosophy. In describing this, Murdoch evokes an impression of early brilliance comparable with A. J. Ayer's or Bertrand Russell's. He is described as belonging to 'the most austerely anti-metaphysical school' (PP 77), and the various titles he has published indicate an incisive intellect. Rozanov is an interesting comment on the aridity of intellectual activity when unaccompanied by a commensurate spiritual–emotional development.

Rozanov, now in his sixties, has begun to doubt the value of his lifelong attempt to organise and order things so as to make truth a little clearer. Perhaps he has been mistaken about everything? *Now* he sees:

> beyond was chaos, the uncategorised manifold, the ultimate jungle of the world, before which the metaphysician covers his eyes. (PP 130)

At this stage to start intellectualising about the presence or absence of the 'other' appears to him futile; there are no clear edges anywhere, only 'an amoebic jelly, an unsavoury ectoplasm of wandering ideation' (PP 130). His mind now helps him precious little; instead, the consciousness of muddle becomes a torment (PP 130).

Rozanov is beginning to realise that while intellectual activity keeps pain at bay for a while by providing a satisfying sense of order, there is a point at which the satisfaction gives way to a range of painful experiences.

The most obvious of these is the intellectual pain of loss of meaning and of admitting that one has been mistaken or deluded. This is painful for the ego unless it has been continually checked and monitored by the spirit to face and accept failure.

Rozanov's state of mind (PP 131–5) evokes the weariness and

satiation of Marlowe's Faustus who has come to the end of certain kinds of knowledge.

Like Faustus pondering the limits of logic and 'physic', Rozanov too goes over the field. He thinks thus:

> Why do thoughts not lose their owners? . . . How does consciousness continue, how can it? Could the curse of money not end and why did it not end? . . . Who could fathom Plato's mind? (PP 130).

Reducing the 'good' to the 'real' (PP 134), he dismisses religion as a different phenomenon on which philosophy cannot pronounce. Eastcote's idea of the real and good contains more than Rozanov's; he can sit still while Rozanov is 'pitchforked' from point to point till, again like Faustus, he dies in despair, leaving a suicide note for Eastcote, one of his few 'real' friends.

Eastcote's refusal to talk philosophy with Rozanov, despite his ability to do so, is indicative of control. Rozanov, on the other hand, needs to discuss these things endlessly. He tells Eastcote that he would like to have someone to talk to. The exchange is as follows (Eastcote is the first speaker):

> 'There must be someone here for your purposes.'
>   'For me to make use of!'
>   'I don't mean it like that.'
>   'Of course not, Bill. Damn it, there's you!'
>   'I still play bridge, but that's not your scene. What about N?' (PP 95)

William Eastcote's polite refusal to engage in such discussions is a comment on their futility, borne out by the two extended, highly intellectual conversations between Rozanov and Fr Bernard. While they make very interesting and difficult reading, evoking marvellously the thrilling pleasure that talk about thought can generate, they project, nevertheless, a picture of two lost and wandering souls, hindered, not helped, by sophisticated intellectual ruminations.

Such is the message if Eastcote is taken as the criterion, but the subtext works against this, and exchanges like the following between Rozanov and Fr Bernard force thought and attention in a way that makes Eastcote's refusal uninteresting. Rozanov speaks first:

> 'When one reaches a certain point, morality becomes a riddle to
> which one must find the answer. The holy inevitably moves
> towards the demonic. Fra Angelico loved Signorelli.'
>   'Perhaps he did. But then didn't Signorelli love Fra Angelico?
> The demonic moves towards the holy.'
>   'No. That is my point. If the holy even knows of the demonic
> it is lost. The flow is in that direction, the tide runs that way,
> water flows downhill' (PP 196).

This is an interesting conversational exchange, and as noted,
Eastcote's silence seems 'uninteresting' by comparison. This is the
point. Good may be 'uninteresting'. What is one to make of
Eastcote's silence? Rozanov's 'Damn it, Bill, there's you' is evidence
of his capacity to be engaged. But he will not play or be drawn
into a game which he senses is harmful. The relationship between
articulated thought and moral goodness is difficult to prise out.
Eastcote *can* talk but will not. Are moral concepts then not to be
clarified? Where does one stop? Or is the clarification to be
undertaken silently by oneself and then practised? Anne and Christ
do talk about these things, but briefly, and from this point onward,
Eastcote's refusal implies that discussion creates an illusion of
progress and clarity: an exciting sense of having understood; or
conversely, an exciting sense of never being able to understand.
Both pleasures are self-regarding and silence is best. Stuart Cuno,
the good figure in the next novel, remarks to the psychiatrist who
wants the interesting conversational exchanges with Stuart to
continue, that 'talking spoils everything'.[9] But Rozanov gives
intellectual understanding the highest possible value by saying
that if there is a place beyond good and evil it is our *duty* to go
there (PP 196). While he claims that his greatest fear is to come to
a point where morality vanishes, he urges pressing onwards to
such a state if the intellect demands it.

So much for Rozanov's problem at the level of thought. At the
level of moral action the discrepancy between mental concept and
actual behaviour is shocking. Despite his expressed dread at the
possible disappearance of morality, and despite N's comment that
Rozanov's 'personal morality had a simplicity which his philosophy
lacked' (PP 134), he acts like one who has not given moral action
and feeling a second thought. Early in the novel the narrator says

that Rozanov was puzzled to find the extent to which his life was
still ruled by vanity (PP 132). The events that unfold reveal that
he is ruled by power-lust, incestuous desire, criminal indifference
and fear of mockery as well as vanity. He is not very different from
the pupil he despises.

His relationship with his former pupil, George McAffrey, gives
the book its title. The portrayal of these two communicates the
failure of philosophy to give order and meaning to life. Rozanov's
cultivation of the intellect has left the heart untouched, and when
his grand-daughter at the end bursts out with

'You have no common sense – no decent feeling at all'   (PP 542)

he has no answer.

His refusal to notice George shows that his notion of morality
remains at the conceptual level.[10] George's wretchedness and rage
stem from Rozanov's early dismissal of him as a mediocre student
who had better give up philosophy. His pursuit of his old teacher
to America, his pleas for an interview and pathetic recall of
Rozanov's statements made years earlier have all happened before
the novel begins (PP 141–6). There is a replay of this obsession in
the novel which opens with talk of Rozanov's possible return to
Ennistone. George's hero-worship and humiliation come surging
back, and after Rozanov's return, he hunts him with energy, but
Rozanov treats him with an indifference much worse than scorn
and tells him to go away.

Rozanov has been a teacher as well as a philosopher. His refusal
to nurture his pupil, and see him as an individual desperately
needing reassurance, shows that his failure as a teacher is no less
monstrous than his failure as a grandparent. Teacher and parent
are related roles; both demand loving attention to the vulnerable.
In both roles Rozanov reacts immorally, refusing to feel in the first
case, and feeling wrongly in the second.

His hardness towards George gives the latter, violent as he is, a
claim to the reader's sympathy which the philosopher forfeits. He
says to George:

'As far as I'm concerned you don't exist.' (PP 224)

That he is capable of saying this shows how far he is from a true
engagement with the moral good or 'the real'. His impressive

capacity to conceptualise deeply and clearly only underscores the shockingly absent humanity. To Fr Bernard's suggestion that he should be kind to George ('Just a little gentleness. You have so much power.' PP 227), he replies with a quotation from Dante: '*Guarda e passa* – Look and pass on.' This indifference, when a word might heal the wounded George, is an exercise in power. Rozanov had inflicted the initial wound assessing George as no good; as a teacher he had to do this, but the pain-inflicting process has been continuous and conscious since then. Finally, after the scandalous reports have appeared in *The Ennistone Gazette*, he turns around snarling in rage at George because now he himself has been wounded.

The assumption underlying the judgement passed above on Rozanov is that it is wrong knowingly to cause pain, the one common assumption that all moral–religious systems share. But if there is to be a choice made between telling the truth (that George is no good at philosophy) and causing pain, what is the responsibility here? There has to be a separation of roles of judging teacher from kind human being – and the two roles have to be played on parallel lines. In this moral task, Rozanov fails conspicuously. His indifference to George is not entirely free of malice. As he throws away George's letter unopened, 'the tiny corner of John Robert's mind which was aware of George' experiences 'a fleeting satisfaction' (PP 427). He writes a hate-filled letter to George, and when Pearl, the servant he employs as Hattie's paid companion, declares her love for him, he looks at her with loathing ('You disgust me': PP 448).

Next, he is capable of lying. Hattie's longing to see Pearl, the maid from whom Rozanov has separated her, is met with a deliberate lie: that Pearl had been glad to see Hattie go. In fact, however, Pearl had begged to be allowed to remain near Hattie and the philosopher because she loved them both.

But then, Eastcote also gives himself permission to lie to Rozanov about the true state of his health. He says he is well when he is actually on the verge of death. Is this different from Rozanov's lie? Both are distortions of fact; so both are lies, and judged by the strictest code, Eastcote also fails. But Eastcote's deliberate decision is taken to spare Rozanov embarrassment, to protect his own privacy. The great difference is in the effect of the lie. Rozanov's is uttered in order to manipulate Hattie as he desires; in saying it he knowingly gives pain to Hattie, and consciously blackens and falsifies Pearl. Eastcote's lie, on the other hand, spreads no ripples whatsoever; it merely helps him to keep a secret which ultimately has nothing to do with anyone else, thereby saving his niece and friends from pain. It might even be seen as a 'good' utterance; it certainly harms no one.

Rozanov's lie is only a small piece of his immoral fabric. Another is his manipulation and arrangement of other people's lives. Rozanov has whisked Hattie in and out of schools, countries, continents, seeing very little of her in all that time. Now he brings her on to the centre of the stage, encloses her in the Slipper House at Ennistone, and *arranges* for her to marry Tom McAffrey. This is shocking in the Western cultural context where it can only be seen as interference and manipulation.[11]

He plans this for Hattie in order to protect her from his own growing incestuous love for her. So is this an honourable motive after all – working against the monstrosity of his own desire? It may be seen that way but he does not have enough control to keep the knowledge of his love for his grand-daughter secret from her (in marked contrast with Eastcote's keeping of his own secret). He babbles of it to her and is reduced to the state of 'a large uncontrolled animal' (PP 471). This is the worst of his 'crimes' – allowing tabooed feeling to spread out and enfold the confused Hattie; nothing less than corruption of the young.

Such feelings and actions attributed to a learned philosopher are intelligible only as comment on the inadequacy of philosophy by itself to bring order out of chaos; or, on the fact that he has not paid any attention to moral philosophy. Partial knowledge is not virtue.

He disliked and ignored his daughter; he dislikes and ignores his pupil; he despises a woman-servant who loves him; he makes Tom McAffrey fall in with his plans; he is in love with his grand-daughter. Consumed by jealousy, anger and sexuality, he is essentially not very different from George except in intellect and worldly success.

Could Rozanov, after all that has happened, set his house in order, and start again in search of innocence? After such knowledge, what forgiveness? Since the Atonement means nothing to him, and since he has no fear of damnation, is suicide the logical outcome of his despair? From one point of view it may be seen as the result of the only real moral struggle he has waged in his life – breaking away from Hattie. Looked at slightly differently, it looks as if, having seen the horror of himself, he could not turn in an outward, upward movement, away from self to contemplation of others as independent beings worthy of respect. In the following novel, *The Good Apprentice*, the tortured young Edward Baltram manages at the end to make that *conversion*, or turning-about, which Eastcote had said could happen not only every day but every moment. If Rozanov could have turned in similar fashion there might have been the prospect of a pilgrim's progress. But till the end his knowledge is clouded; and self, too late attended to, darkens the horizon of clear seeing.

It must be asked why a lifelong attention to philosophy is not in itself an exercise in virtue. If learning a new language can be a path to virtue (SG 89), why has philosophy failed so spectacularly? The answer, I believe, is that non-obsessive activities are helpful only after the consciousness has been rightly directed; they then help to alter it. Also, certain kinds of reductive, analytical thought leave too much out of account. Proper non-obsessive attention has to be accompanied by loving regard.

The other point of complete contrast with William Eastcote is Rozanov's former pupil, George McAffrey. Formal instruction in philosophy has not helped to check and balance the upheavals he experiences from moment to moment, nor reason succeeded in ordering feeling.

George is appalling, yet pitiable because he is so helpless in his own hands, so much the victim of his raging feelings. Intellectual activity is an obsession with him and he 'is consumed by envy of artists and thinkers'. Stella, his wife, also once Rozanov's pupil, was better at philosophy, a memory which enrages George, and the novel opens with George's attempt to kill her:

> There was some deep wound in George's soul into which every tiniest slight or setback poured hurt feelings and obscured his sun (PP 76).

While George's interactions with wife, mistress, mother, brothers and teacher reveal a highly developed narcissism, a tendency to violence and a pathetic irrationality, his state underscores the lesson that we must learn to possess our souls in silence and peace. He weaves in and out of the novel with compelling power, and the title proclaims that he is a centre, but he is a warning, and also a pointer to the fact that he is only a slight exaggeration of the normal. George's abnormality, much discussed by the people of Ennistone, is a questionable matter.

George's awakening to change begins and ends with reminders of Eastcote. In a most extraordinary state after receiving Rozanov's hate-filled letter, he hears in the pub of William Eastcote's death, and though he has had nothing to do with him in the course of the novel, he is affected strangely:

> it seemed to him that this too was a sign, that Bill the Lizard had offered himself up as an innocent substitute for George's death. Love had reached its climax and died in peace . . . (PP 460).

William Eastcote's death as atonement and redemption is discussed in the next section of the chapter. Here it need only be noted that with this event, something snaps and gives way within George, and a relaxing, letting-go process begins. He talks to both his mother and his mistress about Eastcote in phrases usually reserved for Christ (PP 461, 502).

The bad angel has one more triumphant moment in this psychomachia, but though Stella's mention of Rozanov's name is enough to set the old machinery of pain and rage working, and send him out on his murderous mission, after the 'murder' and subsequent blinding, he is a very different person. The references to Eastcote at this point suggest that Eastcote's death is related to, if only coeval with, change in George's life. But as in Plato's myth, too sudden an exposure to the good can be disastrous. It takes a lifetime of preparation and quiet struggle to arrive at Eastcote's station. Rozanov leaves himself no time; George is too suddenly invaded. However, there is hope for George as there could have been for Rozanov. The quiet, shattered George may be at the beginning of a new and better life. Eastcote is associated with quietness and George at the end is, in a dubious fashion, quiet. George's experience on Ennistone Common – the crepuscular light, the strange sun, and the spaceship – may be read both as hallucination and symbol. Both readings project change. When George gazes at 'the strange sunflower sun' he sees it as 'a death thing . . . this is my death'. This points to a death of the old self, a necessary prelude to a new life. It is only after this terrifying sun-gazing (or dying) that the strange spaceship appears. It will be remembered that this 'object' (flying saucer or spaceship) is associated with Eastcote, who had sighted it and seen it as a wholly good visitation. The language used to describe its appearance on George's horizon suggests beneficence. Its silvery brilliance and directed, slow flight suggest a benevolent presence; the blinding ray it emits suggests the stroke needed for the 'blindness' and blotting-out in which alone a patient and proper seeing can begin:

> Then from beyond the Ring and coming towards him, there appeared a brilliant silver saucer-shaped space-ship, flying low down over the Common. It came towards George, flying quite slowly, and as it came it emitted a ray which entered into his eyes, and a black and utter darkness came upon him, and he fell to his knees and lay stretched out senseless in the long grass   (PP 559).

The connecting 'ands' of the last sentence release Biblical echoes, the blinding of Paul on the road to Damascus is remotely evoked, and George is led home as Paul was. The spaceship, it would seem, stands for a composite Christ–Eastcote.

George's temporary blindness leading to a 'cure' of his violent nature, goes back, as Deborah Johnson points out, to Plato's myth of the cave.[12] Too hasty a movement out of the cave, where shadows have been taken for reality, an unprepared gazing at the sun (the good), can blind the gazer.

George's sight is restored after a fortnight and the ensuing quietness, while not entirely convincing of better spiritual health – it could easily be brain damage following a stroke – marks a change. Adam and Zed are mentioned as frequent and welcome visitors (PP 565) at George's house. This may be taken as a good sign, a welcoming of love and innocence.

The placing of William Eastcote requires the consideration of one other figure, the Anglican priest, Fr Bernard Jacoby, who frames the novel. He is present at the beginning on the bridge when George tries to drown Stella; and on Ennistone Common at the end when the blinded George holds on to his cassock and confesses his murder. A tainted 'good' figure, he falls somewhere between Rozanov's intellectualism and power, and Gabriel's sentimentality and weakness. The vampirish aspect of the priest's character, his desire to make the afflicted his spiritual prey, his awareness of his religious magical power (as 'endlessly and thrillingly arcane'), his holding of Diane's hand in the dark church, his yearning over Tom

McAffrey's agile grace, his intoning of beautiful prayers from the Prayer-Book, point to a corrupting romanticism.

The discarding process he undergoes as his understanding of God and the good evolves is a parody of the theme of this present study, serving to show that the movement towards simplicity too can be spurious.

> After messing about with human sexual adventures, he decided to devote his love, that is his sexuality, to God. When God passed out of his life he loved Christ. When Christ began, so strongly, to withdraw and change, he just sat, or knelt, and breathed in the presence of something or in the presence of nothing   (PP 156).

In essence this is not very different from the waiting upon God in the Friend's Meeting House, yet the self-examination and meditation described at length in one section (PP 507) reveal a jumbled, undisciplined conciousness, illustrating very precisely the great difficulty of prayer. His mind is not still, his thoughts fly off at every instant to romantic quotations, sexual associations, and random memories in a manner which most readers attempting prayer or meditation will recognise. From time to time these thoughts are pierced by a sense of unworthiness, but never for long enough.

However, his instincts are frequently good. When Rozanov asks him what he regrets most in his life, he comes back with a genuine and moving reply:

> 'Not to have established unselfish habits.'

The conversations with Rozanov show that his understanding is not inferior. Like Gabriel, George, and Rozanov himself (indeed, like almost everyone in the township of Ennistone), he is too much swayed by emotion.

His dramatic letter to N at the close says some very important things about the abandonment of every kind of magic, the penetration of morality into the moment-to-moment conduct of everyday life, and the infinite simplicity and nearness of the power that saves (PP 571). These are Murdoch's own positions; the fact that she attributes them to a half-crazed priest who preaches to the sea-birds in Greece implies that the realisation of these truths must itself be pure and free of flamboyance. Fr Bernard has progressed some way as a pilgrim but he has far to go. What is needed here is an altered, humbler consciousness which refuses to feed on drama or be thrilled even by the notion of an untainted Good.

Fr Bernard's failure lies in the fact that he has not ordered his life in accordance with the inner light. He is capable of kindness and sporadic single good works (for instance, telling Rozanov to be kind to George), but his life is not governed at every point from a still centre. His whole life has not been a preparation for emergence from the cave and looking at the sun.

IV

This chapter has discussed four characters as foils to William Eastcote but the entire township is the background of disorder against which the value of his life emerges. The words used about him have, in many cases, religious connotations. William Eastcote, like Stuart and Jenkin in the novels after him, is a Christ-figure. Tom McAffrey thinks that he might 'intercede' for him (PP 430); and, as noted earlier, George is quietened down by the death of Bill the Lizard. When he hears of his death, the demons that drive him seem to depart, as if in recognition of William Eastcote's goodness, bringing to mind the New Testament incident when the devils leave the man possessed in the presence of Christ, crying: 'What have we to do with thee, Jesus, thou son of the most high God?'

The language used to describe Eastcote's death is significant:

it seemed to him that this too was a sign that Bill the Lizard had offered himself up as an innocent substitute for George's death. Love had reached its climax and died in peace (PP 460).

That this is clearly a reference to the Atonement is borne out by the fact that on the very next page there is a specific reference to Jesus Christ in George's conversation with Diane:

'Something's all washed away – washed in blood.'
'Like Jesus Christ.'
'Yes. Yes. Nothing less would do. I said the world was full of signs today. And Bill the Lizard dead: God rest his soul. So I

look strange?'

'Yes. Your face is different – more beautiful' (PP 461).

Finally, as mentioned earlier, the spaceship that blinds George with its ray of light evokes the blinding of Paul on the road to Damascus quite consciously, not only in the matter of having to be led away, but also because it effects a curiously ambivalent 'conversion' in George. George is henceforward, quiet, subdued, as if something in him has died.

Eastcote's capacity for effecting change in the lives of people is related to Christ's. The reinterpretation of the Atonement doctrine discussed in the introductory chapter is relevant here. With his death the goodness he incarnated is missed and mourned.[13]

His last words (as reported by Dr Roach) are: 'Pray always, pray to God.' Dr Roach calls him a saint, a wonderful man, not just a comforter, but a living evidence of a religious truth. His niece Anthea realises that her emotional troubles are nothing compared with the loss of 'his goodness and the mystery of his death, his vanished goodness'. The McAffrey clan remember him as 'an example of goodness' and 'a place of healing'. Brian McAffrey wishes too late he had consulted him about his job. Gabriel feels that 'a silent guarantor of the reality of goodness had been taken away from her vulnerable world' (PP 487). Alex McAffrey, the mother of George, Brian and Tom, thinks about him now and realises how much she had loved him and relied on his presence, and how stupidly little she had seen of him.

> He was to be always *there*, making life more significant and secure in a way which did not need to be continually checked (PP 492).

While none of these characters was shown interacting with Eastcote while he lived, they recognise him as a pattern irradiating their lives now that he is dead.

His funeral is described in a separate section of two pages.

At the beginning of the novel Eastcote has just received disquieting news about his health from his doctor and knows he is soon to die. The knowledge stabs him from time to time (PP 292–3), but he does not lose his composure. The faith he has in himself blends beautifully with his faith in something greater than himself. Both are aspects of a 'sober, informed' knowledge that one must control only oneself, and for the rest, look lovingly and patiently at the world outside.

Vincent Newey in 'Bunyan and the Confines of the Mind' agrees with Jungian analysis that a failure to value aright their terrors and sickness is among the major errors of those whose minds are not changed.[14] While this is amply illustrated by the huge cast of characters in the novel, William Eastcote is the one example of the individual truly educated by psychic processes. He is self-possessed, yet non-manipulative. Rozanov remarks:

'Oftener than we think we can make things be the way we desire' (PP 275).

but Eastcote, like James Arrowby, refuses to make things bend to the self's desire. Instead, he alters the objects of desire to begin with, concentrating on things in art and nature in their independence.

Murdoch's novels of the later phase have been larger in scope, the 'melodrama' and 'luridity' (needed for shadowing the truth) spread over a growingly wider canvas. This huge and overpowering novel leaves a number of possibilities open. George may not be saved but only slowed down by a stroke. Stella's loving repossession of George contains elements of anger and cruelty, suggesting the possible unwinding of a whole new chain. Despite the sense of an ending given by Rozanov's death and Hattie's marriage to Tom, the continuance of chaos is indicated.

The overall effect is one of a sad and affectionate understanding of the human potential for good and bad, and more especially, of the absurdity of human life. Small but complete pictures of peripheral figures, such as the one of Alexandra McAffrey, repeat the main theme. Widowed, sixty-five years old, Alex still longs for admiration from an indifferent Rozanov. Her servant's repeated demand for a pension threatens her comfort – may the master–servant relationship be subverted; worse, inverted? Hard and grasping, she loses out, damaged and reduced after her fall to a vegetative condition, an ominous reminder of the shadow that lies over George's 'better', quiet state. Such characters sketched in outline, so numerous, and so caught and pinned-down, ramify endlessly the central picture of blind struggle in the trap of human desire.

Sartre speaks of the enormous unused freedom available to the individual of which he makes no use. Who, or what, can stop me from doing what I want – taking a slow boat to China tomorrow, for instance? *The Philosopher's Pupil* emphasises the futility of such impulsive, willed acts by showing the philosopher and his pupil increasingly imprisoned by their actions. Rozanov exercises his final choice through suicide. In one obvious sense he is free now of the burden of human consciousness, but in another he has acted so as to set aside permanently the question of freedom. George exercises his freedom through murder; yet the manner of its happening points to a remarkable lack of freedom. It is as if when he hears the name Rozanov from Stella's lips, a switch is pressed and the mechanism of rage takes over.

William Eastcote is freer than any of these. He breathes more calmly and easily, and shows that freedom lies not in the movement of the will but in the control of it. His freedom is related to the Protestant view of the individual absolutely alone before God, free to make his own moral choices. No social framework or community can promote or retard his salvation, and guarantees given by the Catholic church in the West, for example, or by the caste hierarchy in India, are missing. There is no structure to absorb the shocks he may inflict on himself; every moment and decision therefore has to be experienced in complete freedom.

As 'moral agent sovereign in his choices', he is characteristic of the Puritan individual *choosing* control and discipline. If William Eastcote were cast into prison for life, he would still be more free than George at liberty in the world, padding along with a hammer in his pocket.

6

Stuart Cuno in *The Good Apprentice*

Stuart Cuno, in the novel that followed *The Philosopher's Pupil*, carries the discarding, purifying process a step farther. William Eastcote was the Puritan; Stuart, the 'good apprentice' of the title, has left Puritanism behind. While the chapters thus far have taken account of the changing role of religion in the Western world, the figures studied have been shaped by different religious traditions. With Stuart the forms have disappeared; he is not moulded by these traditions; he functions without them and is altogether indifferent to their external forms. Alone of all the characters of good, he speaks of *goodness*; not Christ, or *nirvāna*, or the healing goodness of God, but simply the quality goodness itself. The icons and and imagery have been left behind, the theological machinery wholly taken down, and there is no God. But though he is the product of the secular Western world, and entirely free of doctrine and ritual, he is *not* free of moral, even metaphysical, pulls from elsewhere. Not to be located in any visible, defined source, these exert their force in a naked and empty air. Something draws twenty-year-old Stuart Cuno strongly enough to set aside success, fulfilment, whatever, and give himself over to being, becoming, and doing good in a quiet and invisible way.

Murdoch shows here that it is entirely possible to live without religious belief and still acknowledge the force of values usually projected by religious tradition. The need to obliterate the ego is as strong as ever to the seeker of the good, though he has to do it without priestly props or religious consolation.

Section I of this chapter sees Stuart as expressing an intuitive grasp of goodness in the manner of George Moore and encountering charges of emotivism from his detractors. Section II shows how Stuart's blank and decentred personality has an extraordinary capacity for effecting change. Section III indicates that Murdoch's conception of Stuart, haunted by the figure of Christ in the teeth of its non-religious base, suggests a reinterpretation of Christ as pure example. Section IV deals with the Stuart–Jesse encounter as

expressive of simplicity and good versus artistic energy. Section V
suggests that Stuart is an amalgam of the forces that have formed
the West even though he is not tied to any one.

I

The Good Apprentice has two distinct centres. Edward Baltram, who
feeds a drug-filled sandwich to a friend and is thereby responsible
for his suicide, is the centre in terms of the action. Stuart Cuno,
his stepbrother, is the centre in terms of significance.

Though Stuart gives the book its title, he is outside the maelstrom
of events. Yet he alters them in some way; those who blunder up
against him are changed. Edward Baltram says of him: 'He's not
part of the thing at all, he's just an external impulse, a sort of jolt,
a solid entity, something you bump into.' (GA 469).

He gives up the pursuit of a degree in mathematics at Cambridge
to devote himself to 'doing good' in an ordinary way.

Stuart's father Harry Cuno, baffled and enraged, argues with
his son against this apparent folly:

> 'Don't you see you can't do this all alone? Human nature needs
> institutions. You can't do it by yourself, without a general theory
> or an organisation or God or other people. . . . A religious man
> has to have an object and you haven't one.'   (GA 40)

Stuart, considering this, begins tentatively to say that it depends
on what is meant by the word object, when rudely interrupted by
his father. Though not very clear himself, Stuart has an object,
some centre which draws him, something colourless but not
therefore neutral; on the contrary, positively and shiningly itself,
perhaps white, the idea of good itself.

That this idea has a transcendent, semi-mystical nature, that it
is real but invulnerable to the onslaught of reductive analysis, is
made clear through the conversation at the Brightwalton's dinner,
where virtually the entire company of guests turns on Stuart
and attacks him with what are apparently irrefutable arguments.
Against them Stuart can only assert a consciousness that cannot be
explained or bound by empirical scientific method, a consciousness
that points to something above and outside the machine even of
the human brain.

The dialogue sees Stuart at bay for, unlike in the case of Socrates, none of his interlocutors will readily admit either the importance or even the existence of the soul. Midge McCaskerville and Harry Cuno, sensual hedonists, turn on him, claiming the power of technology, and Ursula Brightwalton, the doctor, the neutrality of science. Harry and Midge have just been praising computers ('A computer could run a state better than a human being'), asserting that they offer us a vision of the human mind glorified, clarified and fortified and so on. Stuart begins stutteringly in words reminiscent of Robert Louis Stevenson:

> 'A machine doesn't think' – said Stuart, 'a machine can't even simulate the human mind.'
>
> 'Why not?' said Harry.
>
> 'You mean its syntactical, not semantical', said Ursula. 'Isn't that what they say now? Or that it has mind but not consciousness?'
>
> 'Because we are always involved in distinguishing between good and evil.'
>
> 'Surely not always', said Ursula, 'Not even often.'
>
> 'Who is to judge the wisdom of a machine, another machine? Human minds are possessed by individual persons, they are soaked in values, even perception is evaluation'.
>
> 'But isn't serious thinking supposed to be neutral?' said Ursula. 'We get away from all that personal stuff.'   (GA 28)

The conversation continues in this vein, with the case for science broken up and distributed among all those confronting Stuart. The respect for facts, the supremacy given to a valueless, blank and neutral investigation of the external world are precisely what Stuart, student of mathematics, the most abstract and valueless of all subjects, resists. He falls back on words like 'soul', 'moral' and 'spiritual', 'our knowledge of right and wrong' in order to speak of a dimension unaffected by scientific analysis. Stuart has fewer words, less voluble and eloquent arguments; the best lines are given to his opponents. His father browbeats him:

> 'You want to make everything moral, that's your version of religion, you want to push what's really objective and factual into a corner. But the lesson of our age is the opposite, modern science has abolished the difference between good and evil,

there isn't anything deep, that's the message of the modern world, science is what's deep, Ursula's right, mathematics is the pure case, and that's the point, because mathematics is everywhere, it's swept the board, biology is maths now, isn't that so, Ursula, the language of the planet is mathematics . . .'   (GA 29)

Against such a flood, Stuart, whose decision to give up mathematics, and Cambridge too, so as to do something good has provoked this argument, finds himself unshaken but stammering. It is difficult to speak convincingly of an 'ultimate order', of responsible consciousness, of value-language, when it is all swept aside as illusion, and, much worse, *a matter of style*. Stuart confronts an opposition (well-disposed towards him) which dismisses goodness as superficial, a matter of manner and style.

The psychoanalytical reduction (though significantly not put forward by the psychiatrist Thomas McCaskerville, who understands Stuart and is fascinated by him), is another way of explaining away Stuart's obsession.

'Your religious plan is simply a sexual plan, it's sex by other means.'
'Well, alright', said Stuart.
'You're a—what did you say? Why is it alright?'
'I don't mind if people call it sex, the question is can I do it, not what it's called.'   (GA 41)

Stuart refuses to react to the interest and curiosity meant to be aroused by ascribing a sexual colouring to his intention. Even if all spirit is sex, so what? What is important is that undirected lost spirit is something to be afraid of. Thomas McCaskerville says to him:

'Spirit without absolute, that's what you're afraid of.'
'Yes. Lost bad spirit.'   (GA 30)

An 'unhoused spirituality' (Conradi's wonderful phrase)[1] can turn demonic, as with the Rev. Carel Fisher in *Time of the Angels*. Pseudo-religions and degenerated mythologies are to be set aside. One begins with nothing but a blank awareness of some source of light.

Stuart's great difficulty here is that he has nothing concrete and immense, no institution with a history, not even a spiritual being with a name he can use. The others would be much more comfortable if he had, for they would recognise an old enemy they can effectively handle. But this ordinary (and therefore unusual) way of being apart puzzles and alarms them.

To his father's expostulation that this talk of the ultimate is just superstition ('Anyway, what's fundamental could be evil or chaos') he can only reply 'That can't be so.' (GA 39) His apprehension of good is a matter of intuition. Despite Murdoch's remark that she has 'an absolute horror of putting theories of philosophical ideas as such' into her novels,[2] the conversation at the Brightwaltons' dinner may be seen as a dramatisation of the confrontation between intuitionism, as propounded by George Moore, and emotivism as put forward by his detractors. The skilfully-managed conversation accurately conveys the tenor of light exchange between educated, sophisticated friends, but quite clearly it establishes a division with Stuart on one side and all the rest on the other.

Stuart's statements go back to Moore's notion of good as something to be intuitively grasped, standing above analysis and definition. Alasdair MacIntyre in *After Virtue* says:

Propositions declaring this or that to be good are what Moore called intuitions; they are incapable of proof or disproof and indeed no evidence or reasoning whatever can be adduced in their favour or disfavour.[3]

Moore called good the name of a simple, indefinable property different from that named by 'pleasure' or 'conducive to evolution-ary survival or any other natural property'. The non-definable, non-natural nature of good is beautifully brought out by Stuart's stumbling references to 'our ordinary sense of the world as ultimate' (GA 30), and later, to 'goodness as the most important thing, some sort of spiritual ideal and discipline, like – it's so hard to see it – it's got to be religion without God, without supernatural dogmas' (GA 31). As Stuart gropes towards an expression of his intuition, his tentative phrases communicate the unanalysable nature of what he says.

While Moore in *Principia Ethica* disclaimed using the word intuition to suggest a faculty comparable with the power of vision, he does compare good as a property with yellow as a property in such a way as to make moral judgements seem like simple visual perception. Stuart means something similar when he says:

> 'Human minds are possessed by individual persons, they are soaked in values, *even perception is evaluation*.' (GA 28)

On the other hand, emotivist doctrine which refuted Moore, says that all evaluative judgements and, more specifically, all moral judgements are *nothing but expressions of preference*, expressions of attitude or feeling insofar as they are moral or evaluative in character. Ursula Brightwalton's reaction to Stuart's 'even perception is evaluation' is in line with emotivism:

> 'But isn't serious thinking supposed to be neutral? . . . We get away from all that personal stuff.' (GA 28)

Again Harry says of his son:

> 'Stuart just despises empiricism . . . he's opting for the life of the emotions.' (GA 29)

The implication is that Stuart, by desiring to pursue the good, is merely expressing a personal preference or attitude. But Stuart holds out for the independence of moral thought and its pervasiveness:

> 'It's not just on the outside—Being objective is being truthful, making right judgements is a moral activity, all thinking is a function of morality, it's done by humans, it's touched by values right into its centre, empirical science is no exception.' (GA 29)

Emotivism, according to MacIntyre, states that there are and can be no valid rational justifications for any claims that objective and impersonal moral standards exist, and hence concludes that there are no such standards.[4] Thus Harry's reply to Stuart is that modern science has abolished the difference between good and evil, 'there isn't anything deep, that's the message of the modern world, science is what's deep' (GA 29).

The intuitive–emotive confrontation is taken a step farther when Stuart is accused of manipulating others. Emotive theory implies that in saying 'This is right' or 'This is good', the speaker is not only expressing personal approval but attempting to influence the feelings and attitudes of others. The agent might well think himself to be appealing to impersonal criteria when actually he is expressing himself in a manipulative way. This charge is brought against Stuart by Midge McCaskerville, Elspeth Macran, Mrs Wilsden and Sarah Plowmain. Midge, talking of Stuart's relationship with her son Meredith, says:

'You want him in your power, and you dress it up as morality, as if you were a kind of moral teacher or example.'   (GA 329)

Or again, when Stuart attempts to make Mrs Wilsden stop writing letters full of hate to agonised, guilt-ridden Edward, holding him responsible for the death of her son, her friend Elspeth Macran bursts out with:

'We've heard about you, pretending to give up sex and going round being holy. Don't you realise what a charlatan you are? What you really enjoy is cruelty and power – cruelty like what you're doing to our friend.'   (GA 387)

Stuart's most difficult task is to keep his awareness without letting it degenerate into complacency and self-consciousness. His suspicion of emotion and determined refusal to brood over horror or good action or suffering is Murdoch's underscoring of the mechanism of the ego which may direct all its energy into a degenerate simulacrum of the good and appear to be leading – through emotion-coloured thought – all the way almost to the top (SG 68). Unreflecting, spontaneously good action is what is required. Such reflection as there is must deliberately exclude the self's role in the good act:

Stuart pictured the Good Samaritan as being intently reflective at suitable intervals about the man he had helped (for instance, by sending the innkeeper some more money) but as otherwise dismissing the matter from his mind.   (GA 50)

Interest and complexity arising from either the intellect or emotions are deliberately to be kept out. Stuart and Thomas McCaskerville the psychiatrist have an extended conversation only once. Thomas displays an intense curiosity about Stuart's activities (the personality is beginning to fascinate) and asks him to come again so they can continue the conversation. But Stuart's reply to that is, 'Oh, I don't think we'll ever talk like *this* again . . . it wouldn't do. Things get spoiled by being talked about.' (GA 147)

Murdoch is advocating increasingly a simplicity almost impossible to come by. Can thought ever break free of the subjective, self-flattering self? And if so, how will doing good be different from instinctive action, like breathing? Can it, then, be *good*? It seems as if something may be called good only if a force draws in the other direction, if one has to struggle towards the perceived good. And struggle necessitates a certain drama, a thinking out of issues inseparable from a degree of interesting complexity. The logical end of Stuart's journey is silence; even then one can never be sure of the emotional thoughts that colour the silence. Perhaps a good, pure kind of silence is the ultimate end. Yet that is not what Stuart desires. He wants not only to *be* good but to *do* it, as a probation officer it might be, or a schoolteacher. What he needs is a cage of duties, the right cage of duties (GA 51). He is aware, even as he sorts things out for himself, of the danger of such thoughts. Even so much of drama may be too much.

What Murdoch puts forward through Stuart is a halfway house: neither extreme withdrawal (for that is inadequate and guarantees nothing), nor self-conscious, dramatised dedication (for self enters too much here), but a narrow path, very difficult to find and tread, on which one is and acts, but almost invisibly. The lack of imagination for which his father blames him is perhaps necessary for being good in this particular way. Edward's imagination works feverishly, taking him from horror to horror, preventing him from coming up for air. Stuart works deliberately at curbing this activity of the imagination.

Spontaneous simplicity is what is desired. The deliberate switch from 'Not I but Christ' to 'Not Christ but I' suggests a position farther on than that of Brendan Craddock, himself an expounder of the *via negativa* in *Henry and Cato*. Stuart's way of rejection casts off the beautiful Christian drama. The transcendence within and also everywhere in things outside, seen not as sacraments or symbols but simply irradiated by the good that is in themselves – this is behind Stuart's 'Not Christ but I'. This communicates his feeling that goodness is near, transparent, light, even easy.

Emotional resonances are suspect. However, he likes to sit alone in churches. Is it possible to seek solitude, an interiorisation, without letting in some emotional light? Again the answer seems to be that it must be just the right amount.

The point about treading between too much and none at all is not quite the same thing as the Greek principle of moderation, nothing too much. Here what is sought is not a mean of that kind; rather, a way which is through the world but plainly, simply. This is a delicate and narrow track which, as one learns to keep one's balance, seems to lead somewhere. A quasi-mystical light falls on it, yet it remains merely a plain path. Too much anxious seeking for it may obscure it from the vision for it lies at one's feet ('the simple, close things' of *The Philosopher's Pupil*). Above all, there is to be no drama, no fuss, for that provides only false images. Somehow to be quietly here and at the same time quietly elsewhere – this slipping in and out of sight is essential to the task of the saint. The self has constantly to be left behind; the journey lasts till death. To have arrived at the light is not to have arrived, for that is illusion. Murdoch does not posit the definite mystical experience. There is knowledge of the light, but no experience of it save in flashes. These flashes Stuart calls 'honey-dew', using Coleridge's phrase to describe the happiness he feels contemplating it.

II

In portraying both his person and his actions, Murdoch consciously points to the *decentred* nature of Stuart's personality. To begin with, Stuart lacks charm. This is a very important factor, for Murdoch implies that charm in the individual is an insidious, sidetracking force; it distorts the vision of the gazer who sees only the hazy, attractive veil.[5] At one point, when Edward and Brownie are together in the cottage, Murdoch describes Brownie's face as 'awkward, large and naked, undefended by make-up or pretty hair or charm' (GA 308). Charm, then, is distracting and scatters energy which should concentrate on the real. Stuart is repeatedly described as clumsy, awkward, solidly there. Through this Murdoch seems to say that the aesthetic is *separate* from the moral; purity and holiness are not to masquerade in beautifying appearances. Beauty and charm are dangerous because the spurious too may be tricked out in them. The beautiful *may* be the good, but it need not necessarily be so. In order to perceive the good, the veil of the beautiful has to be set aside. Hence the reference to Stuart's 'curious blankness, so unattractive to some' (GA 83). Murdoch says specifically that there is something dog-like about him with his thick, fair hair and yellow-amber eyes. Elsewhere too she has located the purest kind of good in an animal – Adam's dog Zed in *The Philosopher's Pupil* – suggesting innocence, and absence of drama. The average human response is fascinated by itself and seeks constantly by belittling others to soothe itself. Human interest in others is too often rooted in such egotism. To indicate its absence (an absence which is an essential ingredient of goodness), Stuart is described in canine terms.

Love too has to be watched and purified. Brendan Craddock in *Henry and Cato* observed that this may seem to be the only supremely good thing but it needs to be given up – *that* is love, a loving renunciation of the object of love. Stuart in *The Good Apprentice* tells Thomas McCaskerville that he does not want 'ordinary attachments, intimate friendships or relationships, what's usually called love'; falling in love is 'to go in at the shallow end'. Tentatively, but with a beautiful blurred accuracy, he says about love:

> 'I think it has to look after itself, I mean it sort of has to cancel itself.'
> 'Cancel?'
> 'It has to un-be itself, so it can't exactly be aimed at.'   (GA 145)

Stuart is attempting here to define the nature of the wholly purified Eros. Love is rooted in the ego. It rises from the need of the self; its desire for the other includes a desire to bind, absorb and assimilate the other; it desires the other to cherish it and surrenders itself only because of the reassurance and joy it seeks in seeing that identity picked up, gentled and reflected. This is love at a fairly high level of refinement, but all this is still a kind of self-love. It is this which has to go. It must not arise in this way. In order to be, it has to, in Stuart's words, un-be itself. The self that it asserts has to be unmade. This is next to impossible – how can the self that loves love without its being the agent? If the agent is dissolved, what is it then that loves? One understands that there is a state of loving in which all sense of self seems to have vanished. But Stuart means something more and other than such a rhapsodic release which may accompany the experience of falling deeply in love. What he is demanding is the love of Christ which loves and gives without regard of subject or object, 'the greater love hath no man' kind of love, for Stuart has, by quoting from Tennyson's *The Revenge* in this context, spoken of the willingness to die. He means love of the kind suggested by 'For God so loved the world that he sent his only-begotten son' – i.e. love that is impersonal, limitless and brilliant – that which gives and sustains life and takes such giving as its task. Emotion, in the taking-on of this task, must be present but curbed; must not be allowed to flood the context, and distract attention from the *task* of loving. This is why it is not enough for Stuart to *be* good, or, by contemplating goodness, to have it in some measure. He wants to *do* good, go about doing good, not officiously like a do-gooder, but quietly and without fuss. His vision of goodness is part mystical, part practical; he seeks a brand of goodness which is meant for him as Western man, something bound up with the life of action. When he tells Thomas that there is no God, and Thomas replies, 'As eastern religions have always taught us. . . . Why not?' Stuart interrupts with:

'I'm not concerned with the east. I'm western. It's got to be done differently here.'   (GA 140)

James Arrowby's Eastern distrust of action because of the power and manipulation intermixed with it is not shared by Stuart. He has the missionary's zeal to serve; the ideal of dedicating one's entire life to the service of others is essentially a Western, Christian ideal, eschewing passivity. Salvation by works is crucial to Stuart's programme for goodness. Giles Brightwalton, in a letter dissuading him from giving up academica, expresses doubts:

'I suspect that goodness is too hard even to name and "comes about" infinitely slowly if at all, as a scarcely visible result of watching a million steps. It can't be a programme, can it? (GA 243)

Naive and innocent about good action at the outset ('could he help anybody?'), Stuart finds the task of helping even his brother Edward very difficult. But he keeps at it, and finally, something works for poor Edward. As his tormented consciousness gradually calms down towards the close of this long novel, Stuart's advice

('Ed, I wish you'd go and see Midge, she likes you . . . you could help her': GA 378) at last begins to act. In talking to Midge and helping her to see where her duty lies, Edward for the first time stops thinking obsessively about himself.

Stuart's effect is more directly felt in the case of Mrs Wilsden who has been writing hate-charged letters to Edward, cursing him and holding him responsible for her son's death. Stuart sees some of these. Telling Edward not to hate her in return but to wish her well, Stuart goes to Mrs Wilsden. Mocked and reviled, he stands solidly there, saying she must stop writing those letters to Edward:

> it must be very hard for you to stop hating him, but I feel that you should try – perhaps – because . . .   (GA 386)

He haltingly suggests some sort of forgiving gesture – a few lines, a note expressing forgiveness. She scorns him, calls him sadistic and cruel and asks him to leave her house.

> 'I am sorry', said Stuart, 'I meant well.' He got up, blundering against the lamp.   (GA 388)

The difficulty of acting so, the mistakes it involves and the obstacles it runs into are present in that 'blundering'. But his words bring about change. Later, Mrs Wilsden does write a letter to Edward forgiving him:

> I imagine your state of mind and I pity you. As you may know, I am soon going away, and some peaceful gesture may be appropriate as one surveys one's arrangements and one's life. And an angel has spoken on your behalf.
>
>   J.W.
> Your brother's visit did some good. Tell him.   (GA 504)

This letter, freeing Edward as nothing else could have done, of his terrible burden, has come about through Stuart's action. Doing good has worked.

Midge McCaskerville, caught in the muddle of an adulterous relationship with Harry Cuno, is awakened to an awareness of goodness by Stuart's mere *presence* in the car as they are driven to London in total silence by her lover after the disastrous encounter at Seegard. Stuart's floodlike invasion of Midge's being is a remaking of her poor fallen soul, sensed physically, 'her whole body being remade as if by radiation, the atoms of it changed' (GA 369). Stuart helps her to see the moral mess she is in, and though she thinks herself at first to be in love with Stuart (the dangers of too rapid an ascent from the Platonic cave into the sun?), she comes to see clearly where her duty lies and what her only good course of action can be.

III

The woman taken in adultery – it is this of which one is reminded by Stuart's effect on Midge. Stuart Cuno, despite his rejection of religion, may be seen as a Christ figure, the Christ who is pure essence, a being set apart, wholly innocent and pure. His mother, 'the girl from far away', dead many years since, is described in words which, while applicable at the naturalistic level because she came from New Zealand, are simultaneously evocative of a larger, purer air, of the aerial view of one who is *janua caeli, stella matutina*:

> She had seen the great ocean seals basking on golden seaweed at the end of the world. She had seen the albatross.   (GA 54)

Stuart remembers her dimly as 'an angel. . . . Her mystic form had been a refuge', phrases again reminiscent of the Litany of the Virgin (*Refugium peccatorum. . . . Regina angelorum*).

When Midge, fallen Magdalene and afflicted woman, is aroused from her state of sin by the simple fact of Stuart's presence, she broods over his image in an act of adoration:

> She caressed that face with her thoughts but never in fantasy touched it with her lips or hand; only sometimes she did imagine herself kissing the sleeve or shoulder of his jacket, and this was exquisite.   (GA 462)

The woman who kissed the hem of Christ's garment might have adored him thus. Stuart also experiences a measure of agony in the Underground at Oxford Circus. He seems to be a development of the Christ in *Nuns and Soldiers* – Christ who appears to Anne in a waking vision, denies the suffering that has made him so interesting through the ages by holding out hands on which there

are no stigmata, and tells her he cannot help for she must do all
the work herself. Stuart is a composite of both Anne as Christ
wants her to be and Christ himself. He wants to do all the work
himself; and at one point Sarah Plowmain asks him whether he
has the stigmata (GA 389). Murdoch here is developing Christ as
everyman, or Christ in everyman. Stuart is Christ as everyone can
be if he seeks the good. To do this is not to move *towards* Christ,
but to *be* Christ. He who lives a life in the imitation of Christ is a
Christ of sorts himself, as indeed any enlightened one can be a
Buddha.

Stuart stands for death as Christ does; a dying to wickedness,
'that genuine sense of mortality which enables us to see virtue as
the only thing of worth' (SG 99). Christ in *Nuns and Soldiers* says
to Anne that death is one of his names. Stuart, likewise, is
associated with death, the death of falsehood and wrong. Midge
tells her lover Harry of her recurring dream of a white horseman
who turns and looks at her.

> 'I saw a man on a white horse passing and looking so balefully
> towards me as if he would kill me. Then he went on. I've had
> that dream before.'   (GA 92)

And again later, 'I dreamt about that white horseman again!'
(GA 171). When she begins to recognise the falseness of her
situation, she associates the horseman of her dream with Stuart.
Telling Harry that she has been to see Stuart, she says:

> 'I used to dream about him. At least I dreamed about a pale man
> on a horse looking at me. Thomas said it was death. I just
> realised, when I saw him, that it was Stuart.'   (GA 346)

Stuart himself instinctively identifies with the horsemen on the
Parthenon frieze in the British Museum. He looks attentively at
the frieze:

> He liked the young horsemen. He had always seen himself as a
> horseman, although he had never been on a horse in his
> life. (GA 247)

Stuart's presence in the car, the rays sent out by him in that
silent drive to London from Seegard, transform Midge suddenly

and shockingly. As a witness of her wrongdoing he becomes an obsessive image, a subject to be thought through, meditated upon. She sees in a flash how false and idle her double life has been, and wants now to follow *him*, do anything to be somehow connected with him. He tells her she must return to her husband Thomas, that the good she is destined for is made up of 'dull old familiar things, the duties of her family and her home' (GA 490).

After her decision to choose her husband, son and home, she reflects on the process of purgation she has undergone. It has been a kind of death:

> Death was everywhere; its rays were falling upon herself and upon those she loved and upon the whole earth. She recalled her dream of the white horseman and the curious effect which Stuart had had upon her, the killing of her ordinary life, the annihilation of her instinctive desires, the sense of utter deprivation which had been too a kind of unearthly joy. (GA 491)

Very clearly Stuart stands for the Pauline concept of dying to the old life, the death that Christ in the earlier novel said was one of his names. He himself connects Christ with pointless suffering, the braids of beautifully plaited hair in the Auschwitz Museum. He says of Christ:

> 'I have to think of him in a certain way, not resurrected, as it were mistaken, disappointed – well, who knows what he thought? He has to mean pure affliction, utter loss, innocent suffering, pointless suffering, the deep and awful and irremediable things that happen to people.' (GA 147)

The non-degradable object in the heart of horror – that is what Christ's life and death mean here. There is no hope, no redemption. Life is horror; suffering and meaningless pain are real. But despite that, a pure good walks through the world, broken by it over and over again, but not degraded or changed. This breaking-down does not finally destroy it; the invulnerable essence proceeds unharmed.

IV

Stuart in London is goodness in a world not sufficiently attentive, in a semi-somnolent state. But Stuart at Seegard is another matter altogether. Seegard is the home of the artist Jesse Baltram and his three women – his wife and two daughters. There is an extraordinary scene in this setting where Stuart has come down to see his half-brother Edward who in turn is visiting his old, mad artist–father Jesse in a version of the ritualistic visit to the underworld. Harry and Midge, out on an illicit weekend as Mr and Mrs Bentley, are stranded here and have been recognised. The scene is one of embarrassments, concealments and recognitions, with Stuart as outsider silently seated at one end of the table, watching. Wandering Jesse enters unexpectedly, looks about him, forces away help, *points to Stuart* and says loudly and ringingly:

> 'There's a dead man, you've got a corpse there, it's sitting at the table. I can see it.' He pointed his stick at Stuart. Stuart got up. Jesse went on raising his voice further, not hysterically but in a tone of urgent command. 'That man's dead, take him away, I curse him. Take that white thing away, It's dead. The white thing, take it away from here.'   (GA 292)

This is a very powerful scene. Why Stuart should have such a stunning effect becomes comprehensible only if he is perceived as antithetical to the amoral world of spirit that is Seegard. Stuart is the directed moral sense, checked and disciplined spirit, calling for the death of certain kinds of energies. Jesse, his house and his family, present a world of unchecked spirit, beautiful in parts, but decaying, gone to the bad. Jesse is raw primal energy which takes what it wants: Chloe, May, Midge, Max. Such taking, having and using feeds the creative fire; the artist lives by virtue of his shaping, organising ego – Jesse was a famous painter. But such energy, Murdoch implies, is demonic and finally decays. Seegard is mouldering; the wooden looms are covered with dust, and the great Jesse is a senile, sick man virtually imprisoned. The horror of Jesse Baltram's end, the body caught in the weeds of the river, glimpsed through the translucent wave but left for days, is a comment on the horrors attendant on an undirected life. On the other hand, he has had fame and his inheritors will have money from the many unsold Baltram canvases.

Are we to conclude that only a sweet and virtuous soul like seasoned timber never gives? There is no clearcut lesson. Jesse is power and energy as well as amoral spirit. The point is that Stuart and Jesse exclude each other. The discipline Stuart seeks is death for Jesse – hence the dramatic, instinctive recoiling from Stuart as from a corpse.

The antipathy between Jesse and Stuart goes back to Murdoch's Platonic distrust of art's degenerative power. Art is energy; goodness demands a disciplining of energy, a partial obliteration of strong egotistical strains, a diminishing which is death. But artistic energy will not be bound in this manner; it flies in the face of such censorship.

Seegard, where Jesse lives, is described with the sort of lyrical power and intensity Murdoch reserves for the deliberate evocation of the extraordinary; the power displayed, for instance, in those extended and unforgettable descriptions of sea and horizon in *The Sea, the Sea*. There is an eerie quality to the beauty of the landscape here, a conscious sense of the strange and the magical. Murdoch has said in conversation that it derives from Malory and from the magic and romance of such poems as *Sir Gawayne and the Green Knight*. This is a world in which the polarity of good and bad, the moral orientation of the ordinary world, is simply absent.

Jesse Baltram is the Merlin figure in this world of Seegard. The fact of his being an artist is highly significant. Art is energy, magic and play; it needs to be carefully harnessed to the 'good' if it is to be turned to good account. Does this mean that the ancient quarrel between poetry and philosophy can only be resolved by some version of the hymns and praises of just men allowed in Plato's republic? Is the logical end towards which such an unremitting commitment to goodness moves the silence of the artist?

In 'Art and Eros', a Platonic dialogue about art in *Acastos*, published in 1986 but written a few years before *The Good Apprentice*, Murdoch's Plato takes up a drastically different position and resolves the ancient quarrel. He connects art with real understanding and illumination:

'I don't mean just slick cleverness, I mean something which shakes the whole soul and opens it out into some huge brightness and this is love too, when we love real things and see them distinctly in a clear light.' (*Acastos*, 57)

Later in the dialogue Socrates says that good art tells us more truth
about our lives and our world than any other kind of thinking or
speculation (*Acastos*, 57).

So Edward goes back to the pure joy created by Proust out of
pure pain (GA 521) and Stuart at the end is reading *Mansfield Park*
('It's awfully good': GA 521). Proust and Jane Austen are allowed
into the Republic which is also the Kingdom of Heaven; this is
Murdoch's accommodation of that art which is true, good and
beautiful, in which spiritual discipline has not lessened the energy
but taken it in the right direction towards – what? Truth? By
showing Jesse rejecting Stuart and then Stuart reading *Mansfield
Park*, Murdoch is once again saying something crucial about the
in-between path, the 'having and non-having' relationship which
must exist between art and morality. The truly moral not merely
includes but is intimately related to the finest imaginative activity.
Jesse has to reject Stuart so that the energy out of which art rises
may be communicated. However, there is an arid and false
discipline of the spirit too, excluding the beautiful and joyous.
Stuart will presumably not fall into the trap either; his touching
and amazed discovery of the 'goodness' of *Mansfield Park* indicates
that.

The question is: is this enough? Can the simple response of
Stuart to Jane Austen *take* in, grasp the greatness of great art? How
is he to keep the simplicity so essential to his moral being and at
the same time cultivate the subtlety required to appreciate art's
complexity? Are aesthetic sophistication and the development of
taste ruled out by such a necessary simplicity? Significantly, it is
involuted Edward who, reading Proust, wonders how such pure
joy can be generated by such pure pain and resolves to find out
about it. Stuart contents himself with, 'It's awfully good' and says
he cannot put the novel down. Aesthetic discrimination involves
a certain self-consciousness which borders on complacency, con-
descension and superiority. To be conscious of one's sensibility is
in some sense to cherish it. This on no account must Stuart be
seen to do for it would destroy the carefully developed concept of
good for which he stands.

It is a concept of good which emphasises the fragility of goodness
and the hostility it evokes. Stuart has several moments of disquiet
and doubt. His father Harry, angry that Stuart has seen his liaison
with Midge, angrier that Midge should have left him because of
his son, says:

'Your good and evil are bad dogs better left to lie. Evil has a right to exist quietly; it won't do much harm if you don't stir it up. Everywhere you go you're an intruder. You'll go through life making trouble, you're dangerous.' (GA 442)

Deeply disturbed by his father's remarks and Meredith's wild charges of tampering with his affections and wanting to dominate him (GA 393), Stuart sits alone in a church, pondering the difficulty of his task. He had expected to be somehow immune from doing harm. Very unhappy, he walks wretchedly to the Underground station at Oxford Circus, and as he waits for his train, sees a mouse scampering about on the tracks and thinks naturally of the sad human condition it seems to embody. But as he watches he has a revelation. He realises, as he sees the creature run about, sit up, hold up its paws, that it is in no hurry, it is not trapped, but *lives* there. This brings a sense of homecoming, of the rightness of the here and now, a sense which had been for some time absent. The epiphany afforded by the mouse lifts him up to a state of ecstasy, the scales fall from his eyes, and he sees that shame and loneliness are not a permanent condition. Life may be seen as either a trap or a dwelling-place: it depends on the accuracy of the act of perception, on the seer. The transition involved in 'It was not trapped. It *lived* there' – indicates sudden clear seeing. When he sees rightly and accurately, joy and light fall on him, he is awash in a beatific joy and his entire being seems to be suffused with light and warmth.

Being good and doing it and the accompanying peace and joy are dependent on seeing clearly. It is interesting to note that Murdoch's mysticism in this novel is firmly rooted in clarity of mental perception. There is nothing vague or misty; reason and mind, no less than emotion and body, participate in the exaltation. A semi-mystical joy with such humble materials as a mouse and the Underground station conveys Murdoch's unwillingness to mystify or exalt falsely while simultaneously expressing her faith in the transfiguration of the ordinary by something quite extraordinary. Accurate seeing becomes a means of joyful vision in its other prophetic sense. In moments of clear seeing all things fall beautifully into place and then seem beautiful and joy-bearing.

Stuart's callow youthfulness, his rawness and untried nature, are essential to Murdoch's portrayal of the striving for the good as an endless affair of small beginnings. Nothing final and complete is possible; that would be a falsification, a rounding-off of what is essentially a perpetual process. No one arrives in a Murdoch novel. To arrive is not to be there.

V

In this procession of good figures Stuart is the fifth. His most striking aspect is his capacity for fading into ordinariness; paradoxically, this stands out as his special characteristic. His possible dullness and self-delusion are offered through the thoughts of his greatest admirer, the psychiatrist Thomas McCaskerville (GA 149). But it is immediately followed by a qualification: 'If indeed Stuart were to fade into the dullness with which Thomas menaced him, perhaps that would be his success?' Elsewhere there are references to monotonous ordinary routine as the storehouse of good and innocence (GA 124).

The decentred blankness of Stuart's personality discussed in Section II of this chapter, pinpointed by Thomas's perception of Stuart as an albino, as 'Something immensely solid but without colour' (GA 83), comes more sharply into focus against the background of Edward's frenzy and guilt. The plot, revolving around Edward's experience of guilt, is an elaboration of Cato's state after his killing of Beautiful Joe in *Henry and Cato*, but is carried a step farther because Edward's 'murder' is *wholly* accidental, irrelevant and unnecessary. He gives his fellow-student and friend Mark, a drugged sandwich as a joke because Mark holds out so strongly against drugs; then leaves him asleep in his room while he goes to keep a casual assignation with a girl; and returns to find that Mark, after waking up in a drug-induced hallucination, has walked out of an open window and fallen to his death. All of this is described in the first eight pages of the novel.

Edward's role here, and his experience of guilt thereafter (the body of the novel), is beyond even Cato's, and comparable only with that of the Ancient Mariner:

> 'God save thee, ancient mariner,
> From the fiends that plague thee thus;
> Why lookst thou so?' – With my cross-bow
> I shot the ALBATROSS.

Edward goes through a similar life-in-death.

Edward and Stuart are half-brothers, and Edward's dark and tormented consciousness is the perfect foil for Stuart's innocence. If Edward is the prodigal son, Stuart is cast as the elder brother. Section I of *The Good Apprentice* is titled 'The Prodigal Son', and the novel opens with the 'I will arise and go to my father' verse. There is a direct reference to the parable in the course of the one long conversation between Stuart and Thomas McCaskerville (GA 137–48), and Stuart is lightly identified with the elder brother precisely because there is less dramatic and emotional interest surrounding him. Thomas speaks first:

'Also, there is more in you than you know of. You are not lord of yourself. Put it this way, your enemy is stronger and more ingenious than you seem to imagine.'

'You and your mythologies, how you love these pictures! You think I ought to go to hell and back, you want me to fall and learn by sin and suffering.'

Thomas laughed. 'You want to be like the Prodigal Son's elder brother, the chap who never went away!'

'Exactly – except that he was cross when his brother was forgiven.'

'Which you wouldn't be.'   (GA 147)

The prodigal is by far the more 'interesting' and 'sympathetic' figure, but the ordinariness of the elder brother, his non-dramatic staying at home, is the quality that Murdoch sees as the locus of virtue. There is no attention-drawing separation in his case. Stuart understands intuitively the importance of not being separated. Anne in *Nuns and Soldiers* had not arrived at quite this point, as is clear from her consciousness of apartness and aloneness at the close of that novel. William Eastcote of *The Philosopher's Pupil* is like Stuart, but we see him at the end of his task. Stuart is at the beginning, and Jenkin Riderhood of the next novel, *The Book and the Brotherhood*, in the middle of the task. Both blend and merge with their surroundings, Jenkin even more than Stuart.

Edward, on the other hand, separates himself and gives himself over to his suffering. Thomas McCaskerville tells him that this way of suffering is a desperate cherishing of the damaged self. Edward says to Thomas:

'The whole of creation is innocent as far as I'm concerned, I forgive it, everything except me.'

'So you think you're alone in hell?'

'You want to interest me, to make me think of other people, but I don't want to be cured, and have it all turned into cheerfulness and common-sense by your magic. Your magic isn't strong enough to overcome what I have, it's weak, it's a failing touch. I am permanently damaged.'   (GS 70)

It is only towards the end, after a long period of expiation, when Edward ceases to nurse his separation and lets himself be reintegrated into the human fold, that healing begins for him. This 'absolution' comes, finally, from himself, as he turns to Midge and concentrates on her plight instead of his own. It is true that in doing so he follows Stuart's advice, but he has to do it for himself. Stuart does not play the role of the hermit in *The Rime of the Ancient Mariner*. He remains, instead, a bystander, an adviser.

His understanding of the importance of non-separation from the ordinary is directly projected (at the end of the novel) through his thoughts as he sits in a church 'north of Oxford Street', a place to which he comes frequently. Charges of manipulation and betrayal hurled at him by his father Harry and his young friend Meredith trouble him deeply; all his efforts at being and doing good seem to have turned to harm. He sees now the inevitable mixed nature of things. He thinks:

Am I *deeply* troubled, daunted, by being told that I do nothing but harm? This place used to calm me and encourage me because it made everything that I wanted seem clear and innocent, as if it guaranteed the existence of holiness, or goodness, or something and connected me with it. But I don't need that sort of connection, it's a separation, not a connection, it's a romantic idea of myself, as if I imagined I was robed in white. . . . Do the nearest thing, refrain from stupidity and drama, not just be small and quiet, be nothing, and let the actions come right of themselves. (GA 445–6)

The condition of simplicity desired by Stuart is clarified by contrast with the consciousness of Thomas McCaskerville, the psychiatrist who talks to both Edward and Stuart. He is a magus, a wise man who understands almost everything, but lacks unselfconsciousness. His understanding gives him great power and, like James Arrowby in *The Sea, the Sea,* he cannot help using it. Stuart, by contrast, has no consciousness of power; he stumbles awkwardly along the road as he moves from task to task. That this 'power-lessness' has immense 'power' is illustrated by the fact that Thomas's wife Midge is awakened to a sense of the good (and thereafter, the right) by Stuart's mere presence.

Thomas McCaskerville pays for subtle thought with the loss of simplicity. Reflections and intellectual articulations create his mode of being, to the point that he cannot see that his beloved wife Midge is unfaithful, perhaps unhappy. He regards Stuart's pure-heartedness with awe and envy and affection.

As mentioned earlier, Stuart lives innocently and joyfully in the world, and something about his nature suggests that his actions will not generate disaster of the kind that befalls Edward. One cannot imagine Stuart playing the trick that is Edward's ticket to hell. While Edward is punished far beyond his deserts, the notion persists that 'romantic' and impulsive natures like those of Edward and Cato breed an intensity that invites disaster. Stuart keeps his feelings (for Meredith, for instance) on a lead. And with great simplicity, merely by thinking about it, he elects himself, as Thomas says, 'out of the human condition of indelible selfishness'.

Such an election is Stuart's decision to 'be' Christ. When Stuart explains to Thomas that his apprenticeship to goodness is not something part-time or optional but his whole life, that 'it's all everywhere, as if everything spoke it and showed it', Thomas replies to his stutterings with:

'Steady on. All that sounds like God. You say there is no God, then you aspire to be God yourself, you take over his attributes. Perhaps that *is* the task of the present age.'   (GA 141)

This accords perfectly with Stuart's 'Not Christ but I', and under-lines Murdoch's drastic revision of 'God' and a relocation of 'God' within the human being. The explicit articulation of this has begun with Christ's insistence to Anne that the work is all her own but it reaches its farthest limits with Stuart and Jenkin, who do indeed take on 'God's attributes'. Murdoch seems to feel with Thomas that this is the task of the present age, the only residual religious relic that makes any sense at all.

One last consideration remains. Is Stuart Cuno a Platonist, a

Christian, or a disciple of Moore? It is interesting to note that as one takes each profession of faith in turn, Stuart seems to be not quite that. His explicit disavowal of religion and his constant references to goodness seem to place him with Plato, but the quality of his morality (quite apart from the Christ-figure shadows already dealt with) seems quintessentially Christian. The good as perceived by the pre-Christian Aryan peoples was essentially an acquiescing in the world, a praising of nature and awareness of harmony with it. The hymns of the *Rig Veda* no less than the teleological view of human nature held by Aristotle testify to this sense of being at home in a world which is good. Plato, despite his puritanism, thought that to lie with a lovely boy was a step in the upward ascent. Stuart's resolve to be both dedicated and celibate derives from Christian monasticism. He is not convinced that there can be a final purification of the dark Eros. While undismayed by his sexual feelings for Meredith, he resolves not to yield to them, displaying a Christian distrust of the corrupting flesh. Moreover, when he desires to help Edward he thinks of *love* as only a Christian might do:

> Stuart was aware, and here he did seem to stumble, that only love could wing his words, such words, so as to make them reach that objective. Only in a context of love could talk of sin and guilt effectively take place.   (GA 51)

This is clearly Christian. No other culture or faith so openly states that the angelic tongue without love is sounding brass or a tinkling cymbal.

Yet Stuart openly denies Christianity. His epiphany in the Underground is rooted in clarity, and associated with reason in a way which seems either Greek or contemporary.

Is he then an incarnation of Moore's view of the good? Surely he is too religious by temperament to come under such a label. Moore says in the sixth chapter of *Principia Ethica* that personal affections and aesthetic enjoyment include all the greatest and by far the greatest goods we can imagine and that this is the ultimate and fundamental truth of moral philosophy. But for Stuart these cannot be the only justifiable ends of human action; they are too secular. Besides, Stuart has a programme for doing good.

Clearly he is not any one thing. He seems to be the central, perhaps the only natural quester possible in the contemporary

Western world. Carrying the European inheritance in his bones, he is made by what has been before him. Plato is clearly behind him, but Plato is not all. Christ is clearly of great but not exclusive importance; modern science and analytical philosophy have to be taken into account too. The philosophy, religion and science of the Western world make Stuart Cuno what he is. He is an amalgam, the finest sum of the currents which have produced him, and he embodies the only religious perceptions possible for his generation. Murdoch, citing Tolstoy, affirms that good art is religious, that the best art can somehow explain the concept of religion to each generation.[6] This explains why Stuart Cuno cannot be explained entirely by either Plato or Moore. The impulse behind his creation, indeed the whole novel in which he appears, goes much deeper than any *theory* of goodness can possibly contain. By setting Stuart against the story of Edward's dark guilt and suffering, Murdoch makes room for all that escapes the attempt to control or modify. Edward's world of action and feeling, driven by deep forces from the subconscious, is the world as it is, accepted in its disorderliness by the artist's imagination. Stuart is the religious impulse aspiring upward from that disorder.

Interesting as he is as a representative of currents which have produced him, he functions as a credible human character too. Murdoch succeeds in making him an entirely believable and very touching person. His physical appearance, his direct turns of conversation, his agonising over Meredith after the boy's outburst against him, make him very much more than a vehicle for a particular kind of religious feeling in an a-religious world. Instead, he is a religious *person*, a very human young man with feelings and desires, confusions and conflicts, living in a non-religious society, an environment in which moral philosophy has failed to make ethics a relevant issue.

His innocence, at one level so naive, strikes one as being real and strong; he has not misjudged his moral, spiritual level. Murdoch has triumphed in making him both young and troubled *and* strong and unshaken. His enjoyment of Jane Austen's novel at the end is an unerringly authentic detail, underscoring his youthful innocence as well as his genuine non-obsessiveness. Beautifully, at the end, when his father Harry asks his sons Stuart and Edward to drink to the good things in the world, Stuart asks: 'But *which* good things? We might all mean different ones' – but he drinks to them all the same. That close takes us back to where we began – to the Brightwaltons' dinner and the plurality of goods. Above all of them there – the fallen (Midge), the blind (Harry), the almost-there (Thomas), the desperate (Edward), the youngest (Meredith) – Stuart has shone like a mild sun. In Seegard alone he has no place.

7

Jenkin Riderhood in *The Book and the Brotherhood*

Jenkin Riderhood in *The Book and the Brotherhood*, the sixth in the series of figures representing good, is the one with the least to say about the matter and the one for whom there is a notable absence of background or structure. There is not much explanation of him, and he offers none; there are very few exchanges on the issue of the good between him and the other characters; he is more stripped than even Stuart Cuno. Stuart had spoken of 'seeing' good; Jenkin shows good action that proceeds as a kind of necessity with no expense of words. If the line has been through complex concepts to the simplest good, Jenkin represents the farthest point in such a journey.

At the same time, *The Book and the Brotherhood* fictionalises the welter of contemporary life: the breakdown of coherent religious and moral structures, and the problems confronting the individual living in a society which must take account of technology, Freud, Marx, terrorism, and the impoverishment of a moral vocabulary. What strikes one about this novel is that its flow precludes a strong narrative line. The way events turn into other events, and human relationships form and merge, emphasises the lack of a focal point towards which the action moves. Even Crimond's completion of the book, the failed suicide attempt, and Jean's return to Duncan seem set for other and similar developments, are singularly lacking in finality, and imply that the sort of unity which narrative usually possesses has been deliberately set aside by the author because the concept of meaning and coherence in life has largely vanished from the Western world.

Morality demands a common framework, a shared interpretation of moral terms. But against the array of conflicting explanations offered by Catholic moralists, Sartrean existentialists, logical positivists, Marxists, Stalinists, whatever, contemporary moral philosophy has contented itself with clarifying terms, steadily refusing to absolutise any one available set of moral concepts. Alasdair MacIntyre observes in his *Short History of Ethics*:

the acids of individualism have for centuries eaten into our moral structures for both good and ill. But not only this: we live with the inheritance of not only one, but of a number of well-integrated moralities; Aristotelianism, primitive Christian simplicity, the puritan ethic, the aristocratic ethic of consumption, and the traditions of democracy and socialism have all left their mark upon our moral vocabulary.[1]

In *The Book and the Brotherhood*, more than in any earlier novel, the conflicting claims of different moralities seem to clash and invite the reader to come and choose, underscoring the historical and temporal nature of moral concepts.

Faith in liberalism and democratic processes is trounced through the depiction of the brotherhood, the group of Oxford intellectuals, all once Marxists, but now unable to take Marxism in its modern forms. Jenkin's tentative movement towards liberation theology, a marriage of Christianity and Marxism, is an indication of the possible relevance of a new morality for our time. But the point of the novel is not so much to assert that, as to show how the good man functions in the world today. How does he act? What is he tempted by? If he can neither believe in outworn ancient creeds nor ever entirely shed them, what sort of moral choices does he make, and why? If he is the naked and solitary individual willing and acting, how is he to escape from compulsive and isolated movement? What is the background out of which the good man is to act today when the availability of numerous backgrounds excludes the formation of any coherent one?

Section I of the chapter places Jenkin in his group, 'the brotherhood'. Section II contrasts him with Crimond and Gerard, two prominent figures in the novel. Section III clarifies his brand of ethics, Section IV connects Jenkin with Christ, and Section V re-examines Jenkin as Murdoch's version of the good figure for our times.

I

Jenkin Riderhood's presence in *The Book and the Brotherhood* combines instinctive inner certainty with openness to all that blows through the world outside. He is ready to think about all this, though refusing to conceptualise rigorously. When he acts, he does so without questioning and doubt, almost by instinct, or out of a religious tradition which stubbornly persists though the framework has disappeared from view. In fact, one can see Jenkin as the inevitable development of the figures before him. He is a secularised, ageing Brendan without the charm, the intellect and the mystery; he is a James without the interesting Eastern spirituality; he is an Anne without her struggle, an Eastcote without his stillness and a Stuart without his idealism. There has been a progressive discarding, and Murdoch now presents a figure who is virtually unnoticeable till the novel gathers gradually to his death.

He is thus unnoticeable because the identity-giving forms which at one time or another dominated have collapsed, and in their place has arisen such a multiplicity of ideologies that there is a veritable bombardment of the individual by different calls. Stuart Cuno at the close of *The Good Apprentice* had pointed to this when he asked his father which good things he drinks to: 'We might all mean different ones.' Till this century, Western society lived by some prevailing world-picture or other for at least fifty years at a time. Such coherence, try as Crimond might for a synthesis, is no longer possible. Ideologies have been spawned and modified at such a rate that Jenkin, as everyman, rightly asks for time to think things out before he subscribes to or rejects any of these.

It is this bewilderment and rich chaos that Murdoch evokes in *The Book and the Brotherhood*, the pluralism that besets the modern world and gives terrorism an equal chance with St Augustine. In the face of such confusion the novel offers three possible alternatives. First, to attempt a neo-Marxist synthesis as Crimond does, accommodating everything in a Utopian scheme. Second, to take refuge in the old liberal 'decencies' and retain democratic processes, the old cultural baggage and the value of the individual. And third, to think things out piecemeal without monistic delusions of a saved society, to consider all alternatives carefully, and never lose sight of old moral tenets such as duty, and helping people rather than hurting them.

This last alternative, presented through Jenkin Riderhood, is an assertion of religious values without emotional, spiritual or ritualistic colouring. To place it within a recognisable religious context is to exclude, to impose a scheme, outside which is loss or damnation. To call it a categorical imperative is to separate it from empirical experience and make it idealistic in a way that can be

dangerous. Any kind of idealism can generate dangerous notions
of what conformity with that ideal might constitute. The 'idealistic'
picture might call for the extermination of the Jews, for instance.
For this reason, Jenkin carefully avoids idealism, and is shown as
a man who deals with fragments of experience as they come.

What then is left? An acting-out, after thought for others, of
what seems right: Christian love of neighbour, practised without
reference to the gospels; or it might be Hindu *dharma* without
reference to the scriptures; or the Buddhist eightfold path without
reference to *karma* or *nirvāna*. These references are dropped not
only because they sound antiquated and have become irrelevant
in the world of facts created by empiricist philosophy, but also
because in the wake of a revived fundamentalism, they have often
been used to express the opposite of their innate meaning.

In such a world what is the place of the virtues?

Jenkin's marginal place in his set illustrates a severance of the
virtues from the larger context and the solitary nature of its mode
of existence. Jenkin is the least successful of the group to which
he belongs. Yet the fact that each member turns to Jenkin in a time
of crisis, and that his existence is seen gradually but increasingly
as valuable, points to the crucial importance of the good he
represents and a sense of its lacuna in life. Why, for instance, does
Gerard, the natural leader of the brotherhood, the one who has
everything anyone might want, realise that the person with whom
he wants to share his life is his old friend Jenkin? He has money,
position, friends, a beautiful woman who has waited for him
all her life. He turns instead to this short, stout, middle-aged
schoolmaster. Jenkin, now senior history master in a London
School, has never applied for a headship, and is 'a diffident solitary
man easily pleased by small treats'. Rose remarks that he looks
like a child. Clearly an unselfconscious humility and innocence
deriving from Christian tradition is behind this. Jenkin would not
be good by Aristotelian standards. He talks less fluently and
eloquently than his friends and notably lacks magnificence.

In keeping with the non-magnificent image is the sexual restraint
associated with Jenkin. Murdoch has, in novel after novel, explored
the chaos, irrationality and self-centredness that characterise erotic
love. The toning-down of the sexual colouring in all relationships
pertaining to Jenkin is an indication of the fact that he has a kind
of goodness the soul needs even while it pursues other phantoms.
Not that Jenkin is a sexless being, but the feeling of others for him,

even Gerard's, is less clouded by sexuality. The interactions of almost all the others – Rose and Gerard, Rose and Crimond, Jean and Crimond, Jean and Duncan, Tamar and Duncan, Tamar and Gerard, Tamar and Jean, Gideon and Tamar, Gideon and Violet, Tamar and Fr McAlister, Gulliver and Lily, Gulliver and Gerard, Rose and Jean – all these interactions partake of sexuality to greater and lesser degrees, and are, for that reason, confused and troubled. The narcissistic element can be eliminated from erotic love only with the greatest difficulty; perhaps it can only be transfigured, never entirely written out. And if narcissism is antithetical to goodness,[2] then sexuality is a stumbling block; a doubly dangerous one because it appears to be directing attention outward to another. It may also bring with it the delusion of power. When Jean and Crimond in this novel speak of living on love 'like two gods' (BB 312) we are reminded not only of similar language used by Harry to Midge in *The Good Apprentice* (GA 172), but also of the original delusion in Eden after the loss of innocence. Murdoch in this latest novel surveys the subversive effects of Eros more sardonically than in earlier works. Harry and Midge in *The Good Apprentice* are harmless versions of Crimond and Jean in *The Book and the Brotherhood*.

Jenkin's contained sexuality is therefore significant. Gerard's proposal to Jenkin has its sexual undertow but notably lacks madness.

II

Jenkin's relative freedom from the rich irrationality engendered by sex is sharply contrasted with Crimond's strong needs, and Crimond's apparent strength is revealed finally as weakness. Jenkin, apparently weak, is free and therefore strong. Crimond is as inescapable a presence as Jenkin is 'invisible'. A demonic figure seized by an unbridled force, he is in reality its victim, and the strength he incarnates is a dubious one. His sexual attractiveness – Jean, Lily, even Rose, respond to it – and his mental abilities add up to a virtually irresistible combination. The men dislike him (with the exception of Jenkin); the women are tempted to yield. But he is driven by his drive, if it may be put that way. There is great force here, but it has not been harnessed in the 'right' way.

What is the 'right' way to control the energy of the libido?

Working against the self, controlling the self, have been intimately associated with the right and the good in the novels discussed thus far. Crimond shows no trace of this. He takes Jean; he drops her; he takes her again; he drops her again; in every instance he asserts *himself – his* needs. He uses other things (the money provided by the brotherhood), and other people (Jean, Lily) to stoke and fuel his energy. This is 'an irresponsible and undirected self-assertion' (SG 48), for his will to act and end his life results in Jean's accident, and later, Jenkin's death. Nowhere do we see him examining things and undertaking a checking procedure. Murdoch's language and detail in the passages concerning Crimond (whether in an account of his superb, silent and grim dancing, or of his mad suicide pact with Jean) build up an impression of frenzy under a coldly controlled exterior.

Over against this is Jenkin's quiet, non-dramatic, unromantic figure. Sexuality, as already observed, is 'kept on a lead', not absent, but beautifully controlled. The mind here is constantly checking and rechecking ('The least we can do is try to think': BB 224). He has been for a long time a little in love with Rose but has never spoken of it (BB 370). This is very different from Crimond's wanting, having, holding and discarding.

Crimond is all of a piece, monolithic; there is no give in him anywhere. Jenkin begins with small pieces and details and concentrates on those, avoiding idealism which can so easily be either false or dangerous. It is interesting to see that they are not two polar opposites excluding one another. Jenkin, though killed in Crimond's desperate game, can absorb and contain Crimond, and Crimond weeps uncontrollably for him when he dies.

The Jenkin–Crimond contrast is a clear-cut and necessary one. Subtler, but as important in the clarifying of Jenkin's type of goodness, is the difference between him and Gerard.

Gerard is your highly intelligent, cultivated and sensitive man, reasonably successful in the world. In a sense, he is the reader in response to the chaotic world. One takes one's stand nearest him perhaps because he is the most 'acceptable' kind of upper-middle-class liberal with a proper share of fairness and decorum. He was a Marxist at the appropriate time, and retains faith in a fading version of socialist democracy, the only 'decent' belief in a post-Stalin era. He also has the right amount of extra sensitivity and depth that marks out 'the hero' from the rest, and in any other novel he could easily have been the hero. But Murdoch draws him into her set of the deceived, the slightly absurd, the partly sad, largely happy, near-complacent victims. He is a finer, slightly less comic Rupert Foster of *A Fairly Honourable Defeat* with the same moral and personal vanity, though the comedy directed against Gerard is not so clearly defined. Gerard has to be carefully distinguished from Jenkin; he could almost have been Jenkin: he has both the sense and the sensibility. But he is not, and in his realisation of Jenkin's worth and his longing to have Jenkin, he is again the reader who sees and wants the good. He says so many fine things, and is kind to so many people that the point of his falseness may easily be missed. But measured against Jenkin, the spiritual shortfall is at once apparent. Levquist pinpoints the difference at once to Gerard himself:

> 'Riderhood doesn't need to get anywhere, he walks the path, he exists where he is. Whereas you—'
> 'Whereas I—?'
> 'You were always dissolving yourself into righteous discontent, thrilled in your bowels by the idea of some high thing elsewhere. So it has gone on. You see yourself as a lonely climber, of course higher up than the other ones, you think you might leap out of yourself on to the summit, yet you know you can't, and being displeased with yourself both ways you go nowhere.'   (BB 22)

Idealism of the sort that haunts Gerard is seen here as romantic falsification. It leads to dreams and thoughts about good which are so beautiful and interesting that they hinder the soul in its eternal progressive wandering. The road is more properly the metaphor for spiritual progress than the ladder. Gerard and Jenkin says this to one another. Jenkin says to Gerard: 'You think you are on a ladder going up, and you *do* go up'; to which Gerard replies: 'You think you're on a road going on and you *do* go on.' A little later Jenkin says to Gerard:

> 'You can't by-pass where you are by an imaginary leap into the ideal.'
> 'Alright, but it's better to *have* an ideal rather than just trudging on and thinking how different we all are.'   (BB 128)

Murdoch clearly locates virtue in the road and the trudging rather than the ladder and the leap. The same distinction recurs much later in another exchange between Gerard and Jenkin. Jenkin says:

> 'Don't walk so fast, Gerard. I'm just a practical chap, it's you
> who are religious. Yes, we keep telling each other, we do see
> life differently. I see it as a journey along a dark boggy road with
> a lot of other chaps. You see it as a solitary climb up a mountain,
> you don't believe you'll get to the top, but you feel that because
> you can *think* of it you've done it. That's the ideal that takes you
> all the way.'   (BB 246)

Gerard replies with some dark reference to things looking like
death up there which Jenkin characterises as romantic myth.
Gerard comes back with:

'I believe in goodness, you believe in Justice' (BB 247). This is
an extremely interesting remark – devotion to the idea of goodness
may prevent one from being truly just.[3] It calls out such a play of
sensitivity and contemplation, such stirrings of the heart and mind
that the fat self is pleased by the beautiful notions to which it has
thrillingly responded. Stuart Cuno had better watch his step as he
grows older, or he may fall into a beautiful romanticising snare.

The beautiful can distract from the good. Murdoch has said as
much about charm in *The Good Apprentice*; but here danger is sensed
not only in the charming but in the truly beautiful. One infers this
not only from Gerard's idealism and his compelling images of
death and goodness and the upward climb, but also from his
sensitive reading of a passage from Homer. The choice of the
passage is noteworthy for it is the one from the *Iliad* which Matthew
Arnold holds up as one of the touchstones of great poetry. Murdoch
makes no reference to this at all but describes Gerard's reading
thus:

> Sitting again at the desk Gerard read aloud from the *Iliad* about
> how the divine horses of Achilles wept when they heard of the
> death of Patroclus, bowed their heads while hot tears poured
> from their eyes onto the ground, as they wept with longing for
> their charioteer, and their long beautiful manes were darkened
> with mud, and as they mourned, Zeus looked down on them
> and pitied them, and spoke thus in his heart. Unhappy beasts,
> why did I give you, ageless and deathless as you are, as a gift to
> Lord Peleus, a mortal? Was it so that you too should grieve

among unhappy men? Indeed there is nothing that breathes and crawls upon the earth more miserable than man.   (BB 23)

Arnold includes this among the best that has been thought and said in the world and regards it as a criterion against which whatever we read may be tested. Gerard is alive to the beauty and power of the passage; he reads it well as only one who is so alive can do. By contrast, Jenkin stumbles over the passage from Thucydides.[4] Murdoch is saying something here about the traps that await the aesthetic sensibility. Imagination is suspect, and Jenkin checks the workings of his imagination. He sometimes imagines 'individual other people', people he had never met, but

never imagined stories attached to these people . . . he did not like to speculate about them beyond the formulation of hypotheses necessary for ordinary life.   (BB 131)

Romanticising seems to be the chief obstruction in the way of clear seeing, thinking and acting. The contrast with Gerard makes the point very accurately. Jenkin's simplicity makes him happy; he instinctively avoids muddles, cupidity, lying, exercises of power because they make him uncomfortable. This simplicity seems easy; for Jenkin it is; it is a bare, perhaps less interesting state than Gerard's, and consists of a sort of innocence and cheerfulness. Gerard's more interesting but less pure state is beautifully described by Murdoch with just such imagery as would simultaneously attract, sadden and console Gerard with its beauty and mystery. Jenkin thinks thus of himself and Gerard:

He had become too much at ease, too much at home in his life. Gerard was not at home, made continually restless by a glimpsed ideal far far above him; yet at the same time the glimpse, as the clouds swirled about the summit, consoled him, even deceived him as with a swoop of intellectual love he seemed to be beside it, up there in those pure and radiant regions, high above the thing he really was.   (BB 132)

Longing for and loving the beautiful can have a spiritually deleterious effect. To see the beautiful and extraordinary and thereby experience the illusion of participating in it, the feeling the distance from it, the yearning over it can be a kind of pleasure bordering

on the complacent, different from true joy. Jenkin finds Gerard's
'quasi-mystical, pseudo-mystical Platonic perfectionism' alien.

Jenkin watches for traces of false romanticism in himself. He
wants to go to South America or India, drawn thither by liberation
theology and the thought of working for the poor. He checks to
see whether this is not a large ambition feeding his own self-
importance, and whether the teaching of languages and history to
boys is not the best thing for him. He realises that he is cherishing
his restlessness and his desire to get away, and that this is wrong.
Nothing should matter save easing pain. He suspects that even
the fascination of liberation theology may be romantic, consisting
of a popular picture of Christ 'as the Saviour of the poor, of the
left-behinds, of the disappeareds' (BB 133).

Gerard's imaginative and active mind is well illustrated by his
story of fishing methods in one of the South Sea islands. The
gathering-in of a huge net of flailing, ferocious fish is used naturally
by Gerard as an image of the unconscious mind. Jenkin is more
concerned about the poor dying creatures, and reiterates his oft-
expressed, never acted-upon wish of becoming a vegetarian. We
are told that both Gerard and Jenkin are walkers, but that, while
Gerard walks wrapped in a great dark cloak of his thoughts, Jenkin
walks through a great collection or exhibition of little events or
encounters – such as trees, many dogs, rubbish tips, shop windows,
cars, things in gutters, people's clothes (BB 131). At first sight
Gerard might seem, with his great dark cloak of introspection,
the 'better' one, the one engaged in a necessary kind of self-
examination. But in the light of what Murdoch says in *The
Sovereignty of Good* about the limited value of such introspection
(SG 67) and what she implies here about the dangers of romantic
dreaming, Jenkin's far more ordinary interest in things outside
himself is indicative of better spiritual health. Only the humble
man can be more interested in rubbish-tips than in the comforting-
disturbing cloak of his own thoughts. Jenkin lives in society; Gerard
fails to notice it.

The difference between Gerard and Jenkin is illustrated nicely
by two moments, far separated in the novel, when each is seen
'advising' another. Why is it that when Gerard talks to Violet about
letting her daughter Tamar continue her education, which he is
himself ready to finance, it comes over as moral vanity, whereas
when Jenkin talks to Tamar about waiting and thinking, it carries
the ring of authenticity? What Gerard says is in itself good advice;

it is certainly true that an Oxford education is a supreme kind of excellence for some people. But the author's tone, the use of italics and brackets, the use of indirect speech, clearly communicate Gerard's absurd pomposity. Here is the passage:

> (Gerard) stayed a while with Violet: She told him, and seemed glad to be able to do so, about Tamar's weeping and screaming fits which had preceded her flight. Violet did not know why Tamar was in such a state. Violet was certainly unnerved, upset, frightened, perhaps even shocked into loving concern for her daughter. Gerard took the opportunity of saying to Violet with an *air of authority* that really she *must* allow Tamar to continue her education. Probably Tamar's grief on this subject lay behind her breakdown. Some young people *passionately* wanted to go on learning and studying, and the really difficult things, which would be possessions forever had to be learnt when still young. If Tamar were frustrated now (so Gerard painted the picture) she might fall into depression and lose her job, whereas if she could return to Oxford she would get a much better-paid job later on. Gerard would be very glad meanwhile to help financially, and so on and so on. (BB 371)

The last six words of the passage set the seal on the negative response to Gerard building up within the reader at this point. His flow of talk and advice satisfies primarily himself. He enjoys assuming an air of authority and the chance of playing benefactor as well as adviser. Violet's response of 'quiet amused cynicism' does not come as a surprise.

The truth about Tamar's breakdown (that it follows an abortion), already revealed to the reader through her confession to Jenkin, makes Gerard's reported pontification doubly false and absurd in its irrelevance. Yet it must be reiterated that the point Gerard makes is not in itself a contemptible one; on the contrary, Murdoch has herself spoken of the importance of A-levels and preparing for university.[5] It is, then, the source within the speaker–adviser that is being criticised. Gerard is good, kind, well-meaning. What Murdoch is showing through this is the need to purify the source of good within so that it has less of the self directing it. How is this to be done? Talking too much about it merely strengthens it; what is needed is a comfortable, humble egoism. When Gerard and Jenkin talk about the ego, Jenkin says:

'I don't mind too much. Why destroy the healthy ego? It does a job.'   (BB 128)

The novelist comments later that Gerard was always talking about destroying his ego, whereas Jenkin was quite comfortable with his, never worried too much, and hoped to do better. The answer is not so much annihilating the ego as altering the quality of consciousness through proper attention to the individual. Gerard does not give such attention to either Violet or Tamar; his well-intentioned advice is rooted more in his own need to play the guiding role than in understanding the particular quality of their hell.

This may be contrasted with Jenkin's reaction to Tamar when she comes to him in anger, blaming him quite unjustly, with the story of her aborted child. Jenkin listens to her with complete attention as she rages at him, then tries to take her hand, appalled by what he hears:

In the few minutes she had been with him Jenkin had seen into the hell she spoke of, and although he spoke of helping her he did not see any way in which it would be possible. He wished he could take away her consciousness so that all this pain would cease.   (BB 365)

Jenkin's realisation of the impossibility of really helping is essential to the task of being honest about one's significance. All he does is babble utterly random words in an attempt to soothe:

'we've got to be able to think about it, I'll help you, you don't hate me, you came to me, you must stay with me and trust me, you need people, you need love . . . (BB 366).

He knows that there is more to be mended here than he can possibly accomplish himself. He makes up a bed for her in the spare room, puts out a pair of his own pyjamas, gives her a hot-water bottle and, after she has fallen asleep, makes a private signal of his own over her, committing her to whatever heaven there might be. What emerges from this exchange is the love with which Jenkin *attends* to Tamar and the extent to which he feels not just for her, but *with* her. Such loving attention is part of the limited help one can give. The realisation of helplessness in the face of another's suffering, the refusal to take over, and the performance, instead, of simple acts are indications of Jenkin's humility.

The difference between Gerard and Crimond (both idealists) on the one hand, and Jenkin on the other may be highlighted by a distinction drawn by Gerard Fourrez when, following categories defined by Weber, he speaks of the 'morals of conviction' and the 'morals of responsibility' in his *Liberation Ethics*.[6] Gerard in *The Book and the Brotherhood* clearly upholds the 'morals of conviction'. By this is implied a more or less absolute standard of ethics and 'one single reading of reality', which is not really interested in the challenges offered by more precise analyses and which neglects the real economic, political and idelogical conditions that affect the creation of ethics. Jenkin, by contrast, lives by the 'morals of responsibility' which, says Fourrez, concentrates on the concrete results of action, implying that 'what is important is to act in such a way that one is ready to accept responsibility for one's actions and also different interpretations of one's actions'. Fourrez's *Liberation Ethics* openly declares its solidarity with the struggle of the oppressed and with liberation theology. It is worth noting that Jenkin is drawn by the morality of liberation theology and plans to go to South America.

III

Non-idealistic (unlike Crimond) and non-romantic (unlike Gerard), he has been defined thus far through negatives and contrasts. As a piece of characterisation he emerges as an entirely human and credible character, the nice, dullish man next door whom one would not have suspected to have had so much virtue in him.

But Levquist, their old tutor at Oxford, has always known this about Jenkin. He pooh-poohs Gerard's wish that Jenkin might 'get somewhere' ('He knows several modern languages. As for getting anywhere, he's teaching, isn't he? Riderhood doesn't need to get anywhere, he *walks the path, he exists where he is*': BB 22). Teaching is seen by Murdoch as an exercise of virtue. She says in a letter that some of the most virtuous people she knows are quiet schoolteachers.[7] Similarly, in *The Sovereignty of Good*, she connects the learning of language with moral discipline. Their authoritative grammatical structures command respect, draw the attention away from the self, exist independently, and cannot be taken over, swallowed up or made unreal by the consciousness. Attention to them is rewarded by a knowledge of reality (SG 89). One might add that language carries moral and affective overtones, reaches out to people and alleviates isolation. Jenkin's devotion to languages, his teaching of Greek and Latin and later French and Spanish, and his current encounter with a Portuguese grammar, are clear signs of the good that increasingly spreads out from him.

The next significant sign is his aloneness. It is necessary for him to be alone. After Gerard leaves his flat, he is glad to be by himself, though he was also glad to be with Gerard, and it is suggested that he would never marry because that would prevent him from being alone at night (BB 130–95). How is this solitude to be judged? It is important to see that no interesting complexity gathers around his solitude; we see him, after Gerard has left, putting on the radio, thinking of supper and Gerard, preparing his supper and slowly eating it, reading some Spanish poetry, and then looking at the map and thinking of Christmas in Spain on a package tour (BB 130).

It must be asked whether Jenkin is not put to the severest moral tests by being allowed to be alone. Is he taking the easy way out by not sharing a life and being subjected to the thousand pinpricks of disruption that that entails? The point is that he need not; there is no duty here. Given his society and his world, this is a choice to which he has a right, and he makes it. It is not difficult, moreover, with the picture of Jenkin given by the novel, to imagine how he might have acted within the frame of marriage.

In making him a bachelor, however, Murdoch is implying something about the importance of steering clear of emotional mess. Brendan, James, Anne, William Eastcote,[8] Stuart – now Jenkin – not one is married. Does the marriage structure somehow preclude true virtue? The celibacy enjoined by religious orders the world over would say so. The picture Murdoch draws of family ties shows that she regards such involvement as inevitably binding; its concomitant pain and joy chain down the heart in such a way as to make wholly selfless devotion wellnigh impossible. Tallis Brown and Ann Peronett are two earlier sketches of married people going through moral tests, and of these, only Ann has a child. Her fate is to live within her cage, but she is not free within that cage as Stuart, alone, can be inside his. Stuart Cuno's decision to be single and free of entanglements is intimately connected with his decision to devote his life to being good.

Jenkin's reaction to Gerard's proposal of a shared life is very carefully elaborated with an honesty and accuracy that take full account of the issue – and is then left unresolved. We can never know for certain whether Jenkin will refuse Gerard, though the pointers are in that direction. Even before Gerard puts the proposal to him, Jenkin has begun to feel the need 'to get away from Gerard', not because he is oppressed by him, but because the completeness he offers is a temptation. A perfect resource for Jenkin, as brother, protector, guide, exemplar, he has been 'pure gold'. For this reason he must be given up: 'To test *himself in a Gerardless world*. Reverently to remove something just because it was so perfect.' (BB 133). There is a strong puritanical streak here which needs to break the circle once it gets too perfect, to build and rebuild over and over again, to refuse to be too cosy and settled. This is Jenkin's resolve before Gerard's proposal comes. When it does, he examines it carefully. Gerard is very important to him and the call to share a life carries a beauty fraught with poignancy and possibilities. There is a distinct change, 'a sudden increase of being' (BB 371). The echoing call stirs things in deep places and he cannot help wondering: 'Perhaps after all this changed everything?' He tells himself that this shell must be broken but he finds deep and tender desires running counter to his resolve. For the space of several paragraphs their 'new sense of each other' is lovingly and beautifully described, and Jenkin begins to see how 'easy, natural, appropriate, proper, fated' it may all be. But at the same time, something calls him elsewhere and he sees

the necessity of an absolute departure; and he felt uncomfortably that the voice of duty also spoke on that side.   (BB 449)

He is torn between the prospect of tender human love on the one hand and what seems to be a kind of duty on the other.

In addition to the aloneness associated with Jenkin is also innocence. This comes across strongly in the account of the Guy Fawkes' Day party at Gerard's house. Jenkin takes the greatest delight in organising the fireworks, and experiences genuine, child-like joy in the entrancing whorls and showers of light.

Jenkin's political morality is related to his sense of life's tasks, 'about jobs to be done among strangers' (BB 132). He begins with small pieces and details and concentrates on those, in sharp contrast with Crimond's large all-inclusive scheme for a perfect society. Jenkin has no great plan, only fragments which can be picked up and salvaged. Such a piecemeal notion of good to be done leads him to remonstrate mildly that there is a large lie somewhere in Crimond's synthesis. While Crimond has nothing but contempt for the flat and feeble objections of the others, he says that Jenkin is the only one among them who has a vestige of sense.

It is worth recapitulating Crimond's defence of his book to the brotherhood so that Jenkin's stand may be seen. What MacIntyre calls 'the key intellectual opposition between liberal individualism and some version of Marxism or neo-Marxism'[9] is vividly dramatised in the confrontation. The members of the set have been putting up a defence of liberal decency, Western parliamentary democracy and the value of the individual. To all this Crimond replies with immense force that there is an 'invisible violence' underlying the present social structures and counters charges of countenancing terrorism with the remark:

'Our way of life rests upon violence and invites it.'   (BB 335)[10]

He invites them to look at the real causes of what is wrong with the world, and accuses Gerard of thinking that he and his kind are saved by the idea of the good just because they know about it and of stupidly believing that reality is good.

'You live on books and conversation and mutual admiration and drink – you're all alcoholics – and sentimental ideas of virtue. You have no energy, you are lazy people. The real heroes of our time are those who are brave enough to let go of the old dreamy self-centred, self-satisfied morality . . . what's the use of a soul, that gilded idol of selfishness? Ask whom you identify with, that will tell you your place and your class. The people of this planet are like you, *they* must be served, *they* must be saved, the hungry sheep look up and are not fed.'   (BB 336)

Crimond's arguments are extremely powerful and overwhelming, as he himself is. Breathing fire and energy, he holds up a compelling picture of a Utopian society in which a higher human potential will be realised.

What is Jenkin's reply to all this? The others have renounced their faith in Marxist morality. What has happened to Jenkin? He cannot honestly deny the justice of Crimond's claims. Gerard is upset by what he sees as Jenkin's quiet determination to rescue Crimond, by the image of Jenkin somehow *defecting* to Crimond. To the rest of the set, conscious of the 'wickedness of Hitler and Stalin', communism is an abomination, and cannot be 'done properly' (BB 224).

Jenkin, being a Utilitarian at heart, cannot give up certain aspects of the Marxist explanation; he has to admit that Marxism cares about suffering and poverty and injustice. He connects it with the liberation theology of the Catholic Church in Latin America ('Suddenly people begin to feel that nothing matters except human misery': BB 225). But he cannot take it whole. He remarks to Gerard about Marxism – 'if it could only liberate itself into being moral philosophy' (BB 244). Perhaps his dissatisfaction stems from the separation of means and ends which is characteristic of the classic Marxist credo. He relies finally on Utilitarianism. (MacIntyre observes that in crises Marxists have always appealed to Utilitarianism.)[11] 'Utilitarianism is the only philosophy that lasts', he says (BB 246). By this Jenkin means the importance given by the Utilitarians to the public good over the private. To care about suffering and injustice is another way of asking for the greatest possible happiness for the greatest number in the world. This is why Jenkin wants to go to South America. The cultivation of private good has begun to seem a luxury to him. Gerard sums it up very accurately when he says to Jenkin:

'I believe in goodness, you believe in Justice.'   (BB 247)

Gerard's preoccupation with goodness seems, in this light, to be luxuriating self-indulgence, and Crimond has a strong point on his side when he speaks of the old dreamy self-satisfied morality. When Rose accuses him of having sold his soul, he replies that he is proud to have sold it, for the soul is a gilded idol of selfishness.

Thus far Crimond and Jenkin are in agreement. The relief of the oppressed is the task at hand. However, there is an important difference. Crimond is *wholly* convinced of his cause. It is in his unseeing dedication and *refusal to doubt* that his danger lies. Doubt has always seemed to Murdoch to be an essential ingredient in the development of the moral person. Strong convictions are useful but they must be subjected endlessly to careful scrutiny. Not so much scrutiny as will render action impossible, but just so much as will keep alive an awareness of dangerous rigidity. The difference between 'the morals of conviction' and 'the morals of responsibility' referred to earlier may be recalled here. Jenkin's tentativeness and faith fit well with Fourrez's remark about the latter:

> Moving towards an ethics of responsibility may represent a step forward for individuals who thus, in an act of trust and hope, say, 'This is what I might make of my life.'[12]

In striking contrast with Jenkin's tentativeness and faith, Crimond's sweeping answers to charges of the violence inherent in his scheme highlight the dangers of 'causes' and 'the morals of conviction'. If Gerard's is a false romanticism, Crimond's is a false idealism, and truth seems to lie in the bits and pieces.[13]

In keeping with his checking method, Jenkin re-examines his motives in wanting to get away to work for the poor. Is it possibly a dream of 'feeding on others' misery and making of it a full self'? He recognises that 'nothing matters much saving easing pain, individuals and their histories'. Here is a nice and proper coming together of the kinds of idealism Crimond and Gerard have falsified. The individual, so dear to Gerard's liberal outlook, is concentrated upon and helped by Crimond's socialistic plans.

While Jenkin is greatly drawn by liberation theology, he is afraid as mentioned earlier, that even this picture of Christ as Saviour of the poor in the Third World may be a falsely romantic picture. He comes to the realisation that the truest theology may be *theology broken*, 'smashed by the sudden realisable and realised horror of the world'.

To smash through structures and be in a state of realised horror is a religious experience if an impulse moves from the heart of that horror towards doing good. Such impulses, when generated against a background of comfort, become a luxury, a feeding of self, as evidenced by the 'benevolence' of the set towards one another – the case of Gerard's good intentions towards Tamar and Violet, for instance. But when the walls have fallen and ruin lies round, to recognise goodness and duty, the naked and frail state of oneself and one's fellows – this is truly moral. Breaking the circle of comfort which Gerard provides and offers to make more complete is a necessary part of Jenkin's moral growth. In his loneliness and humanness Jenkin is tempted to accept Gerard, but though one can never know for certain what he would have done, one guesses that he would have gone away. The Portuguese grammar and the book by a Jesuit on *Socialism and the New Theology* indicate a serious and sincere resolve to seek change. Personal change is intuitively sensed by Jenkin very early on:

> He felt, he intuited, that his life was about to change in some way he could not yet determine.   (BB 130)

By contrast Gerard seeks no change, rather, a resettling into, and making permanent, old forms, old friendships. Crimond, on the other hand, wants total change, smashing old structures.

Jenkin sees the need for both personal transformation as well as social change. Hence liberation theology. Merely to change the social structure guarantees nothing. The oppressed today, given structural change alone, become the oppressors tomorrow. Personal change by itself will not do either; it degenerates into self-regard which is doubly insidious because it assumes a quasi-religious aspect. First, personal change – an endless, ongoing affair; then, the other – the replacement of unfair social structures by compassionate ones.

Liberation theologians who have turned on St Paul for his romantic emphasis on the yearning of the human heart towards Christ to the exclusion, it might seem, of social commitment, are realising today that Paul, the builder of churches, placed that emphasis because he recognised that without the transformed heart, no amount of structural change can really bring about *change*. The exploiter and victim merely change places.[14] Jenkin's recognition of the need for change, and his sense of it as a 'large white blankness . . . opening before him . . . a radiant live space like a white cloud, moist and warm', combined with his concern for the struggle in South America, clarifies Murdoch's understanding of the moral task. If Crimond sees the smashing of external social structures as part of his good, Jenkin sees the smashing of inner security-giving structures as part of *his* task. Only such a purification can fit one for the rebuilding of a just society. His inclination is to stay; his duty tells him to go.

This is the point at which Tamar comes to him saying she needs help, extreme help, and as he talks to her, telling her to think it all out, the telephone rings and Jean desperately appeals for help too. She has discovered Crimond's sinister note in Duncan's desk, suspects a challenge to a duel, rings Gerard and gets no answer, rings Jenkin and appeals to him to go at once to Crimond and find out if there is any danger. Jenkin's immediate answer is:

> 'Yes, yes, I'll go at once, don't worry—'
> 'And you'll ring me'.
> 'Yes – I'll fly now!   (BB 454)

That is Jenkin in action. Like Tallis in *A Fairly Honorable Defeat*, when action is called for, he acts at once. Telling Tamar to stay till he returns, he hurries out looking for a taxi.

He never comes back. He goes down to the basement of his flat where the deadly game arranged by the suicidal Crimond is being played. The bullet, fired by Duncan and meant by Crimond for himself, hits Jenkin as he opens the door at the crucial moment and appears in the doorway, and he slumps down dead – killed by accident. This important event is thus described:

> Then, hearing it distantly as in a dream, Duncan heard the odd, the amazing sound of someone's feet on the stairs outside. The sound of approaching feet and then a voice that cried out 'David, David!' The door was flying open and instead of the blue rectangle, Jenkin Riderhood stood there, emerged from the darkness of the stairs. Duncan, in the very moment of firing, adjusted his aim. The report, echoing in the enclosed room, was deafening. Another sound, a heavy, thudding noise, was almost instantaneous. Duncan dropped the gun and put his hand to his head. Jenkin was not there, there was only the open doorway. Duncan walked slowly down the room. Jenkin was lying on the floor on his back. There was a neat red hole in the centre of his forehead in exactly the place at which Duncan had aimed when he was aiming at Crimond. Jenkin was clearly dead. His eyes were open and his face expressed surprise. Duncan closed the door.   (BB 468)

The accidental manner of his death is in keeping with the unplanned nature of his existence and the piecemeal nature of his mind. But it is only with this death that the true significance of his life emerges.

IV

Jenkin's importance is only gradually perceived both by the characters in the book and by the reader. For the characters he becomes important only in their difficulties. Till then, he is on the side of their lives; their actions involve others. Jean, for instance, gravitates between Crimond and Duncan, but when she is anxious for the safety of either, she rings Jenkin and, incidentally, sends him to his death. Murdoch is careful not to overplay this aspect with a heavy hand; she represents Jean as first phoning Gerard and Rose but neither is available. Jenkin is at home and ready to go at once. So, while at the naturalistic level it is accidental that Jenkin goes to the fatal Duncan–Crimond encounter, at the emblematic level, it is highly significant that Jenkin happens to be in when Jean calls. This comes close on the heels of Tamar's turning to Jenkin after getting rid of her child and leaving her home. There is thus a very gradual building up of significance leading to his death. The mourning for him after his death clearly shows his great importance. While he lived it was only just beginning to be perceptible.

For the reader likewise, recognition of Jenkin's significance comes slowly. He is duller than the others, does and says less, and is not involved in the tide of events and feelings swirling outside and making up the bulk of the novel. But by the time we come to the fruitless and bitter grief over Jenkin's death, the reader finds he has been prepared by many small touches – Levquist's praise of him for example, or Crimond's laconic testimony: 'The only one of you who's worth tuppence ha' penny is Jenkin, and he's a fool.'   (BB 338)

The growing perception of the novel's characters matched by the growing perception of the reader is in keeping with Murdoch's usual marginalisation of the good figures. The gradual unfolding of Jenkin as a person implies the slow way in which the good is often recognised. In *The Good Apprentice* others see from the start that there is something odd and different about Stuart Cuno; or they are startlingly affected by him – to wit, Midge's transformation during the drive from Seegard to London. *The Book and the Brotherhood* shows the process differently. That Christ may be the man next door is a truism, but the recognition of Christ in the man next door comes much more slowly and less obviously, in this case only after his death. This matter of recognising Christ is played out at a remove through the thoughts of Gulliver, a hanger-on on the periphery of the set. He sees a tramp shivering in the cold at King's Cross Station and wonders whether he should give him his coat ('suppose he isn't a demon, or an *alter-ego*, suppose he's Christ

himself come to test me' (BB 433). Through such a scene, reflection
on the theme of Christ unrecognised has been raised, and it comes
at a fairly late point in the book when Jenkin is linked in a muted
way with Christ. The Christ-association is nothing new. What is
new is that Jenkin does not suffer; he simply dies. Murdoch's
awareness of the spiritual traps hedging the contemplation of
suffering has already been noted in the chapter on Anne. Stuart
Cuno in *The Good Apprentice* associated Christ with concentration
camps; his suffering was stripped and connected with pure loss
and pointless horror to ensure that it was de-linked from the
beautiful. In *The Book and the Brotherhood* it has been dropped
altogether – Jenkin has nothing to do with suffering. The point, as
Christ says to Anne in *Nuns and Soldiers*, is not the suffering; the
point is love. Jenkin's readiness to help is the expression of love.
He acts out Christ's second commandment without so much as
giving it a thought. In *The Good Apprentice* Stuart was shown
thinking of the Good Samaritan as a practical man who remembers
to send more money to the innkeeper but does not otherwise expend
much emotion on the incident that occurred on the journey from
Jerusalem to Jericho. Jenkin's life and death are an elaboration of
such a picture. He *is* the local good samaritan, like Tallis in *A Fairly
Honourable Defeat*.

The recognition of this gathers slowly in the minds of the others
through the last quarter of the novel that remains after Jenkin's
death. They begin to think of him in terms that one associates with
Christ. This will be discussed in some detail below.

Meanwhile it may be noted that when Jean appeals to him to go
to Crimond's, she says: 'I feel if *you're* there, nothing bad can
happen'. Then, when Jenkin is shot, Crimond, the strong demonic
Crimond, weeps uncontrollably, shedding streaming tears through
the scene in which he and Duncan drag and set the body in a
particular position. Crimond's tears seem to have some symbolic
significance apart from the psychological release that his severe
channelling of will and feeling demands. These extraordinary tears
have surely something to do with fallen human nature (however
apparently demonic) recognising a good much greater than itself,
a good which it might and could have made its own. Crimond
weeps for himself and his sins in the presence of a lost perfect
purity. Though Duncan's hand pulls the trigger, the one responsible more than any other for Jenkin's death is Crimond, for it is
he who has arranged the death-trap for himself.

There is another aspect to the case. The shooting of Jenkin is explained away as an accident during target practice. The police are told that Duncan and Crimond were shooting for practice at the target when the door opened and Jenkin burst in. The story is convincing enough and very nearly true. The point is, if Jenkin had not appeared, and if the unwitting Duncan (thinking the pistol to be unloaded) had shot Crimond (as Crimond desired), then Duncan would have been charged with manslaughter, the love-tangle involving Jean would have come out, and Duncan would have been sentenced for murder. So, indirectly, Jenkin acts as Duncan's saviour. He is a non-dramatic, unpoetic Christ of some kind, an accidental saviour.

The reaction of the others to his death plainly bears out the Christ-association. Each one thinks that he has sent Jenkin to his death, and each one mourns deeply, using, in some cases, the very words: 'He died for me.' The relation of this to the death of Christ for mankind is unmistakable. The deluded nature of the active, self-reproaching imagination and its role in grief is mildly satirised through the mourning of the characters.

To begin with, Rose. Crimond, after Jean's failure in the suicide pact and subsequent departure, had declared himself to be in love with Rose, and been repulsed:

> it came into her mind that Crimond had killed Jenkin, as an act of revenge against her . . . She thought, so I am really responsible for Jenkin's death; if only I had been kinder to Crimond, if I hadn't been so cruel and spiteful.   (BB 477)

But she realises that this is a degenerate kind of fantasy and quickly checks it, remembering instead what 'a wonderful *presence*' Jenkin had been in her life; he had indeed 'given a soul to all things', and she dwells on his wisdom, his particular gentleness, his kindness to her, the peculiar charm of his physical being. Such language, coming after such reflection, invents Jenkin with a hallowed significance.

Gerard also has his moments of fantasy when he wonders about his responsibility. After Jenkin's death there is a malicious rumour afloat that Jenkin and Crimond were lovers and that this was a jealousy-killing. Tormented by images which this story releases, Gerard wonders whether his own proposal to Jenkin had somehow been mysteriously picked up by Crimond, whether something in

Jenkin's demeanour 'had imparted to Crimond that something had happened'.

> If so, then in some sense Gerard was responsible for Jenkin's death.   (BB 484)

This notion of responsibility is repeated almost immediately in the next few pages in the description of Tamar's agonised guilt over her aborted child. She had come to Jenkin to pour out her misery; she wonders now whether contact with her evil had somehow made him die:

> it occurred to her that, whatever might have happened to him, he had been killed *by the dead child*; and henceforth and forever anyone who came near to her would be *cursed* and *destroyed*. So she was responsible for Jenkin's death.   (BB 487)

Tamar cannot forget that on that last occasion when she went to Jenkin's house he had been about to leave. If she had not arrived, he would not have stayed, would not then have received that phone-call, and therefore would not have died. Telling Fr McAlister that she had gone to Jenkin for some sort of absolution for the crime of terminating her unwanted pregnancy, she says that Jenkin had spread out all the evil filth and he took it up and took it upon himself (BB 543). These words allude very obviously to Christ and the Atonement.

This is echoed again in the reflections of Jean and Duncan. Reunited and now in Paris, each has separate and silent thoughts about Jenkin. They both blame themselves for Jenkin's death ('Jean's telephone call had sent Jenkin to the playroom, Duncan's finger had pulled the trigger').

Jean reflects that with this incident Crimond has somehow killed himself, that somehow the worst in him is dead and that Jenkin has achieved something by dying. The choice of words is very significant:

> 'he died for me, she thought'.   (BB 523)

Duncan ponders thus:

> Why did Jenkin have to die? Crimond had offered himself as

victim to Duncan but Duncan had killed Jenkin. So Jenkin died
as a substitute, as a surrogate; he had to die so that Crimond
could live.   (BB 526)

The phrases that Murdoch has used in these passages irresistibly
bring to mind the hymn 'There is a green hill far away', a classic
and popular expression of the Atonement doctrine. It comes as no
surprise to find that the next section of the novel mentions Holy
Week and shows Fr McAlister at prayer. Words from this very
hymn find their way into his thoughts ('We believe it was for us
He hung and suffered there'). The handling of Jenkin's death, like
that of William Eastcote's in *The Philosopher's Pupil*, is Murdoch's
version of the Atonement; that is, the death of a good person, by
creating the sense of a vanished good, forcibly brings it to the
minds of the living, jolting them into awareness out of an inattentive
state.

In the process of thus drawing Jenkin close to Christ, Murdoch
is suggesting different things. First, she is raising questions about
responsibility. The killing of Jenkin is evidence of evil in the world.
Recognising one's responsibility for such evil, one's involvement
in the network of human relationships, recognising that no man
is an island, is an important matter. The members of the brotherhood are shocked into thinking about this, and this is necessary,
however inaccurate and muddled the thought-process may be at
the beginning.

Secondly, through the reactions of the different characters to
Jenkin's death, she is commenting on the difficulty of reacting
purely to the truly pure. The cocoon of self-regarding thoughts
from which each character relates to this Christ-figure and the
inability to break out into the clear light of truth illustrate how
hard it is to relate properly to Christ or the highest good. Jenkin's
death is an independent thing, but each one absorbs it into his
egotistical fantasy. The 'me' comes in inescapably.

Just as Gulliver's thoughts about the tramp at King's Cross
Station play out the theme of Christ unrecognised, in a scene quite
unconnected with the main plot, so too, the problem of relating to
good which these reflections illustrate, is elaborated in an otherwise
unconnected scene where Fr McAlister strains towards Christ in
agony and tears. This scene is not intimately linked with the central
action, yet, like the Gulliver–tramp scene, is presented with a
wealth of detail and made to stand apart on its own. The two

scenes appear to be emblematic presentations of issues that the
novel has raised through plot and characters. What had been
shown in secular terms is now given a conventional religious
framework, and the difficulty implicit there is spelt out in detail.
Murdoch's use of language as she evokes the beautiful haze of
religious response clearly points to a spuriousness in Fr McAlister's
worship. The element of magic is very strong, but though he is
aware and critical, he cannot renounce it. He longs for the Absolute
but finds it impossible to break out of his circling, self-projecting
imagination and mind.

As he pores over the mystery of the Passion he cannot help
wondering about the relativity and accidental nature of his religious
structure. He asks himself:

> Suppose there was nothing of Christ left to us but his moral
> sayings, uttered by some unknown man with not a fragment of
> history to clothe him? Could one love such a being, could one
> be *saved* by him?   (BB 540)

Jenkin is such an unknown man with not a fragment of history to
clothe him, and his life and death are relative and accidental, but
the others in the set realise how much they love him, and the
shock of his death, if it alters the consciousness, can be a mode of
salvation.

Fr McAlister's faith is inextricably woven with doubt. He is aware
of the line of falsity running all the way through his consciousness.
He does not believe in God, or the divinity of Christ, or the Life
Everlasting, but he continually says he does, in order to carry on
the life he has chosen. And even there, who knows how much
and at what times something is believed or disbelieved? Despite
all his questioning, he feels some security ('Behind doubt there
was truth, and behind the doubt that doubted that truth there was
truth').

There is also an awareness of power. The priest thinks to himself:

> 'The power which I derive from my Christ is debased by its
> passage through me. It reaches me as love, it leaves me as
> magic'.   (BB 517)

But this self-knowledge is not enough to stop him from exercising
his power. His interaction with Tamar is in the sharpest contrast

with Jenkin's. Jenkin could do nothing, but he offered her protective
love. Fr McAlister, on the other hand, guided by his ego under
the guise of his Saviour, sets out to heal Tamar and free her of
guilt and torment. The result is a new self-willed, self-centred Tamar
who rejects her unfortunate mother as heartlessly as formerly she
submitted to her in resignation and patience. Fr McAlister's
exorcism in the form of psychological counselling has left her last
state worse than the first. He asks himself whether he has liberated
her not into Christ but into selfish, uncaring power. With these
troubling thoughts,

> Fr McAlister, by a gesture familiar to him, handed the whole
> matter over to his Master, knowing that it would be handed
> back to him later in a more intelligible state.   (BB 510)

Such a movement of faith has been recorded ironically, pinpointing
the self-deception that accompanies the exercise of power. A little
later there is a description of him moving about in his little cottage,
lighting the fire, kneeling and praying, heating his supper. Then
the comment:

> His Master, handing back the problem to him, had informed
> him that his next task was Violet Hernshaw.   (BB 517)

The irony here is unambiguous. Violet is Tamar's mother; he will
now work on her.

The ease with which Fr McAlister falls pray to the lust for power
and manipulation makes it clear how easily this can happen to
anyone. Religion plays its part in the web of deception that the
self weaves around itself. It is even more dangerous than the
secular do-gooding of Rose and Gerard, because it makes a mission,
a cause of such help. The question is: how are we commanded to
love and help our neighbour? Why is Fr McAlister's help so clearly
wrong and Jenkin's so clearly right?

What Murdoch is doing here is teaching several things at once:
the absolute aloneness of the individual, the very great dangers
inherent in attempting to assuage and staunch his wounds, and
the absolute necessity of helping as much as one can, knowing
one's limitations. The difference is in the state of the heart or the
consciousness. Jenkin's has a cleanness and unselfconsciousness
not to be found in Fr McAlister's. He is there, always available,

but not actively taking it upon himself to alter the nature of things. It is through active role-assumption that self-deception and power-lust enter. One must help if one can; otherwise one must let be; and the best kind of help is practical help. To regard oneself as a saviour, or even as a vehicle of the Saviour, is to tread on dangerous ground; at any moment the ground may give, and one may fall into the abyss of self-regard without so much as noticing it.

But how is this state to be attained? How does one become, like Jenkin, as one of these little ones? The kind of thought-process that clarifies such a simplicity works against it. Would Jenkin have thought these things out thus with himself? Or is he what he is merely by a trick of temperament? Is innocence something one just has by chance?

Jenkin's struggle is more innocent than Anne's in *Nuns and Soldiers*. His humility comes to him more naturally. It was his sort of innocence that Anne went in search of, but Jenkin has it without ever having had to look for it.

This argument, pushed to its extreme, asserts determinism, genetic or environmental. There is no other satisfactory answer to the question of why some are purer in heart than others. Perhaps a happy childhood is the secret; the behavioural sciences would have such explanations ready. Calvinism's doctrine of the elect is another explanation.

Murdoch does not set out to explain why or how one is good. She is content here with an ostensive definition, pointing to an example which can help in recognising its nature. As moral philosopher she clarifies the concept as accurately as possible in *The Sovereignty of Good*; as artist, she provides the illustration who, through word and deed, lives out the innocent goodness which she sees as valuable. Jenkin is unobtrusive but loved; unsuccessful but absolutely dependable in an emergency; loving, but in a practical rather than an emotional sense. He sees the necessity of alleviating pain but without interference.

V

Looking at these somewhat 'poor' materials out of which Murdoch has constructed her contemporary saint, one realises that she sees truthfulness, humility and love as the supreme virtues. Faith and hope of a dramatic kind do not seem as important; on the contrary, they are shown to be dangerous (Crimond), productive of the spurious (Fr McAlister), or feeble and false (Gerard). Jenkin has the right kind and degree of faith; inner certainties out of which he instinctively feels and acts.

Jenkin represents morality at both the private and public levels; as a person in a circle of friends, and as a member of society. Through him Murdoch gives the total moral picture.

At the personal level Jenkin is moral because he *attends* to 'the individual knowable by love'. His interactions are free of manipulative urges because his concern has less of self in it. In sharp contrast, every action of Jean's arises out of self-willed desire.

Jenkin's attitude to everyone is much the same. Anyone in pain gets his attention and, if needed, his help. Jean says to him:

'*please* go at once, I feel if *you're* there nothing bad can happen'.

He experiences longing but keeps 'his feelings on a lead' as most people cannot. For this reason he is in less of a muddle.

There is no doubt that through him and through the others who are so different Murdoch is commenting on the irrationality and unreliability of the emotions. Rational man is much more acceptable, but his rationality has a Christian colouring. The model then is rational, humble man, capable of emotion but holding it well under control. The world of the novel is one of emotional turmoil and most of its energy rises from the whirling sources of feeling which *drive* action. While Murdoch evokes the turbulence with the same density and richness as in the earlier novels, her inwardness with it has altered, and her tone is sharper. Cato in *Henry and Cato*, for instance, has the makings of a Fr McAlister, but there was much more sympathy for his religiosity than there is for Fr McAlister's. Cato's religion was not merely observed by the novelist but *lived out*. Having done that, Murdoch is ready to discard it. She has lovingly understood its beauty and appeal, responded to it as Cato and Brendan do, but none of that sympathy lightens her portrayal here. The shades around the human heart are darker; the Easter and Christmas mysteries remain beautiful but aloof from the muddle below.

The difference in the attitude towards Morgan in *A Fairly Honourable Defeat* and Jean in this novel is as marked. Though the self-centred Morgan was clearly the object of criticism, her wild emotional fluctuations and gusts of passion were experienced from the inside. This has disappeared in *The Book and the Brotherhood*. Jean's delusions and the pathetic nature of her emotional vulnerability are delineated in boldly satiric lines. Irony is much more in evidence. Only Jenkin escapes its edge.

At the level of public or social morality Murdoch asserts the need for justice and the recognition of human rights for all. Nothing matters so much as shifting the scales a little in favour of the poor and oppressed, and the references to liberation theology are significant indications of the political morality Murdoch sees as relevant for our time. The figures of good till Stuart were concerned with their private roles; doing the least harm was itself the beginning of the good life – recognising the power-lust within and purifying it. With Stuart Cuno in *The Good Apprentice* there is a shift. Stuart wants to work for society; go about 'doing good'.

Is Jenkin Riderhood Stuart Cuno grown old? Very likely. The excessive invisibility associated with him and his role as school teacher are in keeping with Stuart's wish to be a probation officer, in 'the right cage of duties'. Such a cage Jenkin has found and inhabited; but after a point, Murdoch implies, this is not enough. One's responsibility reaches outwards and onwards. It is necessary to break out of the cage of duties if it has become too comfortable, and find a new one among strangers.

This reflects a shift from the personal to the political. Murdoch has recourse to the ethics of liberation theology surely because of the way it links the spiritual with the material, and aims at imparting a spiritual colouring to Marxist structures. 'If only it (Marxism) could liberate itself into a moral philosophy' says Jenkin; this is liberation theology's claim. The one without the other leads, in the one case, to an inadequate and false spirituality; and in the other, to oppressive tyranny. Murdoch never spells any of this out – Jenkin only thinks of going there. If nothing matters save the easing of human pain and misery, it must be done on a larger scale with the help of an organised movement, and for this the right movement with a true religious colouring must be found.

It must be emphasised that Jenkin's desire to go to South America has little to do with the religion of the Catholic Church. He seeks to affirm his humanity directly. Stuart Cuno attempted it entirely on his own, but by making Jenkin wish to be on the edge of a movement, Murdoch suggests that a political conscience is necessary in the making of the whole moral person.

She also makes an important comment through the manner of

his death. The accident which erases Jenkin indicates her conviction that chance and randomness govern human existence, but equally that that fact does not obliterate the presence of pure good. It is not sovereign in the world of affairs but it exists powerfully and independently outside. Jenkin's death cannot nullify the quality he embodied. Good is sovereign in the fact of its existence in a world so richly antithetical to itself.

The Book and the Brotherhood paints a picture of human life as absurd in even darker colours than anything that has as yet come from Murdoch, but her essential stand has not drastically changed. Ann Peronnet of *An Unofficial Rose* has passed through several forms and developed into Jenkin Riderhood. Jenkin's world is much larger, more uncontrolled and wild than Ann's rose-garden, but his impact, after his death, is much greater. Crimond's new book may be altered by Jenkin's life and death. That death was necessary if Crimond was to change even a little – yet another Christ-association.

As usual Murdoch is saying several things at once. The accidental wiping out of good robs it of force; but none can say what slight alterations it may have effected in the hearts of those among whom it passed.

The question of Jenkin's adequacy has to be faced with the question raised whether he is not too neutral, atomised and ineffective to carry much weight or significance. The morality developed through the novels, however, works precisely against weighted significance. Murdoch seems to underscore, through this, the moral need to stand outside all ideologies; never for too long to live with one, forever to be stepping outside and refusing to crystallise and petrify. The endlessness of the struggle is exactly what makes it truly moral. What is needed is a St Francis of Assisi without the order and the fame – the spirit of quietness and love and an eternal building and demolishing of structures.

There is to be no perfect society; there is no saviour.

However unsatisfying this may seem to the theologian, the moral philosopher, or the political scientist; however much of a non-answer it may seem, it appears to approximate more closely to the nature of things as they are. Murdoch as artist is concerned only with the world as it is; if, as a teacher, she asserts the supremacy of good, she does so with no illusions about its efficacy and power here.

8

The Message to the Planet

Iris Murdoch's latest novel, *The Message to the Planet*, (October 1989)[1] is related to the line of development traced in this study in an oblique but crucially relevant manner. Thus far, goodness, despite the forces arrayed against it, has carried the sense of an inviolable presence; however peripheral, it has had a centrality, an authorial authority; it has been clearly recognisable. Now, however, with this most recent novel, all the pieces are up in the air again as Murdoch concentrates on the connection between the ordinary world and – for want of a better word – the Christ-figure. Marcus Vallar, the pivotal figure of the novel, is not easily recognisable as such to the reader who sees Christ through the mist of Christianity. It is as if Murdoch has come to the end of what may be said about the mystery of simple goodness and now turns her attention to the separation and apartness of the extraordinary, 'holy' individual.

The charismatic spiritual man (the god-man so familiar to the Indian subcontinent) is incarnated in Marcus Vallar. What are the rays that emanate from him? What does he have to do with ordinary human life? Was Christ one such? What could he *do* about his uniqueness and power? Is the only answer to lay it aside and die? Perhaps it is not possible to be powerful, human, and utterly good all at the same time?

The story, briefly, is this. Marcus Vallar, Jew, infant prodigy, mathematical genius at nineteen, and master-painter, outstrips his teacher Jack, turns philosopher and disappears in search of pure cognition, knowledge without concepts, deep foundations, universal language – so it is said. While the world speculates, the group with which he interacted cannot forget him. Jack Sheerwater, who taught him painting, is now unable to free himself of Marcus's painting style. Alfred Ludens, secretly hoarding the painful memory of Marcus's anger at his insensitive rejection of a declaration of love from Irina, Marcus's schoolgirl daughter, still longs to know whether Marcus found what he was seeking, or found even the understanding disciple. Gildas Herne, an Anglican priest, is left without faith as a result of Marcus's criticism. Patrick Fenman, penniless Irish poet, lies dying in Jack's house, as the novel opens,

204

in the belief that he has been cursed by Marcus. Considerable time has passed since Marcus disappeared from their midst.

The friends decide that he must be found, brought back and asked to revive Pat by revoking the curse. Ludens seeks him out and finds him. Marcus 'resurrects' Pat through an act that seems to be a miracle, and it is soon given out that he was responsible for raising one from the dead. Ludens now falls in love with Marcus's daughter, Irina, who, convinced that her father is mad and tired of caring for this genius, arranges to have him confined in an extremely elegant and expensive institution. He is accompanied thither by Irina, Pat (now his devoted servant), and Ludens who loves him and urgently presses him to record the answers – the great synthesis – which Ludens is sure he has found.

From here his fame as a healer spreads and a group of seekers who call themselves the Stone-people, workshippers at Stonehenge, gather to see him daily. Marcus, testing out his own powers shows himself to them in silence, granting what in India would be called *darshan* (showing) in a dignified, mysterious way. Ludens, hating all this, presses him to write, think, speak. At last, Marcus reaches a point where he sees that 'magic' must be abjured. All through this period, and for some time before, he has been meditating on the Holocaust and the suffering of the Jews, his people. As he declares his unworthiness to an enraged multitude, stones are flung at him. On midsummer's day, when a great miracle had been awaited, Ludens discovers him dead on the kitchen floor, his head near the open door of the gas-oven, and a note to the effect that he has died of his own will.

Around this figure the muddled emotions and actions of people who make up the ordinary word swirl in eddying ripples. Irina, Marcus's daughter, serves her father, but *manages* him, bending things to her will, pretending to return Ludens' love but only using him as long as he is needed. She makes a bolt for freedom and 'happiness' with Lord Claverden, her secret Gentile lover, the moment her father dies, displaying a self-centredness which is unsurprising and human but not admirable.

Selfishness marks the lives of almost everyone else, save perhaps Ludens. The solidity and density of the selfish world is projected through the trials of Franca, Jack's wife. Jack is supremely selfish. He must have Alison (his young mistress), and also Franca (his older wife), and he must have them together, in the same house. In the name of truthfulness, openness and simplicity, Jack professes eternal love for Franca and absolute love for Alison in the same breath. Why can he not have them both? Though his colossal childishness is clearly exposed, an interesting inquiry into the moral basis of monogamous marriage is being made. Should one be truthful or faithful? What if one truly 'loves' two people? Whose claim is stronger: Alison's or Franca's? Franca's because she came first? That Jack, however, sees no one except himself, is abundantly clear.

Franca's case is much less simple than Jack's. The fact that she gives her husband *whatever he wants* masks a strong self-centredness. There is a moral problem here: has she, through her Griselda-like patience, contributed to his diminution, colluded to make him a lesser man? There is another aspect to the case. Her selfishness is concealed under an appearance of directed selflessness until it turns unnoticed into resentment and a perfectly masked desire for revenge. She smiles lovingly and calmly, but visions of smashing Jack's head of plunging a knife into his side torment her. What now? Perhaps this outwardly non-violent reaction, the quiet knowledge of her own hatred and anger is the final revenge? Or will she finally turn, through sheer habit, into the saint she appears to be? (MP 44).

Franca is unable to decide whether by simply carrying 'the banner of truth' one can deny the existence of evil, unable sometimes to separate the grain of truth from the surrounding selfish evil in her own heart. There is no simple division into an appearance (saintliness) and a reality (wicked revenge); they seem to be twinned together, facing in the same direction. In the end Alison, tired out by Franca's patience, leaves Jack, and he is back in her arms as she promises to be with him eternally.

France and Jack form the subplot, the material world untouched by spirit. Neither is really *in touch* with Marcus. Jack may have taught him painting, and his own imitations of his pupil's style have made him a popular and rich painter, but of all the group, he is the least involved, relating to him only in a spirit of idle curiosity. Franca, too, is indifferent. With these two, one is in a world made familiar by Murdoch's earlier novels; selfishness as an indelible characteristic of erotic love is an issue explored over and over again.

The world inhabited by Marcus Vallar, however, is another case altogether. The question was raised earlier in this study why Murdoch had not taken Christ head-on, as it were. Here it is in this novel, presented with an extraordinary degree of difficulty and complexity. This is the world of the spiritual, a composite blend of elements, taken from James Arrowby in *The Sea, the Sea*, and remarks about suffering and Christ that appeared in *Nuns and Soldiers*, *The Good Apprentice* (with an explicit reference to Auschwitz) and *The Book and the Brotherhood* (Jenkin's concern for those who suffer in Latin America). That is, the dilemma of the religious leader with power and his relationship with suffering is deliberately being examined. The holy leader has 'power'; those who suffer have no power; what must the good, holy leader *do* so as to relate with the powerless?

It may be easier to approach the question of the significance of Marcus's life and death by taking, in turn, the reactions of others to him.

The believing multitude is represented by the seekers or Stone-people. In the midst of an atheistic technological society, they stand for a non-intellectual readiness to locate sources of power and magic in stones as well as holy men. The need to worship does not die with God. The seekers are reminiscent of the crowds in the gospel narratives, ready to believe or disbelieve at a moment's notice, but all in need of a faith which commands their allegiance. They are easily satisfied. Ludens says of Marcus's showing himself to the crowd, 'It keeps them happy', and to Franca's 'Yes, but does it make them good'? replies, 'It makes them good-tempered' (MP 356). Of all of them, the young girl, Fanny Amherst, who appears and disappears, a glimmering ghost, offers Marcus little stones and wants to touch him, is very like the women in the life of Christ, putting in brief appearances and communicating with him in a *direct* way. Marcus scoops up her smooth stone and looks at her:

> As he held it they continued to gaze at each other, and it was as if, as it seemed to Ludens, in that long moment, they *understood* each other. Marcus released the stone into her outstretched hand. She stepped back, uttering a little cry like the chirp of a small bird. Then she turned and ran swiftly away and vanished. (MP 303)

There are other minor characters who react in more subtle ways to Marcus, and through their mouths a critical picture emerges. Of these, Marzillian, the psychiatrist, and Gildas, the former Anglican priest, are the most important in the sense that they speak very critically, clearly and seriously. Marzillian, who heads the institution to which Marcus is confined, lives by the professional reductionism of psychiatric medicine and watches Marcus with cold interest as he would an animal in a cage. He diagnoses him as a sane neurotic person with paranormal gifts. But that he is not only and merely the total reductionist is implied by his understanding of 'the hopeless doomed limitations of the human soul' (MP 263) and the murmur of contingency that underlies everything. He utters some of the most moving and profound lines in the entire novel (MP 498), lines that subvert the sinister impression of power and knowledge surrounding him. He too recognises dimensions that cannot be enclosed, and the quotation 'There are more things in heaven and earth Horatio' comes twice from his lips. He is not a likeable, human figure (his assistant, Dr Terence Bland, is much more so), but his pronouncements regarding Marcus cannot be ignored; they carry too much weight and authority; are quite close to the 'truth', whatever that might be.

Among the choric figures commenting on Marcus and Ludens, there remain – the feminist (lesbian?) American Maisie Tether and Gildas Herne. Maisie is balanced, clear-sighted and rational, a less sinister version of Marzillian, giving a similar kind of explanation but innocent because she is a bystander, an observer who has no power.

Gildas Herne's many exchanges with Ludens constitute, at times, a critique of Ludens' following of Marcus, and at times a validation of Marcus's significance. He is capable of contradictory stands and makes dialectical interpretations possible for the reader. As a former priest he understands the pull of holiness; as one who has left the priesthood, he demonstrates the pull of rationality. His conversations with Ludens frame the book; he has no axe to grind. He scoffs at Marcus for his megalomania; then kneels in his presence and is healed by his words. But he is no simple convert; even at the very end, speaking of the 'culmination' of Marcus's 'mission', he says in almost the next breath 'Everything is accidental. That's the message.' (MP 562)

When the conversation veers around, in the opening scene, to the possibility of a state beyond good and evil, he says clearly, 'Beyond good and evil equals evil.' (MP 20)

He is not a figure of good of the kind discussed in this book because his peripheral position remains ultimately peripheral.

There is no sense of struggle or victory or emergence; he exists almost wholly as a choric figure, commenting on, criticising and affected by the events but as an observer might be.

Ludens is by far the most important character. He thinks, loves, acts, and interacts with every other character, and as far as the novel as novel is concerned, is the centre of the book. He is also the reader, reacting as the reader might to people and events; flawed but good; mistaken but redeemed humanity. He is our bridge to Marcus. Above all, he is loving and innocent. He believes in Marcus and stays with him till the end; is called sometimes Peter, sometimes the beloved disciple, sometimes John the Baptist. He needs to understand Marcus and learn the nature of his message. He sets aside all other considerations of career and research, and concentrates on the task of 'discipleship'. Through this singlemindedness the urgency of the human search, the need to understand the 'why' of existence, is communicated. His anxiety to record Marcus's thoughts and words (he buys him notebooks and a fountain-pen) and continual hoping that Marcus will write indicate a need as compelling as that of the multitude from which he disassociates himself. They need to worship; he needs to know. He needs written proof, a *written gospel*, something that can codify and make permanent. Such measure of understanding as comes to him is the message that comes to us. He learns that there is no final single message or overriding explanation in the light of which all the random pieces will come together. He learns also that Marcus's confessed inability to love (MP 292) was only a redefinition of love, and that the old muddled concept has to be rejected so that the new one may be better understood.

As this point one must turn to the figure of Marcus Vallar. Iris Murdoch's exchange with the Indian spiritual leader, J. Krishnamurti,[2] suggests that she is interested in the extraordinary human being (*sadhu*, *guru*, religious leader) and the aura that surrounds him. He may manifest 'the rising up of man into the divine' (MP 164) which is a familiar aspect of *avatar*, or he may manifest divinity's descent into the human, which is the Christian notion of Incarnation. In Marcus both interpretations of incarnation merge; he seems to be the one (man pressing onwards towards divinity), but is spoken of constantly in terms of the other. The numerous Christ-references take in his Jewishness, his 'resurrection' of Pat, his regarding Ludens as John the Baptist, his intuitive interaction with Fanny Amherst (a Mary figure), and his appearances to the multitude. Other characters frequently compare him with Christ in a mocking tone. At one point he is tempted to 'let it all pass from him'. There is, however, a marked difference between earlier meditations of Christ and this one. In earlier novels the Christ-pattern shone through unselfconscious, selfless, loving individuals like Stuart and Jenkin. Here, Murdoch explores the predicament of the man who grows towards godhead. If there are unusual powers, what is one to do with them? How does one relate to suffering? Does Christ have to know – and in that sense be – anti-Christ in order to be himself; that is, does he need to identify with evil so as to understand it, and how can this be done without taint?

Marcus as mathematician, painter and philosopher is the composite of all human learning and understanding. Ludens is convinced that if only Marcus will press on past the perimeters of consciousness, he will find the hidden answer. But Marcus realises that this is virtually beyond human understanding. He says:

> 'At the one step *beyond*, where one imagines glimpses of a *final formulation*, thinking is no longer a source of satisfaction or even a rational activity, it is a form of torture, a sacrilege which is its own punishment. And if one could even name it, its name would only ever be understood by very few persons. This too is a doom which must be faced, to know that which only few can know, and which cannot be further explained.'   (MP 162)

To this philosophic mode of being is now added an extraordinary dimension, the spiritual. He has strange power; if he curses, people die; if he touches they come to life.

Is he a madman or is he a god-man? His daughter Irina thinks he is mad; Ludens waits for his articulation of the great synthesis; the multitude thinks he is holy. In the luxurious institution to which he is confined, the realisation of power and his hold over people encourages him to play the holy man's role. How can he know, unless he tries it out, what he must do? He begins to make appearances to the crowd, a silent, robed figure. Ludens is greatly distressed by Marcus's abandonment of philosophy for holiness. But Marcus, as he discusses his 'raising' of Pat with Ludens, says:

> 'Something did happen that day. I felt as if a streak of lightning had come from above and passed through my body and on deep

into the earth, and I felt as if I had become some quite other
kind of being—'

'You mean a sort of divine being. That must be the beginning
of an illusion. Marcus, *don't go that way.*'

'. . . as if a higher power had for a moment violently shaken
me as a warning.'   (MP 341)

This experience seems related to pure intuition, a liberation from
the prison of conscious thought into a realm where 'there is
suddenly nothing between you and what you seek.' (MP 342) For
this reason, when Fanny Amherst, the first of the seekers, comes
to gaze at him he lets her be, much to Ludens's surprise, for he
expects Marcus to go beyond such notions of life-forces and
miraculous cures. The spiritual leader's need to test his charismatic
powers and to know whether they are genuine or spurious, or
even necessary, is a stage to be passed through.

Marcus begins, after several 'showings', to understand his own
enjoyment of the vulgar call to power (Irina, his daughter, says
acidly, 'Dad loved it!': MP 317). He now sees his special role in a
different light; he understands that he must relate differently, not
as one set apart, but as one of them. He still feels that there is
power leading him on, but now teaching him:

'Only now – there are things which I somehow abandoned – like
abandoning children, like abandoning sheep – in the wilderness –
and I must find my own way to the pit, to the dark place –
and not, when I seem to know so little, seem to live like a
god.'   (MP 379)

The link with Christ is unmistakable; the references to sheep and
wilderness prepare the way for the 'dark place' allusion and
Christ's thrice-reiterated statement about his necessary walk
towards darkness and Jerusalem (Mark: 8:31–3; 9:31–2; 10:32–4).

During this period he comes to terms with his human limitations
and confesses to the crowd that he is not fit or worthy and that he
cannot be, though he wished it, a saviour (MP 384). There is rage
and rejection and stones are flung at him. The absurdity of the
scene is underscored by Ludens's pained perception of Marcus's
loss of dignity: '. . . such an impressive figure of silent dignity
and magical power, absurdly shouting and waving his hands about
and having to be removed like a poor madman with his shirt-tails

flying' (MP 385).

The question must now be raised as to how the 'great' 'holy' man is to relate to the ordinary world. Marcus's daughter Irina states the point very sharply to Ludens:

'He hasn't started fasting or lacerating himself, not yet anyway. He just reads about it. He once read a lot of stuff about the Holocaust, you know the murder of the Jews, he got every book on it, read all the books and then burnt them. I suppose that was symbolic, he's great on symbols, maybe that's one way to live without actually doing anything. Well, he did visit Auschwitz and distinguished himself by fainting. He should have remembered he was just a tourist. And he went to India to look at all the suffering on show there, perhaps he thought that *they* would see that he was really a god, but all he got was hepatitis. And another thing is, he's got to be a great sinner and understand evil as well as good and be the victims and Hitler too and Christ and anti-Christ. He wants to enact the spiritual or something destiny of the human soul. He wants to fall into awful depths of suffering and degradation and die a terrible and famous death and be taken to heaven in a fiery chariot, it's all in the mind, just as you say, and, he still expects to get his breakfast on time.'   (MP 105)

This question brings into focus the backdrop of the entire novel: the Holocaust. After such knowledge, what forgiveness? How can the world ever be dealt with or lived in or thought about in terms of 'ordinary morality' after that? By 'ordinary morality' I mean here, not convention and social rules, but even simple goodness of the kind discussed at length in the foregoing chapters. Jenkin Riderhood in *The Book and the Brotherhood* was the farthest point in goodness which is not apart; if he was holy no one noticed. But the point was made at the end of that chapter that he was weightless, as it were, an atomised saint. Can the goodness he embodies stand up to the horror of the Holocaust and the picture of terrified Jews comforting one another as the train draws into the station? That it is still a supreme value is indicated by the fact that Marcus is reported by his friends to have used as a talisman the word *tricotage*. Marzillian puzzles over its meaning, and Gildas finally explains it as *knitting*, knitting in the death-camps, a symbol for a kind of kindness:

'It was a little fragment of real speech. I don't know what it means. Most people didn't live long in the camps. But I see it as improvising, making things for others, being practical and unselfish in *that* situation, the mystery of goodness. It disturbed Marcus.'   (MP 559)

Tricotage is related to Jenkin's mode of being. Its existence in the concentration camp makes it unbearably touching and wholly inexplicable. Is this all, however? *Tricotage*: how slight a thing to place in the balance; yet it seems, in the human sphere, the only source of good.

Through the death of Marcus, however, Murdoch steps beyond the good (and human) to the holy (and suprahuman). Marcus says that for the deepest search, a painful metamorphosis, 'an intense purity and refinement of thought is required . . . a kind of holiness. . . . At a certain point one is compelled to develop a conception of insight, or pure thinking, which is not recognisably "moral", which simulates, or is, the rising up of man into the divine, as if one were being *driven* into the godhead' (MP 164).

Ludens reflects the reader's natural puzzlement at this, and also his sadness when Marcus says he cannot give love ('You want – I know you want – something from me, not just the "secret", but – love, or something like that. I cannot give it – I think I said that before. I am sorry.': MP 286). No goodness and no love? One's thesis is being blown to bits and the ground on which one stands is rocked. *Now what*? If holiness is not the same as goodness and love, does one want it at all?

It is at this point that *The Message to the Planet* goes farther than the previous novels. Marzillian asks, 'where is ordinary morality then, when what is required is the courage of the saint?' (MP 498). Goodness, when it takes on the problem of suffering, changes into holiness. Starting with Anne in *Nuns and Soldiers* and Stuart in *The Good Apprentice*, holiness (bearing the name Christ) is associated with the suffering of the Jews in the Second World War. Anne, talking to Christ, confuses his suffering with the tortures practised on the Jews in the death-camp (NS 288), and Stuart clearly says that he associates Christ with the braids of plaited hair in the Auschwitz museum (GA 147), that is with the worst, most extensive suffering inflicted by men on their fellow-creatures in human history. The deliberate extermination of six million people provides an image of the worst evil that human imagination can devise. The pointlessness of such suffering is internalised by and projected through the awful and pointless suffering of Christ. The agony in Gethsemane is centred around not only pain and fear but the *futility* of his approaching suffering and death. The connection between the Holocaust and Christ is in the act of *identification* through which Christ relived the pain of those who suffer, died to himself, and actually died through loving identification with those who have suffered and died. His innocent and passive suffering on the Cross is related to the guiltless helpless suffering of the Jews who died in the concentration camps.

The fact that Marcus is haunted by the Holocaust (though neither he nor his parents suffered directly) suggests that he strains to understand and identify with it. He says to Ludens:

'When words, even thoughts fail, one might attempt, as it were, an identification, something one might die of' (MP 381)

Later he says again to Ludens:

'When one comes near . . . to the evil which only God could forgive or understand, there are no words, the spirit faints, one must try to think on, onward in silence, with no God, just through a persisting tension of being.'   (MP 443)

There are unforgettable and brief evocations of the horror, forcing the reader to remember what he has never experienced and at the conjuring up of which he is ready to faint. The song of the servant of Yaweh describing the marred, disfigured visage and the dumbness of the one led to slaughter (Isaiah 52:14; 53:6–7) comes to mind when Marzillian speaks of 'that terrible silence of the great majority who travelled dumb from the railway station to the gas-chambers.' (MP 498)

It is as if in the roar of that terrible silence nothing can be heard; the entire convulsed planet is in need of a message. Marcus's death is a sort of message. On midsummer's day, when the seekers had hoped there would be a great miracle from him, he is found lying dead on the kitchen-floor with his head near the open door of the gas-oven. The link with the gas-chambers is inescapable, but the cause of death is left deliberately ambivalent. The note declares that he dies of his own will, not by his own hand; the state of his face rules out the possibility of his being gassed. Is he killed by Irina's selfish desire to be rid of him? She has been referred to earlier as a witch, and Gildas notes the strange coincidence of both fathers dying together (hers and Lord Claverdon's), clearing the way for their marriage. Did he commit suicide? Or did his psychological re-enactment of the experience in the death-camp bring on physical effects causing cardiac arrest?

Or did brooding on evil release dark forces from within which he could not control, so that he died as the result of a psyche at war with itself? All these possibilities are offered to undercut one of the book's central messages: the holy man's capacity for so identifying with suffering that he ceases to be and becomes that which he contemplates.

It is worth recalling Marcus's words quoted earlier: 'When words, even thoughts fail, one might attempt, as it were, an identification, something which one might die of'.

All this is puzzling. What exactly is meant? The decoding of the message may start by seeing this death as yet another interpretation of the Atonement doctrine. Christ's suffering and death, while it plays out the part of the helpless Jews inasmuch as he was himself a helpless innocent Jew found guilty and condemned to death, also lies behind the role of Marcus if his death was the effect of willed and total identification. In St Mark's narrative he is killed; but in St John, he dies through willed surrender ('Into your hands I commend my spirit'). The Atonement here is a literal being at-one-with (At-one-ment), becoming that which is contemplated. Ludens asks Marzillian, 'So you think Marcus somehow entered into this secret, this consciousness, and was able to raise it to such a degree of intensity that it killed him?' (MP 499).

Marcus's death may be read as an intensification of the divine Miranda; in fact, we see Prospero the powerful magician dissolving into the Miranda who suffers with those she sees suffer. His death takes the awareness of suffering to the extremest limit, going beyond the human, stepping out of life into death. Total identification demands powerlessness, a breaking out of the powered self for which the only appropriate image is death. To take it a step further, powerlessness can be manifested only in the moment of actual death. The only helpful analogy is that of Christ.

Murdoch's preoccupation with the need to identify with suffering revolves around the issue of responsibility. No one can be innocent as long as suffering exists; to point to the evil ones and to rejoice in one's own innocence is dishonesty and evasion. There is no innocence in abstention and quiet. Marzillian, discussing this with

Ludens, speaks of the 'co-operation' of the innocent with evil:

> 'When the body and the soul is stripped, who is innocent? . . .
> The evil men knew that their victims would not survive without
> co-operating with them, and the knowledge of that, perhaps
> infinitesimal, degree of co-operation, the simple obedience that
> kept one alive when another, a braver one had died, demoralised
> and shamed those who continue to live, destroying their sense
> of themselves as free worthy beings.'   (MP 498)

The question here is one of responsibility; quiescent innocence
works *with* evil, and ceases then by definition to be innocence.
This problem has begun to worry Murdoch in the novel which
appeared just before this one, *The Book and the Brotherhood*. Jenkin
Riderhood's wish to work in Latin America towards alleviating
suffering there suggests the necessity of active involvement against
evil. This is a question as old as the *Gita*; the substance of Krishna's
answer to Arjuna on the battlefield of Kurukshetra speaks of the
duty to be connected with the world's suffering by fighting the evil
responsible for it.

The death-camps of the Second World War are used as powerful
reminders of suffering caused by evil and permitted to flourish by
the 'innocent'. None here is good. The picture of the condemned
in the trucks that transported them from railway station to gas-
chamber is not merely historical allusion. The Holocaust is chosen
as image because of the scale of its operations: its extent, its
deliberateness and its methods. It carries within it the burns of
Hiroshima and the struggle of the utterly poor everywhere in the
world. The brutality of the Holocaust's directed oppression is only
an intensification of the suffering caused by evil greed, and allowed
to flourish by inattentive 'innocence'.

Love, too, is related by Murdoch to suffering in an intimate way.
It was suggested in the introductory chapter that love *is* justice;
Leibniz's definition of love as justice (*definiemus caritatem justitiam
sapientis*) was cited in an end-note to clarify Murdoch's understanding of love. It is interesting, and initially disconcerting to see that
Marcus rejects love. He says he cannot love Ludens (MP 286); that
he did not love his parents (MP 244); that even the love of God
implied by the ontological proof brings back the confused concept
of desire leading 'back towards individuals and accidents' (MP 244).
Yet, at the close, Ludens says, 'he was certainly able to love'

(MP 558).

Marcus's ability to 'love' offers a blend of Buddhist and Christian spirituality. To put it very simply, Marcus strains towards *karuna*, i.e. com-passion, suffering with. This requires a total emptying of self so that it may be filled with the suffering of the other, an abnegation which is complete. This is, of course, Buddhist. But by exerting the faculty for *karuna* to the fullest, most extreme limit, through complete identification, *he dies*. This is Christian. Murdoch is once again reinterpreting love exemplified by the death of Christ as self-abnegation.[3] The Buddhist light shed on the Christian concept has been discussed in Chapter 2 in connection with Brendan Craddock. The link between Buddhism and Christianity is doubly significant, however, in a novel haunted by the Holocaust because it merges an Aryan concept with a Semitic one. In the light of such a fusion the title takes on an added significance. It is a message to the *planet*, not any one race or people. The extermination of a Semitic people by Aryans who separate a Semitic Christ from his own race underscores the horror and absurdity of the refusal to see that the Aryan and Semitic messages are *one and the same*.

All of this is part of her message, her warning to the planet of the double danger of dehumanised technology and moral chaos. This novel differs from earlier ones in its disturbing projection of the absence of any fixed point of reference or ground. She has remarked in interview that her worst fear is to wake up to a nightmarish world from which morality has vanished.

A second theme of this novel, equally a message to the planet, is the advance of technology, leaving behind all philosophies, religions, moral systems. The result is the Holocaust. The word technology recurs through the novel like a threatening refrain. I give below only a few instances:

What was necessary was a kind of deep thinking . . . the only possible escape from the technology which would otherwise destroy the planet if not by an explosion then by a total deadening of the ability to think.   (MP 54)

'It's *as if*, just before we plunge into a technological world which will reduce us to imbecile dwarfs, the gods were offering us, at the very last moment, a glimpse of—of—.'   (MP 243)

'It was a technological achievement, it was a particular event in the history of our race.' (Daniel Most, a rabbi, talking of the Holocaust: MP 416)

The world to which he had now returned was the world of technology and separation, where steel compartments made impossible the larger movements of the spirit. It was as if they were packed in boxes wherein they could move their eyes only.   (MP 441)

It is clear that technology here wears a horrifying aspect and is intimately linked with the separation of facts from values. This is brought home most startlingly by Dr Marzillian and his institution. Its silent working, luxurious layout, commercial motive, and sinister efficiency (all the cottages are named after English admirals) suggest the way in which the most private and intimate recesses of the individual's mind are invaded and taken over by a professionalised, streamlined technology. Marzillian is, at first, a horrifying figure. Though he gradually reveals himself capable of understanding, even wisdom, he is himself caught in the technological machine; worse, he is a willing part of the monstrous mechanised system. He flies into a cold rage when Ludens fails to keep an appointment with him because forty-five precious minutes of his have been wasted. He inhabits a world where *time is money*; when Ludens asks whether the amount charged is per month, he learns that it covers the costs of a single day. Marzillian's serious (and often moving) understanding of Marcus does not offset the sinister implication that he might use drugs, even surgery, that in fact he does so on other patients, and that all his patients are rich. When Ludens expresses the hope that they may meet again in London, Marzillian tells him that his profession leaves him no time: 'I come to London only on medical business. My place is here where I can concentrate my attention wholly upon my patients. I have, to be quite frank, no time for anyone else. In my trade one must forgo the luxury of becoming fond of people. I would mislead you if I did not, in answer to what you have just said, make this clear. I'm sorry.' (MP 510) This is his response to Ludens's offer of friendship. Poor, loving, loveable Ludens. But thank God for such as Ludens. Marzillian's poverty is far more shocking; it has been created by technology.

  Against this onward-rolling, dehumanising technological juggernaut nothing seems to stand. There is one brief, beautiful experience in which Ludens has a sense of unity with Marcus. This is described lovingly, the still, long, warm summer evening thick with falling stars conjured up by the verbal magic that Murdoch is famous for:

> it was as if they had happened upon one of the great warm streams of the ocean of the cosmos and were, for a moment, being carried onward by it.   (MP 441)

But it passes and they are returned to the world of 'technology and separation' where it is 'as if they were packed in boxes wherein they could move their eyes only. The boxes touched but not they.'   (MP 441)

At the level of voluntary action technology is pressed into service for evil's destructive purposes (the death-camps); and at the involuntary level it sweeps one along, flows all over one, and deposits one on undreamt-of shores (Marzillian's place). Suffering is presented in these terms; hence Marcus Vallar's meditation on the Holocaust and subsequent death.

Murdoch preempts all her critics by providing critiques of her own theme in the novel itself. The several letters written to Ludens after Marcus's death (MP 483–91) take account of different possible points of view. The last exchange between Ludens and Gildas evokes with extreme accuracy the decentred, chaotic world through which Marcus passed in a signal and unusual way. The final exchange between Ludens and Gildas (MP 553–63) is shot through with deliberate ambivalence and contradictions. Whether Marcus was a genius not at home in any ordinary language or just a suicidal type, whether he was brave and selfless or full of *hubris* and a misplaced sense of mission are possibilities that go back and forth as Gildas and Ludens talk. The exchange recalls Christ's question: 'Who do men say that I am?' (Mark 8:27).

Gildas and Ludens have distinct roles. Gildas represents thought at work, though he disclaims all special powers. When Ludens says to him 'there is something you know which I want to find out,' Gildas replies, 'My dear, that is exactly what you were always saying to Marcus. Do you think I've got it now? (MP 557).

In this final conversation Gildas articulates positions that contradict each other not only to show how difficult it is to be certain, but how limiting it is; the 'answer', such as it is, may be located only in the dialectic between opposing explanations. Ludens, on the other hand, is simply the confused, loving, innocent and

helpless human soul. Marzillian's words in another context define
this condition eloquently:

> . . . here below the poor imperfect psyche must travel on,
> carrying this experience, daily relived, of the absolute of human
> frailty, this *secret* which he is not able to convey to any other
> person.' (MP 499)

Ludens is *us*, bewildered and touched, filled with a longing to
know but to whom it is not granted to know, to whom it is said,
'Seek and ye shall *not* find'. As he questions Gildas he gets now
one answer, then another; the only thing that remains constant is
his desire to understand.

One part of the exchange goes like this (Ludens is the first
speaker):

> 'It wasn't a lot of accidents and false starts, he was on a path,
> he spoke of a tightrope, a narrow path, having to find one's
> own way to hell—'
> 'He certainly persevered, but he lacked the intellectual or
> spiritual energy to keep it all in focus. His presence could
> produce in people a sense of significance, understanding, vision,
> even well-being, he was impressive. But he was fundamentally
> muddled.'
> 'So you think his life and death meant nothing, you think he
> died in despair and confusion and—'
> 'Perhaps Christ died in despair and confusion. Any death
> is essentially accidental. As for meaning that is our affair
> . . .'. (MP 557)

Ludens says to Gildas, 'you knelt down to him in the garden, I
saw you kneeling'. To which Gildas replies, 'One may kneel down
anywhere in front of anything or anyone, the impulse to worship
is deep in human kind, it is a natural right.' (MP 557) A little
further on, Gildas recalls that Marcus had found the concept of
love incoherent:

> ' . . . he was a cold fish . . . whom did he love? His daughter?
> His parents?'
> Ludens said, 'I think he loved me'.

'How touching! What you saw was your own love reflecting from a hard surface.'   (MP 558)

When Ludens later says to Gildas, 'So you think he failed', Gildas comes back with, 'who says he failed?' and offers both possibilities, that Marcus's story may disappear without trace, or that he may become a cult figure, a Jewish hero. It is clear from Gildas's near-sceptical reactions to Ludens's tentative affirmations that 'meaning' is a human creation but is none the less religious for that. The ontological proof is the only last resource. He tells Ludens that he may go back to the priesthood, that he has never really left religion.

'I never left it. I *know* that my Redeemer liveth. I know that if I ask for what I love I shall receive it. *Da quod amo. Amo enim. Et hoc tu dedisti.*'

'You think you can make God be.'

'My dear, there is no other way. The soul should stay at home.'

'I envy your certainty. *Statuens in parte dextra.* You know how to pray.'

'Anyone can do it. You move effortlessly, into another dimension of being.'   (MP 561)

These quotations from the text of the novel have been necessary to establish the state of simultaneous knowing and not-knowing that Murdoch predicates of the human consciousness. This same Gildas whose certainty Ludens envies says a moment later, 'Innumerable things could have altered other things. Everything is accidental. That's the message.' (MP 562)

The novel comes to a finish with their singing an evening hymn:

The day thou gavest, Lord, is ended,
The darkness falls at thy behest.

The lines suggest with beautiful accuracy the doubleness permeating and colouring the entire exchange. The *Lord* has *given* the *day* and darkness falls at his *behest*, words connoting authority, certainty and reassurance. But the day has *ended* and *darkness* falls, words connoting uncertainty, loss and desolation. It is as if faith must live in the midst of such unknowing; as if faith can only be itself against the background of uncertainty and doubt.

The closing scene of the novel is similar to the opening scene:

hymns are sung in both. The movement may be cyclical (and futile) but also spiralling (and marginally meaningful). As for meaning, as Gildas says, that is our affair.

Iris Murdoch in *The Message to the Planet* has placed the good and the holy in separate categories, embodying each in a separate figure: Ludens, the good and human; and Marcus, the holy and separate. She suggests that the holy differs in its *assumption* of suffering, while the good attempts to *alleviate* it.

The Message to the Planet is an extraordinary achievement, and a very extraordinary book. It succeeds in awakening the reader to the urgency of moral rearming without for a moment offering any easy way out. The title itself indicates the novel's thrust and scope. The message beamed out to the planet is the same 2000-year-old message, but it is still not understood, and perhaps it never will be. The word message as used in the title implies a certain direction or instruction, or, more neutrally, information. The response offered by the novelistic world is non-understanding, rejection, misunderstanding, half-understanding, inattentiveness and indifference.

Is the message of the novel then chaos, a bottomless pit, cyclical nightmare? Not entirely. Because of the message carried to the planet by religious men things change slightly, temporarily. Ludens, Fanny, even Gildas, have been altered; they are not at the end what they were at the beginning; something has been awakened. That is all the hope there is.

As a novel *The Message to the Planet* is quintessentially Murdochian. Her evocation of a world *in extremis* leaves the reader gasping.

It is only when the characters are pinned and wriggling on the wall that the 'truth' can be ejected from either end. In Ludens, however, she has created a character who very fully represents the aspiring human creature but who is also the riddle and jest of the world. One loves Ludens because he is, with all his frailties, capable of love, and though there is no clear plan of redemption, the existence of such beings leaves room for hope.

This is, of all her 24 novels, the largest in scope and most powerful in thrust.

What next, one wonders?

9

Conclusions

While Chapter 8, dealing with Iris Murdoch's latest novel, *The Message to the Planet*, takes account of her treatment of the separate category of the holy, the rest of this study has traced the evolving concept of good in Iris Murdoch's last novels, and indicated that it passes through different phases till it reaches a high degree of unselfconsciousness. This is not unlike J. Krishnamurti's perception that the *pursuit* of virtue is a trap, a disguised assertion of self. There are striking points of similarity, though the published dialogue between them serves rather to point up the differences.[1]

Krishnamurti speaks of complete attention as the only way of dispelling fragmentation and the 'I-consciousness'. He also says clearly there there is no *path* to truth, but that when one has compassion and is wholly attentive, one will come upon what is eternally true; and, very important, that the truly religious mind does not belong to any organisation, group or sect.[2] Murdoch's gradual shift away from organisations, groups and sects is in line with such an attitude, as indeed is her growing perception of the fact that 'true goodness knows not itself'. This last phrase is from René Fouéré's book on Krishnamurti. It explains Krishnamurti's thought on this subject thus:

> As long as I am simply, naturally, unconsciously good, all is well. But when I start thinking and talking about goodness, when I begin to love it and want it for myself, all goes wrong. I do not want to *be* good, I want to *feel* good, to be considered good by myself and others. To prove my goodness fully I need a background of wickedness which I project beyond myself, discovering and inventing it wherever I look. . . . Thus, by wanting to be good I do not become good, for my goodness hangs on evil, in me and around me. Such goodness is utterly false. True goodness knows not itself; one either *is* goodness itself, without being conscious of it, or one adorns one's badness with goodness.[3]

Murdoch's Gerard–Jenkin contrast, discussed in Chapter 7, comes close to this. However, Murdoch does not go as far as Krishnamurti in seeing the futility of all effort. She retains the notion of a small degree of effort, some shadow of 'ought' as Krishnamurti simply will not do. He maintains that such effort works against itself, that it is an expansion of the self, and that attention and total awareness by themselves can change the consciousness. Both, however, agree on the need to transform the consciousness, on the importance of doubt, and on the falsification to which organised religion is so easily subject. If in the loving attention she gives to different religious traditions she is like Simone Weil, in her eventual discarding of them she is like J. Krishnamurti.

It must also be noted that the later novels, despite their immense cultural and intellectual weight, put forward a notion of the moral life which is far from elitist or obscure, suggesting instead that morality has intimate connections with little nameless deeds of kindness and of love. There is no secret esoteric doctrine here.

II

Finally, one needs to confront what might be called the 'Murdoch problem', for there *is* a problem, an uneasy sense of her work being different and disturbing. Her critics chafe against the flaws; her supporters see the flaws as essential to her intention. If one has to recommend any one novel to someone who has not read her fiction, one is up against a difficulty. It is not merely that the whole oeuvre needs to be read, but that any one novel by itself seems flawed, faulty, unsatisfying. Whichever book one chooses, one feels one has suggested the wrong one.

The unease is related to her characters' lack of freedom. She has been charged with manipulating them, not allowing them to grow and breathe freely, making them vehicles of her ideas. A comparison with Hardy may be useful here. Hardy has a fixed world-picture of life and man as driven by chance, but his characters live freely and independently. The idea of 'hap' does not overwhelm them as *characters*, though it crushes them as human beings. In Murdoch's case, the world-picture is fluid and shifting, but it is precisely this overall picture that dominates. Her characters seem unfree; they are important, of course, and their tones of voice are very sharply defined, but the larger picture is really the subject of the novels. Her primary interest is in the human condition, and only thereafter in the human beings.

There is, undeniably, a presiding intellectualism, a subordination of art's elements to different ideas about life and the world. In novel after novel, starting with *Under the Net*, she turns over possible patterns of behaviour with a clear eye and a detached mind. Because the thought-process of the observing artist is discernible, one misses a surrender to the art-form, a coalescing of form and content which makes the artist momentarily disappear.

But such a coalescence makes for an impression of unity which Murdoch resists. Art usually projects a partial truth as the whole truth through proper management of the parts, the shaped bringing together of form and content. With this, a dominating insight, a coherent vision emerges, and it satisfies, perhaps because aesthetic pleasure has something to do with the security afforded by form and pattern. But the comprehensibility form provides – that coming together in which the artist is invisible, refined out of existence – is, in some sense, a falsification, because the part is presented for the whole. This is what Murdoch struggles against, and one of her ways is to provide an open-endedness, an ambivalence that disturbs at one level, but goes nearer the truth than is possible with that quiet and beautiful acquiescience in a partial aspect which is our usual experience in art.

The Black Prince, with its multiple frames and postscripts, is Murdoch's most elaborate attempt at using form to break form's coherence. In other novels, too, she achieves a destabilising effect by refusing to establish a point of view but calling all into doubt, as, for instance, in *The Sacred and Profane Love Machine*, or *Bruno's Dream*, or *The Italian Girl*, or *A Severed Head*, or *An Accidental Man*, or *The Bell*.

What must be made clear is that the manipulation and conscious incoherence are quite different from the incoherence of inferior art. Every artist perforce manipulates his characters so as to draw them into the scope of a design. What Murdoch does is to manipulate them against the force of the accustomed manipulations so that the randomness of life flows back over the sense of finish (Kermode's sense of an ending) with which every novel closes. For instance, in *A Fairly Honourable Defeat*, things seem to move towards the customary ending; it looks as if the characters have been sufficiently punished and educated and that Rupert and Hilda will now together lead more authentic lives. But that seemingly natural conclusion is not permitted. As mentioned in the introductory chapter, there is another turn, and a whole new set of possibilities is brought into view.

While disorder and breakdown have been dominant themes in twentieth-century art, they have been projected mostly through attention-drawing, aesthetically significant constructs of words governed by tacit notions of beginning, middle and end. Murdoch appears to be falling in line because she *seems* to be writing the traditional realistic novel, but in fact she is not. She is really writing the metaphysical novel, and by manipulating her characters against the artist's usual manipulations, suggests the breakdown of structural narrative codes. This is why her manipulations strike one as an unmasking, as true to the stunning changes and breakdowns that have swept over Europe since the late sixties. Such an unmasking is part of a moral task. Human vision is partial and rejoices in partial pictures, but man's life is thought, and requires a raging, ravening and uprooting in an attempted emergence (never-attained) into the desolation of reality. Murdoch's unsettling conclusions are uncomfortable reminders of the whole that constantly escapes one. To attempt to see that whole and exclude nothing is a moral attitude and a moral task.

The art-work, seen from this angle, needs to be provisional, to draw attention, but also, by virtue of its incompleteness, to point away from itself. Murdoch says in 'Ethics and the Imagination':

Images should not be resting-places but pointers towards higher truth.[4]

And again:

We live by developing imagery and also by discarding it, and when we discard we also develop.[5]

The twenty-four novels, written in a little over thirty years, form a track that twists and turns as she uproots successive images and myths. She says that 'the modern crisis can be seen as a crisis about imagery (myth, metaphysics)'. It seems to me that the disturbing absence of a fixed centre is intimately related to this modern crisis about imagery. It is impossible for anyone today to speak with the weighted calm of George Eliot. Murdoch's task is not essentially different from that of the nineteenth-century novelists, but she has, in Harold Bloom's phrase, 'the style of her age'.

This study has suggested that she offers, in the teeth of the chaos she pictures, an idea of incorruptible and transcendent good — to be approached specifically through selfless loving – as the desirable governing choice. She says:

The good is compulsory, the beautiful is not.[6]

and again:

We are *required* to be good men, not to be geniuses.[7]

Her works of non-fiction set this out with careful sincerity. But she is aware of the inadequacy and possible petrification of intellectually articulated ideas, acutely aware of the false sense of security, of 'knowing-it-all' that such articulation may provide. Rupert in *A Fairly Honourable Defeat*, Marcus in *Time of the Angels*, and Gerard in *The Book and the Brotherhood* are Murdoch's severely critical self-appraisals. Art, with its 'ludic denials', is one way of undercutting intellectual complacency and I suggest that her prolific novelistic output is her way of not being complacent, of releasing a frozen and petrified 'Good', and of remaining close to the 'truth'.

Iris Murdoch is a writer of very great sophistication and intellectual range and, of course, of immense imaginative gifts and verbal powers. Forcing the literary critic to take stands which go beyond the purely aesthetic, her art pinpoints its own inadequacy in the face of the world's intractable and irreducible variegatedness.

Notes

1 Introduction

1. T. R. Wright, *Theology and Literature* (Oxford, 1988), p. 123.
2. J. H. Walgrave, 'Is Morality Static or Dynamic?', *Concilium*, 5 (1965), 32.
3. Cited by Robert Young (ed.), *Untying the Text* (London, 1987), p. 11.
4. W. Frankena, *Ethics* (New Jersey, 1973), p. 66.
5. Letter to the author.
6. Frankena, *Ethics*, p. 108.
7. Ibid., p. 14.
8. D. Helminiak, 'Four Viewpoints on the Human: A Conceptual Scheme for Interdisciplinary Studies', *The Heythrop Journal*, XXVIII (1987), 1.
9. Frankena, *Ethics*, p. 56.
10. S. Radhakrishnan, *Eastern Religions and Western Thought* (Oxford, 1939), p. 82.
11. For the distinction between love as an emotion and love as a task, see Robert Johann SJ, 'Love and Justice' in R. T. de George (ed.), *Ethics and Society* (New York, 1966), p. 39.
12. Iris Murdoch, 'Vision and Choice in Morality', *Aristotelian Society Supplementary Volume*, XXX (1956), 46.
13. C. Flipo, 'L'Amour et L'Ascèse', *Christus*, 22 (1975), 20.

    Only a love stripped of all narcissistic return can divest itself of claims to power, which operates through persuasive pressure or possessive domination. To recognise the other is to wish that he should exist for himself, that is to say, separate from oneself. This change is not effective without the acceptance of certain affective denials, a certain solitude of the heart. (My translation.)
14. Simone Weil, *Intimations of Christianity Among the Ancient Greeks* (London, 1987), p. 109.
15. Ibid., p. 117.
16. Simone Weil, *Gravity and Grace* (London, 1952), p. 42.
17. Simone Weil, *Notebooks, Volume II* (London, 1956), p. 451.
18. Robert Johann (*Ethics and Society*, p. 39) notes that Leibniz defines justice as love: 'Justitiam igitur. . . . commodissime ni fallor definiemus caritatem sapientis, hoc est sequentem sapientiae dictata.' (Unless I am mistaken, we may then define justice most appropriately as the love of the wise man, that is as following the commands of wisdom. My translation.)
19. Frankena, *Ethics*, p. 45.
20. Simone Weil, *Notebooks, Volume I* (London, 1956), p. 244.
21. Ibid., p. 238.
22. J. Moltmann, 'Hope Without Faith: Humanism Without God', *Concilium* 16 (1966), 28.
23. Weil, *Intimations*, p. 137.

24. Ibid., p. 138.
25. J. Hogan, 'Hermeneutics and the Logic of Question and Answer', *The Heythrop Journal*, XXVIII (1987), 264.
26. Ibid., p. 274.
27. Iris Murdoch, 'Ethics and the Imagination', *Irish Theological Quarterly*, Vol. 52 (1986), pp. 81–95; p. 87.
28. Iris Murdoch, 'Vision and Choice', p. 50.
29. Ibid.
30. D. Dubarle, 'Buddhist Spirituality and the Christian Understanding of God', *Concilium* 116 (1979), 68.
31. Ibid., p. 70.
32. Ibid., p. 71.
33. R. Corless, 'A Christian Perspective of Buddhist Liberation', *Concilium* 116 (1979), 76.
34. Ibid., p. 77.
35. P. J. Conradi, *Iris Murdoch: The Saint and the Artist* (London, 1986), p. 224.

2 Brendan Craddock in *Henry and Cato*

1. E. Dipple, *Work for the Spirit* (Chicago, 1982), p. 252.
2. W. James, *Varieties of Religious Experience* (New York, 1902), p. 47.
3. H. Vorgrimler, 'Recent Critiques of Theism', *Concilium* 103 (1977), 23.
4. On this subject see James E. Dittes, 'The Symbolic Value of Celibacy for the Catholic Faith', *Concilium* 78 (1972), 91.
5. Paul Ricoeur cited by Jan Peters, 'Naming the Unnameable', *Concilium* 78 (1972), 71.
6. James, *Varieties of Religious Experience*, p. 229.
7. *The Republic* trans. B. Jowett (New York, no date), p. 255.
8. Peter Conradi, *Iris Murdoch: The Artist and the Saint* (London, 1986), p. 224.
9. Herbert Braun cited by Vorgrimler, *Concilium* 103 (1977), 27.
10. Rudolf Bultmann, *Jesus Christ and Mythology* (New York, 1958), p. 41.
11. Ibid., p. 34.
12. See Chapter 1 for Julius King's relationship with good in the person of Tallis.
13. Bultmann, *Jesus Christ and Mythology*, p. 41.
14. See Chapter 1, Section IV.
15. Robert Johann, 'Love and Justice' in *Ethics and Society* (ed.) R. T. de George (New York, 1966), p. 39.

3 James Arrowby in *The Sea, the Sea*

1. E. Dipple, *Work for the Spirit* (Chicago, 1982), p. 292.
2. Cited in N. Katz, *Buddhist Images of Perfection* (New Delhi, 1982), p. 44.
3. *Dhammapada*, trans. Acarya Buddharakkita Tera (Bangalore, 1966).
4. *Teachings of the Buddha* (Tokyo, 1978), p. 98.
5. Quoted by C. Humphreys, *Buddhism* (Harmondsworth, 1975), p. 81.
6. Ashvagosha's *Buddhacarita*, trans. Edward Conze, *Buddhist Scriptures*

230   *Notes*

(Harmondsworth, 1976), p. 44.
7. A. Bareau, 'The Experience of Suffering and the Human Condition in Buddhism', *Concilium* 116 (1979), 8.
8. Buddhagosha's *Visudhimagga* in Conze, *Buddhist Scriptures*, p. 126.
9. Dipple, *Work for the Spirit*, p. 291.
10. See Humphreys, *Buddhism*, pp. 124–5.
11. Conze, *Buddhist Scriptures*, p. 167.
12. P. J. Conradi, *Iris Murdoch: The Artist and the Saint* (London, 1986), p. 241.
13. Cited in Mahinda Palihawadana, 'A Theravada Buddhistic Idea of Grace', in D. Dawe and J. Carman (eds), *Christian Faith in a Religious Plural World* (New York, 1980), p. 190.
14. See Conze, *Buddhist Scriptures*, p. 230.
15. Cited in Satkari Mookerjee, *The Buddhist Doctrine of Universal Flux* (New Delhi, 1980), p. 240.
16. Ibid.
17. Katz, *Buddhist Images*, p. 52.
18. Ibid.
19. Katz, p. 41.
20. Cited in Humphreys, *Buddhism*, p. 93.

4 Anne Cavidge in *Nuns and Soldiers*

1. E. Dipple, *Iris Murdoch: Work for the Spirit* (Chicago, 1982), p. 328.
2. Dipple, *Work for the Spirit*, p. 329.
3. Julian of Norwich, *Showings*. Translated from the Critical Text with an Introduction, by Edmund Colledge, OSA, and James Walsh SJ (New York, 1978).
4. This is an issue to which Murdoch addresses herself directly in her most recent novel, *The Message to the Planet* (London, 1989). See Chapter 8 of the present study for a discussion of this.
5. Quoted in Jorge Lorrain, *Concept of Ideology* (London, 1979).

5 William Eastcote in *The Philosopher's Pupil*

1. Max Weber, *The Protestant Ethic and the Spirit of Capitalism* (London, 1985), p. 105.
2. See V. Newey, 'Bunyan and the Confines of Mind' in V. Newey (ed.), *The Pilgrim's Progress: Critical and Historical Views* (Liverpool, 1980), p. 28.
3. Cited in Mircea Eliade (ed.), *The Encyclopaedia of Religions* (New York, 1987), p. 131.
4. Weber, *Protestant Ethic*, p. 154.
5. The extended descriptions of the little dog Zed come closer to the purely lyrical and hymn than anything else in the novel.
6. James Hastings (ed.), *Encyclopaedia of Religion and Ethics* (Edinburgh, 1913), p. 143.
7. Note Brendan Craddock's remark about his mother's saintliness and invisibility (HC 370).

8. See comments on Gabriel in Chapter 1 and the reference to W. Frankena, *Ethics* (New Jersey, 1973), p. 66.
9. Murdoch has herself written two Platonic dialogues in *Acastos* (London, 1986). It is worth noting at this point that Socrates in the *Apology* envisages 'heaven' or the afterlife as a continued searching, questioning and examining of people's minds. He names illustrous people, 'to talk and mix and argue with whom would be unimaginable happiness'. Hugh Tredennick (trans.), *Plato: The Last Days of Socrates* (Harmondsworth, 1954), p. 76.
10. Robert Johann says: 'My obligation to be responsive to you not only forbids me to hurt you positively, it also forbids me to be indifferent to you, to comport myself in your presence as if you were not there, to pass by you as if you were some mere thing.' R. Johann, 'Love and Justice' in R. de George (ed.), *Ethics and Society* (New York, 1966), p. 45.
11. In the East, for example in India, he would be seen as a good grandfather doing his duty. Rozanov says as much to Tom when he discusses the proposal with him (PP 276).
12. Deborah Johnson, *Iris Murdoch*, p. 89.
13. Brendan tells Cato: 'We live by redemptive death. Anyone can stand in for Christ.' (HC 371)
14. V. Newey, *The Pilgrim's Progress*, p. 38.

6 Stuart Cuno in *The Good Apprentice*

1. Peter Conradi, *Iris Murdoch: The Saint and the Artist* (London, 1986), p. 134.
2. 'Philosophy and Literature: Dialogue with Iris Murdoch' in Bryan Magee, *Men of Ideas: Some Creators of Contemporary Philosophy* (Oxford, 1978), p. 242.
3. Alasdair MacIntyre, *After Virtue* (London, 1981), p. 14.
4. MacIntyre, p. 18.
5. MacIntyre, commenting on Fanny's lack of charm in *Mansfield Park*, sees it as crucial to Jane Austen's moral intentions. He says 'Charm is the characteristically modern quality which those who lack or simulate the virtues use to get by in the situations of characteristically modern social life' (*After Virtue*, 224). The fact that Stuart is absorbed by *Mansfield Park* at the close of Murdoch's novel is interesting in this context.
6. Magee, p. 242.

7 Jenkin Riderhood in *The Book and the Brotherhood*

1. A. MacIntyre, *A Short History of Ethics* (London, 1967), p. 269.
2. See Chapter 1, Section IV.
3. Ibid.
4. An interesting point of comparison is the contrast Jane Austen draws in *Mansfield Park* between Edward's wooden manner of reading aloud and Crawford's excellent reading of Shakespeare.

5. 'Things that interfere with your education are *prima facie* a pity . . . to be worrying about sex when you ought to be doing your A levels, caring about your work and having a *happy* time.' 'I'm not interested in promiscuity.' *Times of India*, Sunday, 20 October 1986.

6. G. Fourrez, *Liberation Ethics* (Philadelphia, 1982), pp. 81–3.

7. Letter to the author.

8. William Eastcote is a widower. There are references in *The Philosopher's Pupil* to his dead wife Rose.

9. A. MacIntyre, *After Virtue* (Indiana, 1981), p. 261.

10. Crimond's reply and his stand here are related to Paulo Freire, *Pedagogy of the Oppressed* (Harmondsworth, 1986).

11. MacIntyre, *After Virtue*, p. 261.

12. Fourrez, *Liberation Ethics*, p. 217.

13. Milton's mythologising in the *Areopagitica* is apposite here:

> a wicked race of deceivers . . . took the virgin Truth, hewed her lovely form into a thousand pieces and scattered them to the four winds. From that time ever since, the sad friends of Truth, such as durst appear, imitating the careful search that Isis made for the mangled body of Osiris, went up and down gathering up limb by limb still as they could find them.

14. Fr Irudairaj SJ of Premal Jyoti, Ahmedabad, has clarified this point for me. See J. Murphy O'Connor, *Becoming Human Together: The Pastoral Anthropology of St. Paul* (Dublin, 1982), p. 10.

8 *The Message to the Planet*

1. I am very grateful to Iris Murdoch for arranging, at my request, to have a copy of her latest novel sent to me a month before its publication. My colleagues, Dr Sarvar Sherry V. Chand and Dr F. Franco SJ read its 563 pages in record time so as to discuss it with me. I gratefully acknowledge their invaluable help.

2. 'A Discussion: dialogue with J. Krishnamurti', *Bulletin: Krishnamurti Foundation India* (March 1988), 2–20.

3. It is interesting to see that emptying – *kenosis* – is predicated also of Christ. See Phillipians 2:5–9.

9 Conclusions

1. 'A Discussion: dialogue with J. Krishnamurti', *Bulletin: Krishnamurti Foundation India* (March 1988), 2–20.

2. J. Krishnamurti, *The Flame of Attention* (Madras, 1983), p. 26.

3. René Fouéré, *Krishnamurti* (Bombay, 1954), p. 43.

4. Iris Murdoch, 'Ethics and the Imagination', *The Irish Theological Quarterly*, Vol. 52 (1986), pp. 81–95, 87.

5. Ibid., p. 94.

6. Ibid., p. 82.

7. Ibid., p. 84.

Select Bibliography

The works listed below are the references used in the preparation of this book. They include all of Iris Murdoch's novels, a selection of her other writings, and such secondary references as have a bearing on the present work. For the novels, an asterisk marks the editions which I have used and for which page numbers are cited in the text.

IRIS MURDOCH'S NOVELS

Under the Net (London: Chatto & Windus, 1954).
The Flight from the Enchanter (London: Chatto & Windus, 1956).
The Sandcastle (London: Chatto & Windus, 1957).
The Bell (London: Chatto & Windus, 1958).
A Severed Head (London: Chatto & Windus, 1961).
An Unofficial Rose (London: Chatto & Windus, 1962).
The Unicorn (London: Chatto & Windus, 1963).
The Italian Girl (London: Chatto & Windus, 1964).
The Red and the Green (London: Chatto & Windus, 1965).
The Time of the Angels (London: Chatto & Windus, 1966).
The Nice and the Good (London: Chatto & Windus, 1968).
Bruno's Dream (London: Chatto & Windus, 1969).
A Fairly Honourable Defeat (London: Chatto & Windus, 1970; Harmondsworth: Penguin, 1972, 1973, 1975, 1976, 1978, 1980, 1982, 1983, 1984, 1986, 1987*).
An Accidental Man (London: Chatto & Windus, 1971).
The Black Prince (London: Chatto & Windus, 1973).
The Sacred and Profane Love Machine (London: Chatto & Windus, 1974).
A Word Child (London: Chatto & Windus, 1975).
Henry and Cato (London: Chatto & Windus, 1976; New York: The Viking Press 1977*).
The Sea, the Sea (London: Chatto & Windus, 1978*).
Nuns and Soldiers (London: Chatto & Windus, 1980; New York: Penguin Books, 1982*).
The Philosopher's Pupil (London: Chatto & Windus, 1983*).
The Good Apprentice (London: Chatto & Windus, 1985; New York: Viking, 1986*).
The Book and the Brotherhood (London: Chatto & Windus, 1987*).
The Message to the Planet (London: Chatto & Windus, 1989*).

OTHER SELECTED WRITINGS

Acastos (London: Chatto & Windus, 1986).
'A Discussion': dialogue with J. Krishnamurti, *Bulletin: Krishnamurti Foun-*

234   *Select Bibliography*

dation (March 1988), 2–20.

'Against Dryness', *Encounter*, XVI (January 1961), 16–20.

'Ethics and the Imagination', *The Irish Theological Quarterly*, 52 (1986), 81–95.

'The Existentialist Hero', *Listener*, 23 March 1950, 523–4.

'Existentialists and Mystics', in W. Robson (ed.), *Essays and Poems presented to Lord David Cecil* (London, 1970).

The Fire and the Sun: Why Plato Banished the Artists (Oxford: Oxford University Press, 1977).

'A House of Theory', *Partisan Review*, XXVI (1959), 17–31.

'Metaphysics and Ethics', in D. F. Pears (ed.), *The Nature of Metaphysics* (London: Macmillan, 1957), pp. 99–123.

'The Novelist as Metaphysician', *Listener*, XLIII (16 March 1950), 473–6.

'Philosophy and Beliefs' (Symposium), in *Twentieth Century*, June 1955, 495–521.

'Political Morality', *Listener*, 21 September 1967, 353–4.

'Rebirth of Christianity', *Adelphi*, July–September 1943, 134–5.

Sartre, Romantic Rationalist (London: Fontana, 1953).

The Sovereignty of Good (London: Routledge & Kegan Paul, 1970).

'The Sublime and the Beautiful Revisited', *Yale Review*, XLIX (Winter 1959), 247–71.

'The Sublime and the Good', *Chicago Review*, XIII (August 1959), 42–55.

'Vision and Choice in Morality', *Aristotelian Society Supplementary Volume*, XXX (1956), 32–58.

SELECTED INTERVIEWS

Bellamy, Michael (1977) 'An Interview with Iris Murdoch', *Contemporary Literature*, XVIII, 129–40.

Dillistone, F. (1965) 'Christ and Myth', *Frontier*, August, 219–21.

Haffenden, John (1983) 'John Haffenden Talks to Iris Murdoch', *Literary Review*, LVIII, April, 31–5.

Heyd, Ruth (1965) 'An Interview with Iris Murdoch', *University of Windsor Review*, XXX, 61–82.

Magee, Brian (1978) *Men of Ideas: Some Creators of Contemporary Philosophy* (London: Oxford University Press), pp. 264–84.

Mars-Jones, Adam (1985) 'I'm not interested in Promiscuity', *Times of India* 20 October (by arrangement with *The Sunday Times*), 8.

SELECTED REVIEWS, ARTICLES AND BOOKS ON IRIS MURDOCH

Ackroyd, Peter, 'In Murdoch Territory', *The Times*, 28 April 1983.

Baldanza, Frank, *Iris Murdoch* (New York: Twayne Publishers, 1974).

Bloom, Harold (ed.), *Iris Murdoch: Modern Critical Views* (New York: Chelsea House, 1986).

Burke, John J., 'Canonizing Iris Murdoch', *Texas Studies in the Novel*, XIX, no. 4 (Winter 1987), 486–94.

Conradi, Peter J., *Iris Murdoch: The Saint and the Artist* (London: Macmillan, 1986).

Dipple, Elizabeth, *Iris Murdoch: Work for the Spirit* (Chicago: University of Chicago Press, 1982).

Dunbar, Scott, 'On Art, Morals and Religion: Some Reflections on the Works of Iris Murdoch', *Religious Studies*, XIV, no. 4 (December 1978), 515–24.

Gray, Paul, 'Figures in a Moral Pattern' (review of *The Philosopher's Pupil*), *Time*, 27 June 1983.

Hebblethwaite, Peter, 'Feuerbach's Ladder: Leszek Kolakowskie and Iris Murdoch', *The Heythrop Journal*, XIII (April 1972), 143–61.

MacIntyre, Alasdair, 'Good for Nothing' (review of Dipple, *Work for the Spirit*), *London Review of Books*, 3–16 June 1982, 15–16.

Ramanathan, Suguna, 'The Concept of Good in Four of Iris Murdoch's Later Novels', *The Heythrop Journal*, XXVIII, no. 4 (October 1987), 388–404.

Ramanathan, Suguna, 'Danse Macabre' (review of *The Book and the Brotherhood*), *Indian Express Magazine*, 24 April 1988, 5.

Sage, Lorna, 'The Pursuit of Imperfection', *Critical Quarterly*, XIX, no. 2 (Summer 1977), 67–87.

Scanlan, Margaret, 'The Machinery of Pain: Romantic Suffering in Three Works of Iris Murdoch', *Renascence*, XXIX (2) (Winter 1977), 69–85.

Todd, Richard, *Iris Murdoch* (London: Methuen, 1984).

Updike, John, 'Books: Back to the Classics' (review of *Acastos*), *New Yorker*, 18 May 1987.

Welden, Margaret, 'Morality and the Metaphor', *New Universities Quarterly*, Spring 1980, 215–28.

Wolfe, Peter, *The Disciplined Heart: Iris Murdoch and her Novels* (Columbia: University of Missouri Press, 1966).

Background

Bapat, P. V. (ed.), *2500 Years of Buddhism* (New Delhi: Publications Division, Government of India, 1976).

Bareau, André, 'The Experience of Suffering and the Human Condition in Buddhism', *Concilium* (*Buddhism and Christianity*), 116 (1979), 3–10.

Boyd, James W., 'The Path of Liberation from Suffering in Buddhism', *Concilium* (*Buddhism and Christianity*), 116 (1979), 11–27.

Bartsch, Hans W. (ed.), *Kerygma and Myth* (First English edition London: SPCK 1953; New York: Harper Torchbook, 1961).

Brandt, Richard B., *A Theory of the Good and the Right* (Oxford: Clarendon Press, 1979).

Buddharakhita, Thera, trans., *Dhammapada* (Bangalore: Buddha Vacana Trust, 1979).

Bultmann, Rudolf, *Existence and Faith* (New York: Living Age Books, 1960; London: Meridian 1960, Hodder and Stoughton 1961, Fontana 1964)

Bultmann, Rudolf, *Jesus Christ and Mythology* (New York: Charles Scribner's Sons, 1958).

Coleman, John, 'Values and Virtues in Advanced Modern Societies', *Concilium* (*Changing Values and Virtues*), 191 (1987), 3–13.

Conze, Edward, trans. *Buddhist Scriptures* (Harmondsworth: Penguin Books, 1959, 1960, 1966, 1968, 1969, 1971, 1973, 1975, 1976).

Coomaraswamy, Ananda K., *Hinduism and Buddhism* (New York: The Wisdom Library, no date).

Corless, Roger, 'A Christian Perspective on Buddhist Liberation', *Concilium* (*Buddhism and Christianity*), 116 (1979), 74–87.

Crossin, John W., *What are they Saying about Virtue?* (New York: Paulist Press, 1985).

Dhavamony, Mariasusai, 'The Buddha as Saviour', *Concilium* (*Buddhism and Christianity*), 116 (1979), 43–54.

Dittes, James E., 'The Symbolic Value of Celibacy for the Catholic Church', *Concilium* (*Celibacy in the Church*), 78 (1972), 84–94.

Dubarle, Dominique, 'Buddhist Spirituality and the Christian Understanding of God', *Concilium* (*Buddhism and Christianity*), 116 (1979), 64–73.

Edwards, Philip, 'The Journey in The Pilgrim's Progress', in V. Newey (ed.), *The Pilgrim's Progress: Critical and Historical Views* (Liverpool: University of Liverpool Press, 1980).

Eliade, Mircea (ed.), *The Encyclopedia of Religion* (New York: Macmillan, 1987).

Fernando, Merwyn, 'The Buddhist Challenge to Christianity', *Concilium* (*Buddhism and Christianity*), 116 (1979), 88–96.

Flipo, Claude, 'Ascèse et Amour', *Christus*, 22, no. 85 (January 1975), 67–77.

Frankena, William, *Ethics* (New Jersey: Prentice-Hall, 1973).

Fouéré, René, *Krishnamurti* (Bombay: Chetana, 1954).

Fourrez, Gerard, *Liberation Ethics* (Philadelphia: Temple University Press, 1982).

Hastings, James (ed.), *Encyclopaedia of Religion and Ethics*, Vol. VI (Edinburgh: T. & T. Clark, 1913).

Helminiak, Daniel A., 'Four Viewpoints on the Human: A Conceptual Schema for Interdisciplinary Studies – II', *The Heythrop Journal*, XXVIII, no. 1 (January 1987), 1–15.

Hodgson, Peter and Robert King (eds), *Readings in Christian Theology* (London: SPCK, 1985).

Hogan, John, 'Hermeneutics and the Logic of Question and Answer', *The Heythrop Journal*, XXVIII, no. 3 (July 1987), 263–84.

Humphreys, Christmas, *Buddhism* (Harmondsworth: Penguin, 1951, 1952, 1954; Second edition 1955, 1958; third edition 1962, 1964, 1967, 1969, 1971, 1972, 1974, 1975).

James William, *Varieties of Religious Experience* (New York: The Modern Library, 1902, edition authorised by Longmans Green and Company).

Johann, Robert S. J., 'Love and Justice', in R. T. De George (ed.), *Ethics and Society* (New York: Doubleday, Anchor Books, 1966).

Johnson, Deborah, *Iris Murdoch* (Brighton: Harvester Press, 1987).

Jowett, B., trans., Plato's *Republic* (New York: The Modern Library, no date).

Julian of Norwich, *Revelations of Divine Love*, (ed.) Grace Warrack (Methuen

1901; 1907, 1909, 1911, 1914, 1917; 1920, 1923, 1927).

Hampshire, Stuart (ed.), *Public and Private Morality* (Cambridge: Cambridge University Press, 1978).

Katz, Nathan, *Buddhist Images of Human Perfection* (Delhi: Motilal Banarasidas, 1982).

J. Krishnamurti, *The Flame of Attention* (Madras: Krishnamurti Foundation India, 1983).

Leonardi, Claudio, 'From Monastic Holiness to Political Holiness', *Concilium* (*Models of Holiness*), 129 (1979), 46–55.

Lillie, William, *An Introduction to Ethics* (London: Methuen, 1948, 1957).

MacIntyre, Alasdair, *After Virtue* (Indiana: University of Notre Dame Press, 1981; second edition, 1984).

MacIntyre, Alasdair, *A Short History of Ethics* (New York: Macmillan, 1966; London: Routledge & Kegan Paul, 1967, 1987).

Moltmann, Jurgen, 'Hope Without Faith: An Eschatological Humanism Without God', *Concilium* (*Is God Dead?*), 16 (1966), 25–40.

Moltmann, Jurgen, 'The Crucified God', in P., Hodgson and R. King (eds), *Readings in Christian Theology* (London: SPCK, 1985).

Mookerjee, Satkari, *The Buddhist Philosophy of Universal Flux* (Calcutta: University of Calcutta, 1935; Delhi: Motilal Banarasidas, 1975, 1980).

Newey, Vincent, 'Bunyan and the Confines of Mind' in V. Newey (ed.), *The Pilgrim's Progress: Critical and Historical Views* (Liverpool: University of Liverpool Press, 1980).

Niebuhr, Richard H., *The Responsible Self* (New York: Harper and Row, 1963).

Ogden, Schubert M., 'The Christian Proclamation of God to Men of the So-called "Atheistic Age"', *Concilium* (*Is God Dead?*), 16 (1966), 89–98.

Peters, Jan, 'Naming the Unnameable', *Concilium* (*A Personal God*), 103 (1977), 69–79.

The Teaching of Buddha (Tokyo: Buddhist Promotion Foundation, 1978).

Vorgrimler, Herbert, 'Recent Critiques of Theism', *Concilium* (*A Personal God*), 103 (1977), 23–34.

Walgrave, Jan H., 'Is Morality Static or Dynamic?', *Concilium* (*Moral Problems and Christian Perspectives*), 5 (1965), 22–38.

Weber, Max, *The Protestant Ethic and the Spirit of Capitalism* (London: George Allen & Unwin, 1930; Unwin Paperbacks, 1985).

Weil, Simone, *Waiting for God*, trans. Emma Craufurd (New York: G. P. Putnam's Sons, 1951; New York: Harper Colophon Books, 1973).

Weil Simone, *Gravity and Grace*, trans. Emma Craufurd (London: Routledge & Kegan Paul, 1952).

Weil, Simone, *The Notebooks* Vol. I, trans. Arthur Wills (London: Routledge & Kegan Paul, 1956).

Weil, Simone, *The Notebooks*, Vol. II, trans. Arthur Wills (London: Routledge & Kegan Paul, 1956).

Weil, Simone, *Intimations of Christianity Among the Ancient Greeks* (London: Routledge & Kegan Paul, 1957, 1976; ARK edition, 1987).

Wright, T. R., *Theology and Literature* (London: Routledge & Kegan Paul, 1987).

Index

242 *Index*

a

a

panna (wisdom), 80
Paul, St, 27, 141, 191
Peronnet, Ann (*An Unofficial Rose*), 15, 186, 203
Peter (NS), 114, 116–19
Philosopher's Pupil, The, 1, 6, 7, 26, 27, 37, 102, 122, 124, 125, 146, 147, 155, 156, 167
philosophy, failure of, 133–5, 138, 139
Plato, 4, 46–7, 170–71
power, 15, 53, 204, 207, 210, 211, 215
powerlessness, 15, 53, 207, 215
priest, priesthood, 39, 42, 43, 47, 56, 66, 123
Principia Ethica (Moore), 151, 170
Protestantism, 98, 122–5
Proust, Marcel, 164
prudentialism, 10

Quaker, 23, 122, 123–5

Radhakrishnan, S., 14
Reede, Tim (NS), 117, 118
realism, and IM, 226
religion, IM's demythologising of, 3, 10; and morality, 14–15; and the outsider's advantage, 23; IM's engagement with Buddhism and Christianity, 23–6, 62; and aesthetic component, 29
religious experience, 40–45, 56–60, 223–4
Republic, The (Plato), 46
Resurrection, the, 23
Revelations of Divine Love (Julian of Norwich), 98, 99, 103, 106, 113, 115, 119
Riderhood, Jenkin (BB), 1, 5, 6, 21–2, 28–9, 36, *173–203*; unnoticeable nature of, 175–6; contained sexuality of, 176–7; and morals of responsibility, 185; aloneness of, 186–7; political morality of, 187–91; death of, 192; as Christ figure, 193–8; as contemporary saint, 202–3
romanticism, 3, 45, 111, 179, 181–2

Rozanov (BB), 123, 129–30, 133–9, 142, 145, 146
Russell, Bertrand, 133

Sacred and Profane Love Machine, The, 1, 15, 225
salvation, 10–11, 34, 98, 113, 123
samādhi, 80
samsāra, 67, 70, 78, 87, 88, 96
samsāra sāgara, and *The Sea, the Sea*, 68–9; as common Indian phrase, 69
Samyutta Nikaya, 69
Sartre, Jean-Paul, 145–6
saviour, 11, 31, 32, 49, 86, 94–5, 109, 195, 203
sea, the, 68–70
Sea, the Sea, The, 1, 6, 37, 67, 68, 69, 70, 76, 84, 102, 207
Seegard (GA), 158, 162–3, 172
self, 20–21, 61–2, 68, 72, 75–6, 78, 94–6, 112, 115, 118, 205
semitic, 217
Severed Head, A, 225
Shakespeare, and Charles Arrowby, 73–4, 80
Shaw, Gertrude (NS), 116–17, 118
Sheerwater, Jack and Franca (MP), 205–6
Short History of Ethics (MacIntyre), 173
Showings (Julian of Norwich), 103
sila, 80–81
Sovereignty of Good, The, 4, 8, 9, 15, 31, 65, 99, 101, 109, 118, 119, 120, 126, 182, 185, 200
suffering, 27–8; as *dukkha*, 74–5; sentimentalisation of, 108–12; in the Judaeo–Christian tradition, 109; as task, 112–13; and Jenkin, 189; of the Jews, 213–14, 216; Marcus Vallar's identification with, 215–16; assumption of by the holy, 222
sūnyata (emptiness) 33, 95

tanha (desire), 76
technology, 217–19
teleological stand, 10–11